THROUGH THE OPEN DOOR

THROUGH THE OPEN DOOR
SECRETS OF SELF-HYPNOSIS

BY
KEVIN HOGAN
AND
MARY LEE LaBAY

FOREWORD BY
DWIGHT DAMON

PELICAN PUBLISHING COMPANY
Gretna 2000

*The word "Pelican" and the depiction of a pelican are trademarks of
Pelican Publishing Company, Inc., and are registered in the
U.S. Patent and Trademark Office.*

Library of Congress Cataloging-in-Publication Data

Hogan, Kevin
  Through the open door : secrets of self-hypnosis / by Kevin Hogan and Mary Lee
LaBay ; foreword by Dwight Damon.
    p. cm.
  Includes bibliographical references.
  ISBN 1-56554-785-3 (alk. paper)
    1. Autogenic training. I. LaBay, Mary Lee. II. Title.
RC499.A8 .H643 2000
154.7—dc21

                                                                    00-028476

Printed in United States of America
Published by Pelican Publishing Company, Inc.
1000 Burmaster Street, Gretna, Louisiana 70053

To
Quincy and London,
Katie, Jessica, and Mark.
The loves of our lives . . .

Contents

Foreword

As president of the National Guild of Hypnotists, I am also editor of the Journal of Hypnotism, the largest circulation hypnosis publication in the world. Kevin Hogan is a staff writer for the Journal which is read by over 6,000 professionals in 40 countries and his columns draw a tremendous amount of readers' mail and interest.

At the National Guild of Hypnotists, for the past forty-nine years we have been concerned with bringing an awareness and understanding of this unique profession to the public. We want people to know that by using hypnosis and the power of their minds, they can make big changes in their lives.

We recently launched a new publication for the public called *Hypnosis Today*. This magazine is designed for you, the reader of this book, the person who wants to utilize the tools of hypnosis and self-hypnosis to optimize various aspects of your life. And, once again, Kevin Hogan's articles in this new magazine bring knowledge and arouse interest of the readers.

Hypnosis is not a panacea. Hypnosis certainly doesn't cure all ailments, nor does it turn everyone into geniuses. Hypnosis does, however, help you do just about anything you do, better. People who use self hypnosis before and after surgeries tend to heal faster. Hypnosis is also positively correlated to accelerated learning, enhanced performance in sports, improvement from chronic illnesses, easier childbirth, and dozens of other major life issues. What a wonderful tool resides in all of us for self-improvement and better health!

Self-hypnosis, as presented in the book you are about to read, includes a wide range of techniques and strategies that can help you make big and lasting changes in many areas of your life. The reason the authors present such a vast arsenal of tools is because there is no single "magic bullet" for change or for health. The authors have worked hard to present every imaginable solution to a multitude of challenges and they are to be commended. It is rare that you see a self-hypnosis book, or any book for that matter, meet such a standard.

Mary Lee LaBay has acquired a reputation as a dynamic instructor of hypnosis and a fine hypnotherapist. She has been working in the field for over 10 years and has really made a name for herself in the Pacific Northwest. Her writing style is not only elegant but instructive. I think you will really enjoy her immense contribution to this volume.

Kevin Hogan is an emerging star in the field of hypnosis. He has helped create a bridge between complementary medical practitioners and those in the traditional medical field. His work with people who suffer from chronic illnesses is widely recognized and his contributions to the field of hypnosis are impressive.

As you read this book you can know that your authors are not only fine teachers but people who really want you to achieve all that you aspire to.

Mary Lee and Kevin offer easy to understand step-by-step instructions in handling many of life's most challenging experiences. This book sets a new benchmark not only for self-hypnosis books but for self improvement books.

DWIGHT DAMON, D.C.
President
National Guild of Hypnotists
Box 308
Merrimack, NH 03054
http://www.ngh.net

Acknowledgments

This book was written by Mary Lee LaBay and Kevin Hogan, yet it represents the work of not just two, but many, people.

We both would like to gratefully acknowledge Dr. Dwight Damon, the president of the National Guild of Hypnotists, for writing the Foreword to this book. His support is always gratefully appreciated.

We both would also like to acknowledge the three key contributors to this book. Chris McAtee wrote the chapter addressing pain relief. Melissa Barnes wrote the chapter discussing childbirth. And Lee Ater designed our beautiful cover. Your work will now live forever.

We also would like to thank all those who contributed their stories to this book. Katie Hogan, Kim Johnson, Giavonne Mitchell, Jeanie Taylor, Susan Hedrick, Rose Rockney, Monica Piechowski, John Sayre, Rebecca Phifer, Peter Gravestock, Craig Lang, Liz Heidenger, Mair Llewellyn Edwards, Jo Ann Sunderlage and Sam Zeiler. Thank you for sharing your personal and private experiences with the reader. They are transformed because of you.

We both would like to thank Elsom Eldridge, the NGH Convention Director and president of the International Guild of Professional Consultants for his support for our work.

We also want to thank Dr. Milburn Calhoun, the owner and president of Pelican Publishing, for suggesting this project.

Special thanks to Lynda Moreau, our publicist at Pelican. You are the greatest, Lynda.

Thanks to Joseph Billingsley, Pelican's sales manager. Know that your work is deeply appreciated. Thank you.

We also want to thank our friends and family who watched us fall off the world while we wrote this. We're back!

I (K.H.) want to personally thank a few people who I have both taught and that I have learned from. Their friendship, support, encouragement, dedication, and love is always appreciated. Devin Hastings, Will Horton, Elizabeth Nahum, Holly Sumner, Wendi Friesen, Roy Hunter, Terry Watts, Lee Freed, Joe Vitale and Richard Brodie.

I also want to thank Joe Keaney in Ireland for bringing me to Dublin to share my work with all of his wonderful students.

I (M.L.) would like to personally thank my parents, Maurice and Marge LaBay, and my brother, Jim, for always being there in so many ways. I also want to give my special appreciation to David Thusat, Mike Garrett, Nancy Adams, David Miller, Terry Musch, Kim Ambler, Jack Swaney, Julie Mason, Patricia Baumann, Carol Jacobson, Nancy Parks, Dr. Patti McCormick, Tess Sterling, Don Parks for your continued encouragement, inspiration, support and opportunities. You have all made such a difference in my life!

I want to especially thank Kathleen Jones and Jann Finley-Epps who insisted I attend the event where I first met Kevin. It has changed my life!

And a special thank you to all our clients and students.

Introduction

Through The Open Door: Secrets of Self-Hypnosis

The Door is open. The door to your unconscious mind is The Door to your future. Your unconscious mind is that part of your mind that is unaware of what is going on at this moment. However, the unconscious mind has been conditioned over the course of your life to pursue certain goals and ignore others. The fact is that your unconscious mind brings into your life virtually everything that you have and most of what you experience. Therefore, our job in this book is to show you how to teach your unconscious mind to pursue that which you now want, and stop pursuing the people and things it wanted when you were much younger.

Miracles happen. A miracle is an unusually positive result or experience. Miracles are more likely to happen when you can set the stage for miracles to occur. We will show you how to prepare your life for these potentially extraordinary experiences.

Dr. Milburn Calhoun, the president of Pelican Publishing Co., contacted me (K.H.) and asked me to write this book. There is a universal need for tools, strategies, and techniques of change that people can put into real life use. I asked my partner Mary Lee LaBay to share in this labor of love and she agreed. This book is a little different than most self-improvement or psychology books. Here is how to get the most out of this book.

This book is like having an owner's manual for you life and mind. You will learn about what works in life as far as improving your health, overcoming pain, and raising your self-esteem. We have been careful to cover every major aspect of your life including relationships, prosperity, and your psyche. We carefully map out specifically how to make a change in your life and then we give you at least one strategy or technique to create that change in your unconscious mind. When you do the self-hypnosis exercises in this book you will notice a fundamental shift in your mind and body. This is how you know that changes are taking place in your life.

You will notice that there are many pages of guided meditations. These self-hypnosis exercises are set off from the main text. We suggest you record these on audio tape for your personal use. This will allow you to experience certain trance experiences each and every day. Meditations are different from other self-hypnosis techniques like the swish and the circle of confidence that you will learn about. Meditations include stories and structured scripts of suggestions that have been carefully designed for your unconscious minds.

IMPORTANT: Notice that when you record a guided meditation that it should be done in a slow, gentle voice. Please pause for several seconds during the breaks and between paragraphs. The unconscious mind is not to be rushed! Enjoy the experience and allow it to integrate into your mind gently.

There a number of remarkably effective techniques that are easy to use throughout this book. Do these exercises and you will reap the rewards of your investment here.

Finally, we have included a number of stories throughout the text from people who have had their lives changed from learning and using self-hypnosis. It is our hope that these stories will inspire you to attain greatness and lasting health!

THROUGH THE OPEN DOOR

CHAPTER ONE

Understanding Hypnosis

Do You Remember When You Forgot This?

You are driving your car to the office or work. Somehow, you arrive safely, even though you are a bit surprised that you do not remember much of anything that happened from the time you left your driveway to the time you pulled into your parking space. How is that possible?

You got into the car and you drove. You should be able to remember the turns you made, the signs along the way, and the exits you took to get to work, but you do not. The reason? You were in trance. You may have always wanted to ask a hypnotist if he could make you forget what happened while you were in trance. Now you do not have to wonder because you do it every day on your own!

There are several kinds of "trance" (what some people mistakenly call hypnosis). One kind of trance is what we call the "dissociated trance." This means you have two very distinct "tracks" going on in your mind at the same time. In the case of driving your car to work and not remembering the commute, you do not remember it because you were partially dissociated from the driving experience. The unconscious part of your mind was pretty much driving the car and the conscious part of your mind was "sitting in the passenger seat," maybe having an imaginary conversation with your boss, your spouse, a customer, or your kids. Whatever the conscious part of your mind was doing, it was not driving the car or you would remember the signs, the roads, the commute, and the other cars, but you do not. The reason you do not remember is because your conscious mind was distracted by thinking about other things it considered more important than driving.

When someone asks what a hypnotic trance is like you can say, "It is like when you are driving a car and you can not remember how you got where you were going." The unconscious mind drove the car to work and your conscious mind sat in the passenger seat having conversations with others or maybe watching movies of what the day would be like. The conscious mind was in deep thought. The unconscious mind was driving the car. We call this experience "dissociation" or "divided consciousness." This is a common, everyday trance experience that nearly everyone is familiar with. It is that simple!

What is very interesting is that if someone had pricked you (once) with a pin, or pinched you, while you were driving, you almost certainly would not have consciously felt a thing! Most people experience these dissociated states of mind each and every day. We will talk about using dissociation for some kinds of pain control and the temporary relief of other symptoms later in this book.

What are some other examples of the dissociated trance state?

Have you ever read a book or an article and at some point you realized that you did not remember what you had just read and had to go back and read it again . . . and again? (Your conscious mind was focused on something other than the book and your unconscious mind was trying to read the book!)

Can you recall a time when you were listening to someone talk to you, but you were really involved with your own thoughts and weren't able to keep up with the person talking to you? (Your conscious mind was busy at work and your unconscious mind was nodding your head, but your attention was not really "all there.")

Have you ever cut the lawn or made dinner, only to barely remember the experience as you were busy "inside," thinking or talking to yourself? (This is like driving to work and not remembering how you got there. Two very distinct tracks going at the same time and you did a good job at both.)

It is worth noting, by the way, that in some cases the unconscious mind does a good job when the conscious mind is busy doing something else. When does this happen? When the unconscious mind is guiding an activity that is primarily physical in nature or an activity that has been done many times, the conscious mind can attend to other, more thoughtful projects on the "inside." Unfortunately, when most people try to do two different "thinking" activities at the same time, the results are usually not as good. It is very difficult to keep track of two conversations at the same time. It is also difficult to be "inside," talking to yourself, while listening to someone talk with you and then attempt to process both sets of communication. In fact, it just does not work.

The Power Trance and Other Everyday Trances

The everyday trance of "divided consciousness" is the ideal trance for managing pain and reducing the effects of symptoms. It is necessary to experience divided consciousness if you are going to ride a bike and think about other things at the same time. There is another kind of trance that is experienced by many people everyday—it is called the "flow state" of mind or the "associated trance." You might also call it the "Power Trance" because of the amazing things that people can do while in this state of mind.

This kind of trance happens when you are thoroughly engrossed in some activity that you obviously are challenged by or simply love to partake in. You may have found yourself reading a book and being oblivious to the world around you. Maybe you remember a time when you were watching your favorite TV show and found yourself crying because of the reality of the fictional drama. Perhaps you have played a game and lost track of everything outside of the game, to the point where the rest of the world just "disappeared."

During these experiences, you become completely wrapped up in whatever you are doing. What's going on in the outside world just becomes unimportant. You lose track of anything outside of your desired experience. These periods of everyday trance remind us how easy it is to associate to, or step into, a different reality than our own. Remember this as you read on!

An excellent chess player will play an entire game of chess and not think of anything but that game. We call this being associated. The chess player has no other thoughts, no other distractions. The chess player's mind is only in the game.

A great tennis player is completely "in the zone" when playing the game. There are no thoughts of what to make for dinner, the trip home, or paying taxes. Her thoughts are completely involved in the game, and when the tennis player is really good, the thoughts almost seem to disappear and she is simply playing the game as if she were a part of the game.

Two things happen when you are completely in the moment. The first is that the world dissolves around you and you become part of the experience. You do not experience the game, you are the game. The other thing that happens is that you are completely focused. You do not worry about what other people think of you, you do not think anything that is not relevant to your actions, you simply experience the moment as you are.

This "flow state" is the optimal state for peak performance and one we will return to repeatedly throughout this book. When you are in flow, everything you experience in flow is like making love. It could go on forever, and you would be happy and successful, never wanting to leave.

Your Real Biorhythms

Many years ago, the idea of biorhythms became popular. There were supposedly three cycles of time that everyone experienced, beginning at birth. These cycles would give you various high and low points, say emotionally and intellectually, every few weeks. Over time, it became obvious that these specific biorhythms simply did not exist.

There are biorhythms, however, that do exist. Most women, for example, have a periodic menstrual cycle, though it is by no means predictable from month to month. There are also daily rhythms that almost everyone experiences called Ultradian Rhythms. These cycles begin about every 90-120 minutes, and they vary from person to person, both in when they begin and how long they last. These periods of "spacing out" happen to just about everyone, every day, several times per day. Using these cycles can benefit your health, happiness, and can completely change your life! The Ultradian Rhythm phenomenon will be discussed in some detail midway through this chapter.

What is Hypnosis?

Hypnosis comes from the root word *hypnos,* which means sleep. Sleep, however, has nothing to do with what hypnosis is. "Psychology," by analogy, literally means "study of the soul," and of course, psychology is nothing of the kind. Similarly, the word "hypnosis" is a misnomer, meaning nothing like what its literal origin is.

Hypnosis is the ability to access specific every day trance states.

Hypnosis is the ability to access specific every day trance states of mind at will, both dissociated (divided) and associated (possible flow state).

Hypnosis is also the umbrella field of study of altering states of mind and consciousness, to create change in your mind, which will ultimately create change in your body and your life. Hypnosis will help you heal, create change, and help you pursue your life's dream. Come join us on the journey to the deepest parts of your mind and change your life forever.

Hypnosis: An Everyday Experience

What is a trance? A trance is a narrowing state of attention. Trance experiences include a simple everyday daydream, "spacing out," being completely "into" an erotic experience, or being worried about something that might happen. In each of these cases, your attention is focused in a specific area and you are not consciously thinking about everything else that is going on around you.

> *A trance is a narrowing state of attention.*

Each and every day you experience many trances. On any given day, you may live through trances of frustration, annoyance, depression, anxiety, and a host of other unwanted experiences. All of these trance states can be changed through self-hypnosis. Self-hypnosis is a process whereby you take control of the trances you experience on an hour-by-hour and day-by-day basis.

In this book you will learn how to de-hypnotize yourself from the trances (states of mind) you no longer wish to experience. You will also learn how to hypnotize yourself so you can experience those states of mind you do want to enjoy. Your mind is for you to take control of—and this book shows you how.

In the remainder of this chapter you will learn a great deal about your mind. You will also learn many terms that we will use throughout the book to help you understand how to run your mind and create the life you desire. Before we go to work on meeting your mind, let us do a little bit of open eye trance work. Ready? Enjoy!

Create Your Future

Allow yourself to relax in a quiet environment, if possible.

Clear your mind. You can imagine all of the worries and problems of the day getting smaller and eventually becoming granules of sand that slip from your hands as you try and hold them . . . ever tighter . . . with less success . . .

Go out into the future . . . ten years . . . and imagine a specific day that you will be living . . . living a life that makes a difference . . . and experiencing the rewards of that living.

Imagine clearly who is with you and how they look. Notice what others in this vision are wearing and how they see you. Look around in this vision and in your mind's eye see how positively people respond to you. Notice what you hear. Notice what you feel . . . the air temperature. Relish these moments.

Notice how you feel inside.

Now, bring these feelings back with you, to today . . . and realize that this is your future and that your future is now, in part, in your present. How does this make you feel inside?

When you are ready, take a deep breath in . . . and then out . . . and then focus on the words that come next on this page.

This experience uses a hypnosis technique called "pseudo-orientation in time." Pseudo-orientation in time is a common trance experience that includes clearly seeing a future scene or event. You may see yourself getting married or divorced. You may see yourself getting audited by the IRS or making a big sale. Whatever you are seeing, you are not experiencing something in this moment or from the past. You are in the future. If you were going to direct your mind to focus on a desirable future event, you would be using this experience on purpose, and then you would experience one kind of self-hypnosis.

Each day you can go out into your future, and bring back to the present the pleasant feelings and experiences that you expect to happen there. The more rich and real they become, the more your unconscious mind will seek out specific life patterns to achieve your desired future. The unconscious mind, though childlike, is very much the goal seeking part of you. Therefore, when you regularly experience sensory rich (everything you can see, feel, hear, touch, and taste) experiences in your imagination, your mind will become directed toward making those creations a reality. The unconscious mind has a tendency of finding ways to make the pictures and images it experiences real, for better or for worse. This is the first lesson of self-hypnosis.

The unconscious mind tends to find ways to manifest its imagery.

The simple images of going ten years into the future can help you make dramatic changes in your life. The reason is simple. The unconscious mind accepts these images as virtually real. The unconscious mind then begins to seek out paths that will ultimately lead to the experiences you set forth. It is not quite magic, but it comes very close!

Imagine what would happen if you could learn the power of hypnosis and use it in your everyday life. What would you do? How would you act? Would you change yourself in some way? Would you think about changing others around you?

In the remainder of this book you will learn how to use the power of self-hypnosis and you will learn how to create the life you desire. You will find that you can improve your health, your happiness, your intelligence, and even your income . . . all through the power of hypnosis.

What is Self-Hypnosis?

Self-hypnosis includes a variety of experiences that involve shifting your state of mind from one state to another. Self-hypnosis encompasses the creation of inner reality and fantasy, using the power of the imagination, for purposes ranging from simple relaxation to killing cancer cells. Self-hypnosis can include experiencing one, two, or all of the "senses" in the mind's eye. Self-hypnosis can be experienced with your eyes open or closed. There is no single definition of self-hypnosis. There are a various methods, depths, and intentions involved in altering states of consciousness that we term self-hypnosis. Self-hypnosis, by implication, is directed by the self, and, therefore, we say that a part of the self is always in consciousness, even when a large part of the self is active at the unconscious level.

The Power of the Mind

Your mind can do some very remarkable things. It can calculate answers to problems at speeds only exceeded by the person in the car behind you as he honks his horn when the light turns green. (The brain cranks out rapid-fire answers to questions like these: Should you hit the brakes? Should you pick up the stranded motorist? Should you donate to the person collecting at the front door?) The unconscious mind decides all of the answers to these questions so you do not have to think about it at the conscious level.

If you had to consciously decide what to do in every single situation in life you would be completely overwhelmed and never get anything done. The wonderful thing about the unconscious mind is that once it understands something, it will take care of it for you without asking for further advice from the conscious mind. Your unconscious mind automatically brakes when necessary, and drives by the motorist as you call 911 on your cellular phone. The unconscious mind has learned over the years what to do, and it continues to do those same things over and over again until intentionally taught to do something differently.

Using the power of your mind, you can learn how to lengthen your life, perform better at work, lose weight, stop procrastinating, learn faster, physically look better, be happier, and create virtually any kind of lifestyle you can imagine for yourself. Your mind is the control panel of your life, and it is completely in charge of altering the overall health and function of your body.

Take Care of Your Mind for the Sake of Your Health!

This book is for you, a person who wants to maximize all of your physical, mental, emotional, and spiritual strengths. In the early pages of this book, you learned about two kinds of trance (associated and dissociated). Now we can go to the next level and learn the basics of hypnosis. First, we will learn how to create new states of mind. Then we will learn how to access states of mind that have created health, happiness, and reward for you in the past and use these states of mind once again for even better experiences!

Everything that we experience, including our health and behavior, has, in part, some effect on our genetic and evolutionary history. Your physical size, your height, your eye color, your intelligence, whether you are balding or not—all are predisposed to a great degree by genetics. It is very difficult to fight genetic predisposition, but we can make headway with self-hypnosis. In some cases, we can win battles that we never thought possible.

Most of the experiences we have, our character, our habits, and our choices can all be improved or changed with self-hypnosis. Your character is partially determined by genetics. Research exists that show that some people are genetically predisposed to become a criminal or get divorced. However, we can take control of these aspects of our life with hypnosis. We can also take charge of our health with self-hypnosis, although many of the diseases and disorders people experience are influenced by our genetic makeup. Our genes definitely bring us the gift of life, and they bring us many of challenges that we must overcome as well!

Self-hypnosis has been shown to improve the longevity of some people with breast cancer. Self-hypnosis can improve health in people with both chronic and psychosomatic illnesses. That said, please be clear that just because hypnosis can help improve the health of the chronically ill individual, it does not follow that psychosomatic or chronic diseases are not "real." Psychosomatic illnesses are very real and often deadly. There is good news though! Hypnosis can frequently "unplug" psychosomatic illnesses completely and can sometimes give new life to the sick or dying people who suffer from these terrible ailments.

People who suffer from tinnitus, environmental illness, fibromyalgia, chronic fatigue syndrome, multiple chemical sensitivity, and numerous other disorders can make great long-term gains with hypnosis. Many of these illnesses are not just physical or psychosomatic—they are, indeed, both of organic and emotional origin.

In situations of great stress and distress, a hormone called cortisol is released into the body. Cortisol release is directly related to reduced effectiveness in the immune system. Even though an immune system that is too strong can be dangerous, most people can use a bit of an immune boost, and we show you how to do just that later in the book.

When Should You Do Self-Hypnosis?

A recent discovery in the field of hypnosis is that almost every human needs about a 20-minute break every 90 minutes after working or being active. These cycles appear to happen across all cultures and are evident in men, women, and children. Recognizing just when we need to take a break can help us use that time most effectively. The best way to use that time appears to be with hypnosis.

If we work during break times, we are actually creating stress that is completely unnecessary for our lives. In the rest of this book you will learn how to take 15-20 minute breaks that will help you heal and excel in your personal life. Certain activities are good for you during these break times, while others are not. One of the world's greatest hypnotherapists

(Milton Erickson) used to wait until the beginning of his client's mental "break" before putting his clients into a trance. He knew something at an intuitive level that we now know to be a fact—there is a best time to do hypnosis and that is at the beginning of this important break called the common, everyday trance.

If you are reading a book, you will know when you come to this part of your cycle because your eyes will get "fuzzy" and "gloss over." If you have ever re-read a paragraph or a sentence several times and did not understand what you read, then you have read into a break time that your body is demanding. The left brain essentially is shutting down, and is not interested in taking in any more information until it has taken a mental rest. You will learn more about effective ways to relax in short periods of time later in this book!

These rhythms have been evident for centuries, but recently Ernest Rossi, Ph.D., author of *The Twenty Minute Break,* has championed the optimizing of the natural experience of these ultradian rhythms in every-day life. When people go into these short periods of being "spaced out" they could maximize these moments by listening to self-hypnosis tapes or just taking a 15-20 minute break.

So, how do you know when to start playing that self-hypnosis tape? The signals are easy to identify. When you yawn, or go back and re-read that sentence for the third time, or you start to get up unconsciously from what you are doing, you are ready for an ultradian break. Now it is time to put the tape in the cassette player, sit back, and enjoy a self-hypnosis session that encourages calm, quiet, and restfulness. This is probably not the time for self-hypnosis that is goal directed or something that requires a change in life. The 20-minute break has nothing to do with goals. It is the 20 minutes of healing and meditation that you need for optimizing your physical, emotional, and spiritual wellness.

What are Some of the Advantages of Self-Hypnosis?

Self-hypnosis is not a synonym for relaxation, although relaxation is one benefit of self-hypnosis. Self-hypnosis is relatively easy to learn. Once you know how to use self-hypnosis, you can literally change your life for the price of a few books and audiocassettes, in contrast to thou-sands of hours of therapy and counseling. There is a time for therapy and counseling, but the one drawback to therapy is that you can not take your therapist with you everywhere you go. You can take the power of your mind with you everywhere and always. This book teaches you how to tap into that power!

Self-hypnosis is something you can do on your own time. You do not have to have an appointment. You can do self-hypnosis in the car or in the office! While someone else is smoking a cigarette on a break at work, you can be quietly programming your life for success, happiness, and fulfillment.

A Thumbnail Sketch of the Mind and Brain

One simple over-generalization we want to make about the brain is that it is divided into two parts. The thinking part of the brain we will refer to as the cortex. We will refer to the emotional part of the brain as the limbic system. The cortex is the part of the brain that helps us act rationally in the face of emotionally charged circumstances. The thinking part of the brain keeps us out of trouble by stopping us from doing harm to others when we get angry. It is also the part of the brain that helps us make good decisions for ourselves when the emotional part of our brain would have us do otherwise!

The emotional part of our brain, the limbic system, plays an important role in psychosomatic illnesses. The negative emotions are important to experience, but it is also equally as important to discharge them when the time is right. Self-hypnosis helps us do this as well.

The limbic system is where the emotional/irrational part of us lies. It is from here that the flight/fight response is generated. We want this part of our brain to make only the decisions that are absolutely necessary. The limbic system, for example, is the part of our brain that makes us run faster than we normally can when a dog is chasing us. It is the part of us that recognizes that "thing" crawling across the floor might be a snake. It does not know that it is a snake, but it knows that it might be a snake and so it makes you act swiftly. The emotional part of our brain is very important to our survival but it can also cause us all kinds of problems.

Phobias (often single trial and always fear-based learning) are created in the limbic system from incorrectly associating a trigger to a fear response. For example: Claustrophobia (a fear of being in tight quarters or closed in places) might start when someone is physically punished in their bedroom and then told to stay there for the rest of the night. The person then unconsciously associates being in the room with feelings of sadness, pain, and hurt. A phobia has been created.

When we talk about the conscious mind, we are talking about everything that you are completely aware of at this moment. When we talk about the unconscious mind, we are talking about everything that you are not aware of at this moment. All of the memories, experiences, and emotions that you are not experiencing now make up your unconscious mind.

> *Your unconscious mind encompasses everything that is outside of your current state awareness.*

For example: You are reading the words on this page. You see the black and the white on the page. You are sitting or lying down and know that. You are aware of any sounds around you—these are all conscious thoughts. Whatever you are focusing on right now is in consciousness. Your conscious mind is where you put your attention. As we change what we pay attention to, we change what is in our conscious awareness. As we focus more intently on what we are paying attention to, we automatically reduce our awareness of the other things happening around us.

Our conscious mind generally can hold about seven bits of information at any particular moment. A telephone number is usually about the maximum that most people can hold in consciousness at any given time. Everything else that is going there is not going to be coded into our conscious awareness without our forgetting the telephone number we were thinking about. Try this experiment. My telephone number is 612-616-0732. Got it? Now listen to all the other sounds that are going on around you. Focus on how you feel inside. Look at the environment around you.

It is very hard to remember new information without "coding" it into your brain. Coding means that some kind of association or rehearsal of information takes place. Some people code phone numbers by saying them over and over again. Other people use mnemonic devices to remember them. Most people write them down and put them in a phone book! The reason for this is that it is hard to remember new information without having something to associate it to. That telephone number that you read really is my phone number, but you probably will not remember it because numbers are very difficult to remember. People do not have much to associate numbers to.

Now, what was my telephone number?

Later, we will show you how to learn new information rapidly and remember it so that it is always easy to access that information!

Now you have an idea of what the conscious mind is and what we mean when we say those words. The conscious mind changes from moment to moment, and it is what you are aware of now.

The unconscious mind is very different from the conscious mind. The unconscious mind is the repository for every piece of information you have ever learned and experienced. Some information that you have learned or experienced is very difficult to recall. Memories such as these are called repressed memories. Repressed memories are very common.

Did you go to college? Can you quickly name four professors that you had in college? Most people over thirty cannot even name two of their professors from college. Most people over twenty-five cannot remember the names of all of their teachers from elementary school. Can you? Who was your first grade teacher? Can you remember your second grade teacher? What was the name of your third grade teacher? Fourth grade? Fifth grade? Sixth grade?

If you can not remember, do not worry about it. Most people do not recall all of their teachers. In the chapter that teaches you how to use self-hypnosis for memory, you will learn how to remember all of your teachers and information that is eminently more practical!

CHAPTER TWO

Accessing the Unconscious Mind

The Anti-Suggestive Barrier: The Castle Wall of the Unconscious Mind

All attempts at hypnosis and self-hypnosis (including autosuggestion) will come nose to nose with the anti-suggestive barrier of the mind. Georgi Lozanov synthesized a model of the mind in 1971 that is still useful as a tool to understand what kinds of suggestions your mind will take hold of and what suggestions will be ignored or even repelled.

The anti-suggestive barrier is the part of the mind that "protects" the unconscious from suggestions that seem to be dangerous, whether from media or individuals. This barrier does not always identify truly dangerous problems. It only repels what the mind has been conditioned to believe is dangerous. For example, the anti-suggestive barrier of a fundamentalist Christian might perceive literature about the occult as dangerous, when in fact the material is nothing more than words in a book. The anti-suggestive barrier is also the part of the mind that tunes out the ideas of others who are very different from the self in race, creed, politics, religion, ideology, etc.

The anti-suggestive barrier deflects and rejects virtually all potential input and ideas that do not create confidence and a feeling of security in the individual. It also rejects that which is unethical to the individual. Finally, the anti-suggestive barrier rejects input that is not perceived to be well intended on the person's part.

> *The anti-suggestive barrier rejects input coming into the mind that is not consistent with what already resides in the unconscious mind.*

At any given moment, the conscious mind makes up a tiny portion of the whole mind. This could be analogous to the moat outside of a castle. The castle's outer wall is something we call the "anti-suggestive barrier," while the inner buildings and courtyard would be the unconscious mind. The inner buildings are where repressed memories are stored. Memories that are easier to access are located in the courtyard.

The castle wall is made up, in part, of various stones, or what we call "states" of mind. There is also the mortar that holds these stones together, and it represents "conditions." We wish to keep the analogy simple, so we will name the castle wall the "anti-suggestive barrier" of the mind. It is this anti-suggestive barrier that determines how information will pass from the conscious to the unconscious mind.

Parts of the Anti-Suggestive Barrier

Character, temperament, ideas, emotions, will, memory, thought, and perceptions all make up the person and his or her personality. They are components of the anti-suggestive barrier, as are the "mediators" that will be defined below. According to Lozanov, the author of *Suggestology and Outlines of Suggestopedy,* the following mediators also comprise the unconscious mind and protect the unconscious in the manifestation of the anti-suggestive barrier. Where possible, we use Lozanov's brief definitions of each of these mediators.

All of these components of personhood have an effect on how suggestions will be accepted, or not accepted, by the mind. A few of the important mediators are:

Set Up—Our "set up" is the unconscious organization of readiness for a certain type of activity. People are genetically wired for certain dispositions, or not. Environmentally, our early experiences do, or do not, prepare us for certain life experiences.

Attitude—An "attitude" is one's conception of the value of a given phenomenon, a conception built in one's life experience.

Motivation—"Motivation" is the augmented desire, or lack of desire, to achieve, or live through, something. Motivation implies that something additional is in place that was not in place before the motivation began.

Expectancy—"Expectancy" is the belief that something is about to be achieved or lived through.

Interests—Your "interests" help form the direction of your personality's search for self-realization.

Needs—Your "needs" are the things that are vitally important to you as an individual.

The castle wall is composed of many conditions and states. As noted above, the anti-suggestive barrier is made up, in part, of genetic predispositions. Interactions of the "biological person" with the early environmental experiences around them are what we call a "set up." It is this early period, or the first four to six years, when the person's genes and environment mix together to create the little person who will grow up to be . . . a big little kid.

Generally speaking, we say that if information passes from the conscious mind to the unconscious mind without debate, critical thinking, or argument, it resonates with the anti-suggestive barrier. This means that we experienced or heard something that was "okay by me." When you hear something you disagree with or think is nonsense, your critical faculty triggers the, "What a bunch of hooey!" response. The unconscious mind does not act on information that it thinks is nonsensical.

The Three Key Anti-Suggestive Barriers

There are actually three barriers within the larger anti-suggestive barrier. These are the logical, emotional, and ethical barriers.

The **logical barrier** allows the mind to protect the self by not doing anything that is not logically well motivated. You should understand that this specifically means that which is logical to the self, and not necessarily to a mathematics professor at a university.

The **emotional barrier** allows the mind to protect the self by not partaking in any activity that is apparently going to hinder the security or the confidence of the self.

The **ethical barrier** allows the mind to protect the self by not partaking in any activity that breaks the ethical morals of the individual.

In self-hypnosis, and even in hypnotherapy, it is a key goal to "overcome" or "resonate with" the three suggestive barriers to create internal harmony and peace.

Learning to Bypass and Resonate with the Barriers

When you learn to use self-hypnosis, you will learn how to construct messages to yourself that will resonate with the anti-suggestive barrier. Then they will bypass or pass through the barrier so that everything you say to yourself goes straight to the unconscious mind. Subsequently, the message can be acted upon and implemented into your daily life. In the old days, we thought we could just say, "I am 110 pounds, I am 110 pounds, I am 110 pounds." What happened was that we did not lose the weight or make the changes we wanted to make because the anti-suggestive barrier said, "What a bunch of hooey! You are not only fat, but your nose is growing longer too!" The mind will act on that which it believes, not on that which it knows to be a lie.

What is even more interesting is that the mind will not necessarily act on your own words as quickly and effectively as it will someone else's! Sometimes we do not trust ourselves as much as we trust others. When this is the case, self-hypnosis is actually more difficult to do than hypnosis with a hypnotherapist. However, using this book will help you change that. By improving your self-esteem and self-confidence, and then fine tuning your intuition, you will begin to experience a renewed sense of self-efficacy.

Autosuggestion (What to Say When You Talk to Yourself)

Self-hypnosis is as powerful as it is because it is the ultimate experience of self directed choices. You can give yourself the gift of experiencing the feelings that you choose and creating the reality you want to live. You can teach yourself to visualize what you want to see and to hear the sounds and voices that you want to hear. So, what do you want to say when you talk to yourself?

In 1923, Emile Couie became one of the first writers who would write in detail about a form of self-hypnosis called autosuggestion. Autosuggestion makes up the words that we say to ourselves to create the life we desire. There are several components to effective self-hypnosis. Autosuggestion is the first we will deal with in detail.

Autosuggestion is an area in human development that has been popularized by some and bashed by others. This portion of the book will deal with a few powerful modes of talking to yourself at the conscious and unconscious level. You will discover that this kind of self-hypnosis can help you design your life and create a bridge from dream to reality. It certainly is true that language is a powerful tool. Its use for the acquisition of those things we want to have in life has been recorded for millennia.

Affirmative Autosuggestion

There was a time in our pre-history when the spoken word was considered magical. It is interesting that a book as old as the Bible discusses the use of language in conjunction with faith and belief, in a manner that is consistent with what we know to actually work in self-hypnosis in the 21st century.

Autosuggestion is considered to have three components. The three are **language, faith (or belief),** and sometimes **ritual.** In other words, you will say something to yourself, know that it will become a reality, and do some physical activity during the suggestion.

Autosuggestion can be used at any time of the day, while you are performing virtually any activity. You do not have to have your eyes closed or even be breathing deeply. You *do* need to utilize the proper language and be absolutely truthful and certain about what you say. If you do this, your mind will begin to act immediately upon your autosuggestion and go to work for you.

The Bible, written several thousand years ago, discusses all three of these components, from Genesis to Revelation. We will touch on a few typical thoughts from the Bible, as the words, written so long ago, still resonate with truth today. Consider the use of language, faith, and belief as a means of acquisition in the following passages.

When Jesus healed a blind man, note why Jesus said he was healed.

Jesus: "What do you want me to do for you?"

Man: "Lord, that I may receive my sight."

Jesus: "Receive your sight; your faith has saved you."

What saved the man's life? Faith. Interesting, isn't it? Now, consider this next example.

When Jesus' brother, James, explained how to gain wisdom, he told the readers of his epistles to do the following:

"But let him ask in faith, with no doubting, for he who doubts is like a wave of the sea driven and tossed by the wind. For let not that man suppose that he will receive anything from the Lord; he is a double-minded man, unstable in his ways."

In the above passage, what degree of certainty is necessary to acquire wisdom? How does James describe the man who has any doubt at all?

Here is yet another example that is worthy of consideration. In the final Biblical passage below, Jesus notes one of the ultimate potentials of man.

So Jesus said to them, "Because of your little faith; for assuredly I say to you, if you have faith as a mustard seed, you will say to this mountain, 'Move from here to here,' and it will move; and nothing will be impossible for you."

If Jesus were correct, what would the key to our human potential be?

We like the Biblical model for language and belief because, in the 21st century, we know that prayer really does improve a person's chances for healing and language really can change the results we get in life.

When using autosuggestion you should remember these key thoughts:
- Doubt creates fear.
- Fear creates mental, emotional, and spiritual paralysis.

There can be no mention of doubt in our autosuggestion. There can be no fear if we are to make our future as bright as we want it to be! Where there is doubt or fear, and faith or belief intermixed; a paradox is created in the unconscious mind. The paradox is difficult to solve for someone who is not skilled in the various forms of autosuggestion that are discussed in this chapter.

When using autosuggestion, we will use the Biblical model that is enhanced by what we call hypnotic language patterns. (We will discuss how to use hypnotic language very shortly!)

Here are the three keys to successful autosuggestion:
- Utilize statements of faith, which is the certainty or knowledge that something is, although we do not see it yet.
- Utilize statements of goal-directed language. These words imply that the acquisition of a goal or desire is becoming a reality.
- Utilize statements that are made in the present or "near future" tense. Some things simply are not true today and the uncon scious mind will reject lies. Other things can be stated with a sense of ownership in the "now" sense because the changes can be real now.

These three keys are what make autosuggestion powerful. How long will it take for the results to begin, though? When will you actually "get" what you are suggesting to yourself?

The answer is simple. When all three keys are met, the solution will begin to materialize. Its manifestation could take one second, one year, or a century. Interestingly, many people who have used some form of affirmative self-talk in the past were convinced that they only needed to believe to acquire their desires. What they left out was the doing that goes along with the believing.

A farmer can plant seeds and know they will grow to the time of harvest. If the farmer cares for his crop, waters his fields, and ultimately harvests his crop, he realizes his objective. If he fails to do any of these elements, he will not realize his objective. When you want to make change in your life, your mind will help you focus your attention to where you are going, but you will always want to take the necessary action in getting there!

After you read some powerful autosuggestions, you will learn how to formulate your own. Autosuggestions must be believable for the unconscious mind to take action. They must also be framed with conviction and belief. With this in mind, here are some autosuggestions created to help you get what you want and help you live a more fulfilling life.

1) I learn more about my life purpose every day.
2) Each day I live more purposefully.
3) Today I realize I am becoming in love with life.
4) Today I find myself liking more and more.
5) Today I begin to make positive changes in the world around me.
6) I imagine that people love me more every day.
7) I give more of me to those I love, now, every day.
8) I now perceive of problems as challenges.
9) I now consciously decide how to use my time.
10) Each day I am coming closer to the weight that I will feel comfortable at.
11) I happily am responsible for my life.
12) Today, I am the person I choose to be.
13) I know that the world would be a very different place if I were not here.
14) I now consciously decide what I will think about.
15) I am beginning to find it easy to move toward the realization of my thoughts.
16) I am mentally designing a healthier body today.
17) Today it is becoming clear as to how my life is in alignment with my life purpose.

18) Because of the spending habits I am now changing, my net worth is rising rapidly.
19) When I look in the mirror, I find that I am beginning to like myself more and more.

There are at least two optimal ways to use autosuggestion. First, you can make your own audiocassettes and listen to them two or three times per day, every day. Second, you can write these autosuggestions down on paper, in your own handwriting, and read them to yourself both out loud and silently as a meditation, three times each day.

Autosuggestions become imprinted in the mind when they are linked to emotions. Therefore, it is best to match each statement with the proper emotion. If you want a passionate belief imprinted, state the autosuggestion passionately.

If at any time there arises an internal conflict in reading your autosuggestions, it is very important that you create a happy resolution to the conflict you are experiencing. In order to be aligned internally, we must integrate those "parts" of you that are not currently in alignment with your optimal future and true life purpose. Almost everyone needs to make internal alterations if they are going to successfully live by design, and not chance. Later in this book, you will learn how to do just such an alignment with yourself!

Words that Get Past the Castle Wall

You probably noticed that words like "now" and "because" are regularly used to open the door to the unconscious mind. These are words that, because of our childhood upbringing, make everything around them believable to the unconscious mind. For example, do you remember this dialogue:

Child: "Mom can I please stay up late tonight?"
Mom: "No, honey, go on up to bed now."
Child: "But Mom, please can't I stay up late? Please?"
Mom: "No, honey, I said get on up to bed."
Child: "But Mom . . . "
Mom: "NOW!" (Child goes immediately upstairs.)

Hypnotists and hypnotherapists love to use the word "now" because they know it gains almost immediate compliance with most reasonable requests. "Now" has become a stimulus for us to do almost anything that we are directed to do. After all, "Imagine Yourself in a Mercury Now."

Here's another dialogue that shows how yet another word opens the doors to compliance (for ourselves and others) in an almost unbelievable fashion.

Child: "Mom, can I go next door to the Johnson's?"
Mom: "No, honey."
Child: "But why, Mom?"
Mom: "Because I said so."

The child hears the word "because" so often that the child no longer asks for more information as to why a behavior must be followed. "Because I said so," or "Because anything," are good enough for the child, and as the child grows up they are good enough for the adult. The word "because" becomes a seemingly logical and rational reason for people to do anything they are asked to do. Therefore, when we use autosuggestion, we like to use the word "because" in almost any context that we can.

There are more words that are like "butter in the brain" that make it easy to slide suggestions along. The word "don't," for example, is very powerful.

Here are some interesting thoughts for you not to think about!
"Don't think of the color of your car."
"Don't think of the President's face."
"Don't think of the stars in the American Flag."
"Don't think of puffy white clouds in the sky."

We call the word "don't" a directive. The reason is that it directs people to consider specifically what they are told to "don't" do. As you grew up, you were told "don't" over, and over, and over. Ultimately, the mind began to focus on what it was told to "don't" do and since then it has done the same. Therefore, if you say, "Don't feel obligated to take me out to lunch," the person will feel obligated to take you out to lunch. It sounds unbelievable, but this is how we have been programmed since childhood, and it is exactly how we respond as adults.

There are many more words and phrases that just slide right past the castle wall, and you will read about many of them throughout this book.

Metaphors and the Stories That Change Your Life

Another common way hypnotherapists bypass the anti-suggestive barrier of the mind is to use metaphors or stories to share ideas with the client, and, more specifically, the unconscious mind of a client. Stories and metaphors are useful in creating change because they are "only" stories and therefore little resistance is offered by the anti-suggestive barrier. Metaphors and stories help us learn lessons and gain life experience without actually having to live through real life events. They also help us to make sense of current circumstances in a safe manner. When we listen to a story, a fable, or a metaphor, we will identify with characters or circumstances in the story—and we will discover ways of creating change that we may not have accepted consciously or unconsciously without the aid of the story.

In this book you will learn not only from the real life stories of people just like you, you will also learn through guided imagery and metaphors that are constructed by the authors to help you make changes in your life in an easy and simple manner. Some of the stories you read or record for your own self-hypnosis will actually help you make several changes in your life at one time. This occurs because there is often more than one lesson in any given story or metaphor. Repeating the reading of or listening to a metaphor can be useful, too, as you can learn something different from a metaphor when you have gained more real-life experience. Take advantage of the metaphors in this book and allow them to speak to your unconscious mind!

Gazing Into Your Future . . . Again

Now that we have a little more understanding about what the unconscious mind will respond to, let's do a few minutes of self-hypnosis with your eyes open. Read the following guided meditation slowly. Experience each moment fully and completely.

Go out ten years into the future and select a different day than you did before . . . Select a day that will represent the future that you want to have. And when you are imagining this special day, use bright colors, lots of sounds, and experience lots of physical sensations. Go there now . . .

Carefully notice how positively people respond to you on this day in the future.

Notice how people talk and pay complete attention to their facial features. Observe the colors and kinds of clothes they are wearing. Notice all of the sounds in the environment.

Pay attention to all of your internal feelings as you experience this future day more clearly by the moment . . .

Take your time and enjoy this time . . .

Be fully in the experience . . .

. . . and now as you bring this experience to a close for now . . . .bring those images, sounds and feelings back with you now to the present . . . feeling just as wonderful now as you do in the future . . . realize how wonderful your life is and then prepare yourself to shift your conscious attention to the words of this book so you can learn even more about yourself and your future!

CHAPTER THREE

Overcoming Procrastination

Procrastination can be one of the most devastating of all the problems you face. We often call procrastination practicing for death. Why? Because when you procrastinate you are not partaking in the life that you want to live. Procrastination commonly happens because part of you believes that you do not deserve the rewards of the actions you need to be taking. Procrastination often is the most seemingly benign form of self-sabotage you will experience.

> *Procrastination is a common form of self-sabotage.*

Until 1987, I was a procrastinator of the greatest magnitude. I had written two books, but never got them published. I did not even send the final manuscripts to a publisher. I just set them aside and worked on other projects. I was working very hard. I invested hundreds and hundreds of hours into researching and writing these books. Then I self sabotaged my entire life by failing to get the books to print and into the hands of an audience that could really use the information I had written about. Why?

I was sabotaging my work! There was a part of me that believed it was not good to earn a lot of money. Up to that point in my life, I had lived either in near poverty as a child or deeply in debt as a young adult. I began to identify with being poor—it was part of who I was as a person. There was a part of me that felt I did not deserve to have more than anyone else in my family. I would work hard, but then, when it was obvious the work would come to fruition, and that I might become successful, I would get lazy and stop being productive. I would just sit back and click the remote control around and around and around. I procrastinated. I sat in front of the television and started clicking the remote at channel 02. Then I would click the up button to 03, 04, 05, and all the way up to 69, which was how many channels we had. Then the next click was 02. I went around and around the channels, and, at age 25, I was clicking away my productive years.

I went to see a motivational speaker one day—Zig Ziglar. "You've got to have goals," he said over and over. Heck, I had goals and I had potential. I could see that much. Then, at some point in the program he said, seemingly to me, "You have to stop being a wandering generality and become a meaningful specific." The key words for me were "wandering" and "meaningful." I knew I was wandering in life. And I also knew that I couldn't be what I was here on earth to be if I *kept* wandering. I knew that I had so much to share (as evidenced by the written manuscripts). Then, as Zig was talking, I looked at my lap that held the book, *See You at the Top,* which Zig wrote. I remember thinking, "You know, Zig, you *will* see me at the top!"

From that moment on, Zig's program faded from my conscious awareness and my possible futures started to flash before my eyes. I saw one future of being very poor. One future was remarkably mediocre. Another future was successful. I liked the successful future. There were wonderful people, a nice house, a nice car, books in print, and appreciative people, and I decided, *this is what I want.*

I started to think, *What do I have to do to change?* I knew that everything I had done in life brought me to where I was on that day. If I was going to go anywhere else in life, I had to make some decisions . . . now.

"I have to stop procrastinating (wandering), and I must start to get my back side in gear and not just work on, but *finish,* projects." Already, from the start, I was able to see the end. I could already believe in myself. I was setting goals. I was writing about what I knew the most about!

Zig's presentation ended. I went home with everything Zig had ever written or uttered. The first thing I did when I got home was to not begin reading any of Zig's books, however. Instead, I grabbed books from the bookshelf, and started to learn how to reprogram my brain so it would no longer procrastinate. I found several books that taught some techniques of hypnosis and NLP. I took the best ideas I could find and I spent the next hour and a half doing what I am going to teach you right now.

Step One
Identify the Behavior You Want to Change:
Do It In Your Mind

I sat down in front of the television and held the remote control in my right hand. I then proceeded to do a hypnotic technique called "swish patterns," repeatedly. Here is how it worked (and how it has worked every time I have used this powerful, life-changing pattern!).

I closed my eyes and envisioned the television in front of me. I envisioned my right hand clicking the remote control. In my mind's eye, I saw the cable box changing from number to number . . . 34, 35, 36, 37, 38 . . . 69, 02, 03 . . .

Step Two
Decide What Behavior You Want to Do Instead:
See Yourself Rewarded

That was what I no longer wanted to experience—that was the endless loop of procrastination I needed to stop. Now I had to figure out what behavior I wanted to do instead—what specifically did I want to do instead of clicking the remote control?

What I wanted to do was to take action by writing to publishers. I wanted to write books that would change people's lives and I wanted to see the appreciation on the reader's faces . . . and I wanted to be paid very well for the work that I would do. How could I convert all of these "wants" into one short mental video that I would enact in real life? How could I create a behavior that I would do instead of continuing the clicking?

I decided that my new behavior would be to get up, go to the computer, and take action every time I saw the number 02 on the remote control. That would be my "stimulus" or "trigger" for the new behavior. What about the reward for changing the behavior, though?

My new video must go something like this—I see the TV. I see the 68, 69, 02, and, as soon as the 02 clicks on, I immediately get up and go to the computer. I start typing, and shortly I see the rewards that I really wanted coming out of the computer. I hear all the words people say as they come out of the computer. I see the money. I feel the sense of self-satisfaction. It all feels perfect. That is the new video.

Now we have to install the new behavior. I have two very specific videos that I have to splice together in a way that will create lasting change. That means as soon as I see 02, I have to get to work on something productive that I have been procrastinating about.

The Splice and The Swish

Now I see the new behavior in my mind. I see the cable box at 02 and the TV is on. I see myself getting up, going to the computer, starting to type, and I begin to experience the rewards I want to experience. That is the new behavior. I shrink this image so that it fits into a little tiny picture-in-picture box in the lower right-hand side of my mind's theatre. On the big screen is the movie of the procrastinating behavior. I see myself watching the movie of procrastination. I see the numbers 66, 67, 68, 69, 02 and then *swish!*

Immediately the tiny box in the lower right hand corner *explodes* onto the big screen. The old movie that was running has shrunk down to the picture-in-picture box at the bottom of the screen. You can not even see what's going on in that tiny picture. But you do see yourself going to the new behavior. In my case, I saw myself going to the computer, doing the work that would be productive, and receiving the rewards I wanted.

Then I let the small picture of the old behavior enlarge itself onto the screen again. I saw the old behavior. Lying on the couch, I click . . . 66, 67, 68, 69, 02 and *swish!*

Immediately the tiny box in the lower right hand corner *explodes* onto the big screen. The old movie that was running has shrunk down to the picture-in-picture box at the bottom of the screen again. You can not even see what's going on in that tiny picture. But you do see yourself going to the new behavior.

I did this 40 times in one hour. By the end of the hour, I now had a new response to seeing the 02 on the cable box. Until that day, I always just kept clicking. But now, I literally found myself getting up off of the couch and walking to the computer, beginning the projects that would richly reward me.

For me, I never had to reinforce this new behavior. I simply did it. Just like Pavlov's dogs, when the stimulus arrived, I responded! One hour of self-hypnosis changed my life. I have not procrastinated in over ten years. When something needs to be done that I deem productive, I simply get up and do it.

What Happens When the Swish Does Not Work?

It is going to happen to someone! No hypnotic technique works all the time. So, what do we do when this great swish technique does not work?

Self-sabotage that manifests itself in the form of procrastination is often the fear of success. As I noted earlier, this commonly occurs when a part of you does not believe you deserve success. You will find yourself needing to do some introspective self-hypnosis work if the swish does not work for procrastination. We will talk about this below.

Internal Dialogue

Internal dialogue is the sum of all the talking that goes on inside your mind. Internal dialogue should be composed of productive "discussion." Unfortunately, we often discover that as we use other hypnotic techniques they do not always work, usually because there is some unfinished business that has to be taken care of first!

If the swish pattern did not work for some reason, it is probably because there is what we call a "parts problem." These problems are generally easy to resolve.

Imagine you are beginning a weight loss plan, and you say to yourself as part of your autosuggestion program, "I see myself as twenty pounds lighter." Imagine that there is another part of you that says, "No way do I see myself as twenty pounds lighter. I have been this weight all my life." This is called incongruence.

The goal of internal dialoguing is to resolve this paradox. This is precisely why most self-talk programs and affirmation tapes do not work. When there is incongruence, there will be no change made. Affirmations or autosuggestion alone will not overcome incongruence.

The following self-hypnosis pattern will help establish a productive internal dialogue and make you more whole and integrated as a person. Whenever these incongruencies come to consciousness, you can deal with the incongruencies easily, as long as you use the general pattern that follows.

Internal Dialogue Problem Resolution Pattern

1) Close your eyes and say to yourself quietly, "Will the part of me that

does not want to stop procrastinating (or whatever the issue is) tell me why that is? It is important to me to be focused on my goals."
2) The part will tell you why it does not want to stop procrastinating.
3) Ask yourself, "What positive intention does this allow you to accomplish?"
4) The part tells you what the positive intention is doing for "you."
5) Another question: "First, I'd like to thank you. I appreciate that. Would it be okay from now on to still help me get that (positive intention) along with helping me to stop procrastinating?"
6) Part either agrees or airs the alternate point of view.
7) You say to yourself, "Thanks, and let me know if I ever seem to be letting you down!"

This is of course a very simple outline and many variables can come into the mix. If you run into problems with this quick, self help approach, a good hypnotherapist will be happy to help you resolve the issue for you in what normally takes only one or two sessions. These kinds of incongruencies are essential to resolve because you want to be able to do the things that are important to you. By the way, there is nothing wrong with talking to yourself. However, there is no benefit in having parts that create paradoxes in yourself!

In the vast majority of cases, these two procedures will overcome your procrastination. However, on a rare occasion your self-hypnosis techniques may not succeed in helping you reach your goals. In these situations, you will want to turn to the resources section at the back of this book and contact a professional hypnotherapist near you.

A Metaphor

I walk up to the closed door. It is wooden with three panels and a gold knob. I have been here before, and it feels familiar. I have a strange feeling as I take the knob and open the door. I step into the dark room. All around is lumber and unfinished projects. It is a small room and everything lays around, unfinished.

I look at the walls, and out the window, because there is not much to do in the room. Actually there are many projects, but I am just not sure where to begin or what to do. So I stare out the window—outside the window there is light and trees with leaves. There is a road and a walkway. There is a sense of freedom and adventure when I look out the window.

But I am inside. My attention turns back to the room. There is a closet on one wall. When I open the closet door, I find it is empty. I close the closet door and look around the room again. There is a picture on the wall. It is bright and colorfulan abstract in blue, red, and green. Yet still this room is dark. There is not much happening.

With nothing else to do, I start to clean up the room. I add a little color by hanging more pictures and bringing in a live plant. While I am decorating, I stop once in a while to work on one of the many projects that are waiting for attention. It is not so important that they get finished, only that they get attention. They give me pleasure and I feel a sense of satisfaction just in touching the materials and seeing the progress.

The room begins to feel more livable, more cozy, and warm. I do not want to add too much light—just a little indirect lighting against the wall, projecting upward. I will add another small lamp near the window. It feels so warm and inviting.

Now I bring a few books to read, along with a love seat, a table, and a chair. I vacuum and dust. Coats and tools will be placed in the closet. I will even change the curtains so that more light can pass through. I will be able to see more of the outdoors. It is so inviting that I want to spend many hours here, relaxing, in my own little world. I can do what I want to do, when I want to do it. I have a blanket and a pillow on the love seat. They make me comfortable when I relax there, reading books.

I open the window and enjoy hearing the wind blowing. I see leaves rustling in the wind, and feel the sunshine pouring into the window. I am not worried, but rather so relaxed. I am finally so cozy, content, and satisfied.

CHAPTER FOUR

Fear No More

Our bodies come equipped with the necessary tools for survival. Since the beginning of the twentieth century, great progress has been made in the study of stress, fear, and the body's "fight or flight response." It is now known that when the brain perceives a danger, whether real or imagined, it sends a signal to the hypothalamus, which is the regulator of the body's stress response. The hypothalamus sends a signal to the sympathetic nervous system that then prepares your body for a sudden response. Your blood rushes to the center of your body, increasing heart rate, blood pressure, and muscle tension. Your senses are sharpened as your digestion slows, your pupils dilate, and your hands and feet get cold and sweaty. Your body is prepared to go to battle or take flight and escape.

This is a very important ability required by the body to survive in cases of accidents, emergencies, battles, muggings, intruders, and even in competitive sports performance. However, when this type of stress continues over the long term, it has a destructive effect on the body. The adrenal glands continue to secrete corticoids into the body. These are adrenaline, epinephrine, and norepinephrine, which inhibit reproduction, growth, tissue repair, digestion, and the immune and inflammatory systems. Your health is endangered as these vital functions begin to shut down. In the long term, this can lead to a long list of chronic diseases and early death.

When the danger has passed, your brain sends a new signal to the nervous system instructing it to relax and return to normal functioning. However, if a person maintains a life filled with stress and fear, the wear and tear on the body will persist. Therefore, it is vital to your health to reduce stress and eliminate unwarranted fears. We will define "fear" as an ongoing, persistent irrational response, as opposed to "fright," a sudden, event-related experience.

F.E.A.R. = False Evidence Appearing Real

Fear is a projected negative assumption about an anticipated future event—it is an extraordinary alarm that goes off in response to a thought, not in response to an event that is occurring in the present. You may feel it, you may be reacting to it, but it is not based on anything connected to the present time/space. Therefore, in the strictest sense of the word, fear is not real.

While experiencing fear, you are not capable of enjoying the present moment. In fact, you may not be in touch with the experience of the present moment at all. You are projecting into the future in anticipation of a negative event, thereby also ruining any chance of pleasure in the now. If you take it one step further, you cannot really be fully alive while under the influence of fear.

Take a moment right now to think about something that you fear. While you are totally concentrating on the fear, how much of your present environment, activities, feelings, and experiences are you actually aware of? How much of the present reality do you miss while focused on your fears?

If it is true that we attract what we think about, fear is a surefire way of insuring the eventuality of a dreaded outcome. If we are consumed by the fear, we are pouring immense amounts of energy into actualizing the very thing that we fear.

People tend to experience reality in a way that confirms their beliefs.

Humans tend to perceive their reality in a way that confirms their belief system. If you believe something is true, you tend to notice the events and experiences in life that support, resonate, and confirm that reality. So not only might one be attracting that dreaded outcome, but one may also be oblivious to all the evidence that would conflict with their gloomy worldview.

The Nature of Fear

Fears differ from phobias. Phobias originate as a response to an event, most likely an alarming one, and then similar triggering events continue to bring on the same response. On the other hand, fears are conjured from the imagination concerning possible future events. And although there may be supporting evidence that helps to keep that fear in place, the effects of it are manifested *from* the mind and not a simple response to stimulus in the moment.

Fear is a form of worry—only stronger.

We all have fears. We are rational beings with conscious minds that allow us to remember the past and anticipate the future. It is when healthy concern for our survival and safety turns to irrational terror, or, at the very least a pervading stress, that it becomes a matter to be dealt with and healed.

In observing children, it is obvious that one is not born with fear. We come into this world innocent, trusting, and fearless. Fear is something that is learned. It is not innate. It is not the natural human condition, no matter how comfortable or familiar it has become.

Where Do Fears Come From?

There can be many sources. It may have been something you were told, or warnings or threats given. You may have seen something on television or heard it on the news. You may have grown up in a difficult neighborhood, had bullies in your class, or older siblings that liked to frighten you. You may have adopted these thought patterns from your parents and other environmental sources. Simply witnessing an event may have later created a generalized fear response.

Those who taught you fear may have had your best interests in mind at the time. Your teachers of fear may have been ignorant themselves, and were only repeating what they had learned through indoctrination. They may have wanted you to be safe and, therefore, bombarded you with loud protestations against certain risky behaviors. Their well-intentioned warnings may have become generalized over the years, to become a message that the world was not a safe and secure place in which to live.

A person who simply wanted to gain control over you or the situation may have also instilled fear in you. Fear can provide a shortcut to thinking by instilling an unreasoned response to a situation that becomes automatic over time. If you fear punishment for a particular behavior, you may avoid the behavior out of fear, and not because you have made a choice concerning a moral dilemma. In such a case, oftentimes you may not even be able to say why you avoided the behavior—you may have no reasonable explanation. You just know that it is not the "right" thing to do, and perhaps you will not mention the uneasy emotion that accompanies that automatic response.

The initiating cause of the fear may not appear to be directly linked to the continuing response until deeper scrutiny reveals the underlying sense of life of the person. A person's sense of life is acquired from the moment of birth, and perhaps from before. It is our sense of whether life is a safe or dangerous place to live. Our sense of life gives us our perspective, our colored glasses through which we view life. It contributes to our pessimism, optimism, confidence, and fears. It is an unconscious emotional response derived from the accumulation of all of our experiences.

If you were continually beaten or ridiculed, if you were sexually abused, or always left out of activities or decisions, your sense of life would be shaped in a different way than someone who was encouraged, supported, praised, held, and comforted.

Parents who continually criticized and withheld support for their child may have instigated what is now a fear of failure. The cause of a fear may be something more recent, such as a delay in a project giving way to uncertainty about its success, leading to fear about starting it up again.

How Do Our Fears Serve Us?

What purpose do we have in carrying our fears around? All too often, the fear response remains long after the initiating indoctrination has long faded from memory. Primarily, there is a part of us that thinks that maintaining the fear will somehow help us survive or stay safe. After all, that was the reasoning when it all began. We may consider it to be a vigilance that will prepare us for an eventual situation.

Our Fears are Familiar

Some people find their fears are comforting, familiar. There is an emotional element to fear that is distinct. It can certainly mask other feelings that are being neatly tucked away out of reach, such as sadness, loneliness, despair, inadequacy, and abandonment. Fear may even give a person an excuse to do or not do certain things. It may actually give them a sense of control over other parts of their lives where they would otherwise feel powerless.

By living in this fear condition, one is taken out of this present moment. Their mental focus is moved ahead to the imaginary future possible event, bringing into this moment a portion, or all, of the emotional stress that would accompany the real event. This translates into the person experiencing the reaction on a continual, or at least frequent, basis, with the irrational "rationality" that this will prime them for the actual event so that they are prepared for it or can avoid it.

> ***Living in fear takes you out of the present moment.***

We may try to pass off our fears as careful planning or practical apprehension. But, when it is accompanied by distinct bodily reactions, what was rational in the thinking stage, becomes a part of the fight or flight reaction of the autonomic nervous system.

Releasing our Fears

Perhaps you are ready to give away one or more of your fears. How would you like to ask someone else to carry it for you? The following is a guided meditation that will allow you to relax—find a safe space and ask for assistance from a heroic guest. He or she will come at your invitation, and you are welcome to hand over your fears to them for disposal. You may record the following meditation to make it easier to use. Record it, speaking slowly.

Find a quiet place to sit or lie down, free from distractions. Begin by giving yourself permission to set aside your fears for a while. You know that there is nothing to do about them for this moment, and it will be just fine to relax and rejuvenate yourself. Now, take a deep breath . . . and hold it . . . and now release . . . allowing the tension in your body to just float away with that breath. And again . . . breathe in . . . hold it . . . and now release . . . again relaxing even deeper. It feels so good to just let go . . . relaxing and releasing the tension. Breathing in . . . hold it . . . and out . . . even deeper . . . relaxing . . . Feeling so good . . .

Now imagine yourself in a safe place. It might be a place you have been to in the past or it might be a creation of your imagination. A safe place, that is just for you. A very special place, where you can relax . . . and unwind . . . and release . . . and let go . . .

What do you notice about your special safe place? Is it day or night there now? Are you alone or with others? What else do you notice about this place? How do you feel now that you are here? What would you like to do now that you are here? You can do anything that you want to do. It is your place, and you are safe here.

In this place, your personal safe space, you can invite a guest if you wish. That guest could be a hero that could remove from your life that which you fear. If you are willing to give up your fear, this hero would be willing to take it away and protect you from it forever. What would your guest look like? Would they be a man or a woman? How old do they appear?

Imagine that they are there with you now. Would you like to have a conversation with them? What would you say? What would they say? Allow yourself to discuss your fear with them. Tell them all about it. It is safe here and nothing can hurt or harm you in any way. How can your guest help you with your fear? Would you be willing to give over your fear to them now? Do that now. It is good to release yourself from that fear—from those thoughts and feelings.

It feels so good to be free of them . . . so free. Your guest leaves now, taking your fear with them to be dealt with and resolved. Watch them leave. Release them from your safe space. And, now here you are . . . free and light . . . feeling so good.

What would you like to do next? Would you like to stay in your safe space a little longer? Allow yourself to enjoy this time. Relaxing . . . so calm . . . so peaceful. Take your time . . . enjoy it . . .

When you are ready to return you will simply want to count from one to three. One . . . aware of this room . . . two . . . coming up . . . three . . . wide aware, relaxed and returned to the present moment.

Physiological Response to Fear

Typical physical reactions to fear include a prickling sensation, goose-bumps, an icy chill down the spine, weak knees, a tightening of the throat, constricted breathing, and heart flutters, pounding, or palpitations. One may also experience a quickening of the breathing, blood pounding in the throat or temples, nausea, and feeling paralyzed or disassociated from the body. Events and time may feel slowed or warped. One's hands may become clammy, the stomach clenches, and one may break out in a sweat.

Further body language may include flaring nostrils, dilated pupils, and wide, darting eyes. The person's movements may become constricted or jerky. The voice becomes high and strangled, and may crack.

Naming Our Fears

It is important when dealing with fears that you do not eliminate healthy caution along with the unwanted thought patterns. You do not want to become reckless. If you have a fear of being mugged, for instance, you will want to redesign your autonomic nervous system to relax in normal conditions, and yet be able to respond quickly and appropriately when danger is perceived. It would not serve your best interests to "heal" so well that you flirt with danger to the point that you willingly walk down dark deserted alleyways in high-risk neighborhoods. The goal is to bring balance into your life, not create a pendulum swing to the opposite pole.

Sometimes we walk around with a sense of fear and are not fully aware of it. Or we may be aware of the sense of fear, but can not (or have not) really named it. It could be perceived as background noise, or perhaps it is overpowering all other awareness . . . and yet we are not really sure what it is exactly that we fear.

In working through fears, the first step is to identify them. Oftentimes, in naming them, they lose their power over you. What fears do you have that you are aware of?

> *Naming your fears can render them impotent.*

Do not worry how silly or insignificant they seem to be. We have seen clients that had the following fears, for example: fear of not being liked, being hit, being yelled at, abandonment, not having enough food, coming home and finding everyone has moved, something happening to their children/spouse/parents, not having enough money, embarrassment, dying, loss, sex, intimacy, or being "found out" to be a fraud, to be seen, to not be seen . . . just to name a few.

Sorting Out Problems From Fears

Remember that fears are not real. If you have named something that is actually happening now, it is a problem, not a fear.

A word about problems—a problem is something that is occurring at present. It has presented itself and has not yet become resolved. A situation is only a problem if there can be a solution. If there is no possibility of a solution, there is no problem. Then it simply becomes a condition of life. There is nothing to be done about it.

For example, if your spouse has a history of physically abusing you and you are concerned about him coming home after a drinking binge, that is not a true fear. That is a problem. There is a real event happening, and there *is* a solution that you can act upon.

A life condition is something like the weather or the terrain of the country where you live. A condition might also be a health problem. For instance, if you have appendicitis and are required to remove the organ, this is no longer a problem. You have no choice. It will happen or you will die. Your focus and concern can turn from the issue of the operation to the problem of choosing the proper physician and hospital.

So separate out any "problems" and life conditions that mistakenly ended up on your "fear" list.

Resolving Fears

Once you have named your fears, you can begin to resolve them. Taking one listed fear at a time, and we will take it to its complete anticipated end. Writing one of the fears on the top of a piece of paper, or perhaps in your journal, answer the following questions:

- What is the very worst thing that you expect to happen concerning this fear?
- In what ways are you contributing to this fear becoming real?
- If that feared event were to actually happen, what would you like about that experience? (This seems odd to ask, but there may be some part of you that would enjoy or benefit from an aspect of that experience.)

Describe the process of what you expect to happen that will take you from this moment to that anticipated outcome. Provide as many details as possible.

Write a detailed story about what would take place, from beginning to end, if that event were to actualize.

Does this event possibility still seem that bad? That possible to happen? Even that likely to occur?

When you think of this fear, what do you notice about your physical body? What changes occur? Where do you notice any tension, pain, or sensations? Do your body movements change, such as increased blinking, hunching, or rigid, jerky movements?

When you think of this fear, what do you notice about your emotional responses? Are there tears, butterflies in your stomach, chills, or rapid breathing?

If you were to look even deeper past the fear, would you find any other emotions such as sadness, aloneness, or grief? Do you find any other mental reactions such as anger, repulsion, or vindictiveness?

A Writing Assignment

Write another story, with you as the main character, moving through the episode. Imagine the worst-case scenario. While writing, identify as closely as possible with the story, feeling the emotions, and noticing the visual and auditory details. Allow yourself to totally be immersed in the experience and in the fear. Continue to write these stories until you notice that your reactions to the scenes are not as intense. Perhaps you feel more prepared to deal with the possibility of this event occurring. Perhaps you have learned a new way of dealing with the situation that would avert any chance of it actually happening. Perhaps you come to realize that it would never really happen.

How has writing the story changed how you feel about that fear? Have you become desensitized to the subject? Are you bored with thinking and writing about it? Continue to write stories about that possible experience until your reaction to it has distinctly subsided.

Kinesiology Technique

As you begin to think about the subject that brings about your fear response, allow yourself to totally connect with the sensations and emotions that accompany it. Try to fully immerse yourself in the thoughts, feelings, and energy of the fear. As you connect with that intensity, take your hands and place the first two fingers from each hand on the corners of your forehead and gently pull outward. The corners of your forehead are along the hairline, above the temples, where the sides and crown of your head meet your forehead. Hold this "pulling" touch until you physically feel a distinct shift in your emotions and thoughts. You may release a sigh, and/or you may find that your mind cannot continue to concentrate on your fear. You should find that the level of intensity of the fear will not return to the same magnitude.

Relaxation Techniques

Fearfulness and relaxation cannot be accomplished at the same time. If you are concentrating on relaxation techniques, including self-hypnosis, visualization, or meditation, you will be unable to simultaneously focus on your fears. Give yourself permission to set aside your negative thought patterns for a period of time, and allow your mind and body to take a break for rejuvenation, clarity, and rest.

Taking a deep breath, allow your body to become relaxed and flaccid. Softening your muscles, relaxing even deeper. As you close your eyes, imagine you are looking at a dot of light. That dot is white. It just rests there in front of you, calm and still. Continuing to look at that dot of light, you notice that it begins to turn yellow. It appears like the sun now, bright and clear. It feels like it radiates warmth all around you. Now the dot of light begins to turn blue, like a small patch of sky. Clear and cool . . . so tranquil, so calm.

As you continue to gaze at the dot of light, it changes to purple. The color of a delicate flower . . . fragrant and fresh. So lovely. Now the dot of light changes back to white. Radiant and pure. The dot begins to grow larger and larger. It is as big as you, and now even bigger. Growing and surrounding you in its radiant warmth. Like being surrounded in energy from the sun. It feels so good to be here. So warm and safe. That light will stay with you for as long as you want. You only have to will it to stay. It will surround you and protect you and remind you to stay this relaxed. As soon as you feel that the light is solidly around you, you may open your eyes and return to the present moment . . . now once again in your wakeful state of mind. Knowing that you may return to that serene state of mind any time you choose to close your eyes and imagine that white light around you.

Turning to a Higher Power

Fear often shows its face in the areas of our lives that we feel we cannot control. When we fear that we are losing control we begin to restrict ourselves so much that, eventually, we feel we are about to burst! When fear becomes overpowering, we may turn to alternative ways of liberating ourselves from those feelings. These may include alcohol, drugs, sex, relationships, illness, thrill seeking, food, compulsions of all sorts, and even murder or suicide. Even losing our minds—insanity—may seem a more comforting alternative than living in the fear. We may subscribe to cult groups or organized religions because they offer some semblance of hope or an answer we can cling to, however irrationally, that alleviates the intensity of, or diverts our attention away from, the core fear.

> Even though I walk through the valley of the shadow of death,
>   I will fear no evil,
> For you are with me, your rod and your staff, they comfort me.
> —Psalm 23

Turning to a higher power, setting your sights on the bigger picture, having the knowledge that there is assistance from something more powerful than you, are helpful avenues to some degree. However, these are not the preferred methods of dealing with fear. They often only mask the real problems, and drive the anxiety and responses deeper down inside of you. The healthiest way of dealing with fear is to face it head-on. Name it, work through it, and, in some cases, seek it out and conquer it.

I would like to share with you a message I (M.L.) received from a friend recently:

"I flew yesterday. It was really windy with lots of wind shear. I know I have come along a bit because it would have scared me a couple of months ago, but I quite enjoyed it yesterday! Believe it or not, and I have not told anyone this, I decided to learn to fly because I felt myself becoming afraid of flying! As I got older and more aware of my mortality, I started to grow fearful of situations I perceived as hazardous, like flying! So what better way to overcome than to confront it! Now I love to fly!!! I'll sky dive next.

"I think confronting one's fears is the best way of dealing with them. When you are up close you can see them for the paper tigers that they are. I have also found the converse to be true. Letting fear dictate your actions invariable leads to a place you do not want to go."
—*Peter Gravestock*

The degree of fear a person has will often indicate how much they feel separated from the process of life. Fear can occur when a person lacks trust that they are exactly where they should be in their life. They have doubt that the lessons they are experiencing are beneficial to their spiritual growth and that with proper planning and preparation, things will turn out in the best possible way. Additionally, there is a doubt that they will be able to handle the situation if it were to actually occur.

> *Fear often occurs when a person is not comfortable with who, what, or where they are.*

Gaining clarity of your path, knowing your spiritual purpose, taking control of what is happening around you, and directing your own life will all support you in a way that will give you greater confidence and less fear.

Empower Yourself

Getting rid of a fear can be a simple, quick process or it can be complex and take time. It will be helpful to use the following empowerment technique to bolster courage and maintain the energy to carry you through to the complete dissolution of that fear. Placing yourself in increasingly challenging, yet non-destructive or life-threatening, situations can foster your self-confidence and sharpen your skills in handling difficult situations.

Take a deep breath and close your eyes. Envision yourself standing erect, wearing a talisman around your neck that covers your whole chest. It is so large that it forms a shield. You may design this shield in any fashion that you desire. Make it from any metals that you prefer—in a shape that suits you perfectly.

Embedded into this talisman shield are stones. Each one represents a strength that you have. Perhaps it is the courage that you showed in facing an earlier challenge. Perhaps there is stone that represents the perseverance that you exhibit in life. You might add one in for cunning, charisma, or for being quick witted.

What other characteristics do you have that would serve you well in your shield? Add them all in. What colors are your stones? How many are there?

Your shield may be etched with designs that represent past feats that you have accomplished, or that inscribe encouragement into your shield. Just be sure that it is designed exactly the way you want it.

As you stand there wearing your shield, what powers are you reminded of? In what way do you feel braver, stronger, or sharper?

While visualizing yourself in this shield, think about the fears you used to have. Imagine facing them while wearing your shield. Do they shrink in size? Do they fade in magnitude? Do they seem as potent?

Remember that you may visualize yourself wearing this shield anytime you feel it would be of help in facing and banishing a fear.

When there is still doubt about being able to handle an event, visualization of the situation is often the best method of overcoming the apprehension. For instance, perhaps you are a person who goes to single's dances, yet is afraid to ask any of the ladies to go for a cup of coffee afterwards. Perhaps you are not afraid to ask them, you are just afraid that they might say no. This is commonly referred to as fear of rejection. There are many underlying causes that might surface that have led to this fear of rejection, and those, too, could be addressed at some time. However, it will be simple enough to work directly with the presenting problem of how to muster the courage to ask some of these ladies to go out after the dance.

In utilizing visualization, simply sit quietly, closing your eyes if you like. Begin to imagine yourself at the dance. Feel the dance floor beneath your feet and hear the music. Notice the numbers of people socializing, dancing, and walking around. Smell the air of this place and notice the temperature. Then allow yourself to notice one of the women. Imagine starting up a conversation with her. What do you notice next? What does she do? Does she respond or does she find a way to move away from you? How do you feel? If she walks away, continue approaching different women until you engage one in a conversation. Then go ahead and ask her if she is interested in getting a cup of coffee after the dance. What occurs? How do you feel about it?

If she says yes, how do you feel? Even if she agrees to go, move on to another women and ask her out for the following evening. Continue until you have asked at least ten ladies to go out with you. Out of the ten, how many said yes? How many said no? How many were undecided or had other plans? How did you feel in each case? Did it become easier to do with each attempt?

While doing this exercise, you may come to realize that a "no" response does not necessarily mean that you are being rejected as a person. It may only mean that that person is not interested in the activity, not available, doesn't know you well enough to accept, or is not comfortable about going out with you. You are still a worthy human being.

Repeating this type of exercise will greatly increase your confidence in actually going out and doing it! It desensitizes you to the emotional reactions of the event. It allows the experience to be one that feels normal and one to which you are accustomed.

This is exactly the same process a salesperson would have to go through in order to overcome any fear of being turned down on a cold call or a sales pitch.

A Personal Visualization

Let us tailor a visualization that will be specifically suited for your own fear(s). Begin by choosing one of the fears from your list. Imagine yourself going through the entire scene of the actualization of that fear, from beginning to end. Use colorful details, including sights, sounds, smells, tastes, feelings, and emotions. When you have visualized yourself going completely through the scene, see the scene move backwards quickly, all the way to the beginning. Begin again through the scene to its completion. When you get to the end, rewind the scene to the beginning again. Continue to do this, forward and backward, until you can move through the situation with ease and confidence.

How do you feel about this subject now?
Has some or all of the emotional charge been dissipated?
How do you view this subject differently than you did before?
What will you do, or not do, now that you have completed this exercise?

On Being Frightened

Fear is different than dread in that the latter is something you do not want to do, but feel obligated to go through with anyway. With dread, the anticipated event is a known factor, while the projected events that bring on fear may or may not come to pass.

Fear is different from fright. Fright occurs in the moment of the event. Generally, it takes you by surprise at the instance that you are engaged in a terrifying experience. Fear, on the other hand, is a pervading reaction to the thought of something happening (or not happening).

Some people enjoy being frightened. In fact, a great majority of people enjoy some degree of fright. If not, why would horror movies and roller coasters be so very popular? Why else would Stephen King be a best-selling author or Alfred Hitchcock's movies be such popular classics? There is something about a good thrill that is alluring to large numbers of people.

In seeking out thrills, we get to test our reactions, we get to experience that adrenaline rush that may be absent for the most part in our everyday lives. In ancient times, there were constant threats to a person's life. A tiger wandering into the village, inescapable weather conditions, and attacks from warring tribes. We continually had the opportunity to face real danger and have our survival skills, dexterity, and bravery challenged and proven. There were plenty of occasions to get a dose of adrenaline. In modern times, we participate in sports or board games, gambling, or playing the stock market. We can find ways to sharpen our focus, hone up our agility, and drive our energy levels.

To the extent that a person refrains from such challenges, self-doubt and trepidation have the opportunity to creep into the psyche. It has been stated that if you fall off a horse it is best to get back on and ride as soon as possible. Facing our fears and moving boldly through them build our self-confidence and courage. It reminds us of how brave, strong, and capable we really are.

And remember that it is the telling of these stories about our close encounters with death, our heroic responses, our death-defying antics, and our brush with the monsters of life, that give us our own unique characters. These experiences color our lives, animate us, and set us apart from every other human on this planet. Therefore, if there are no monsters to slay, no adventures to set us apart, do we create them in our minds? Do our fears take the place of real dangers so that we find ourselves less boring? Do our fears help to remind us that we are still alive?

If we no longer felt the rush of the fear, would the neutral stance be too free of sensation?

A Metaphor

I stand just outside the castle wall. A young maiden, unsure yet curious. I lean against the wall, feeling the warmth it radiates from the rays of the sun. I want to sit down and relax, not walk or move on. Beginning to sense chatter, my attention turns towards the trees. Suddenly I become nervous, feeling that perhaps I am doing something wrong. I sit down, and huddle up, wrapping my arms around my knees. Perhaps I should not be found here.

The noise of the voices grows and it beckons to me. I follow the voices, tentatively but ever more curious. I do not want to move, but perhaps it will be worth it. As I walk into the trees, I do not see any people. Rather, I see figures of light. They surround me under this canopy of trees. They form a circle and ask me to sit with them, as they have made room for me to join them. I start to grow in stature to match their size. I am still physical, yet I too have the qualities of glowing light. The energy circles the group, around and around, in both directions at the same time. I have a deep sense of happiness and joy—an experience of tranquility and knowing. I feel as though I am a baby cradled in my mother's arms.

As it slows down, the energy flows just inside each figure of light. I sit there, feeling anxious as though there is something that I should be doing. So I stand in the middle of the circle, and begin to ascend, floating ever higher. As I move my arms, light swirls all around them. It feels so good. Everyone is smiling and nodding.

I become as a fire in the middle of the circle. I smile and am content. I want to touch the ground and know that I can. I float until my feet touch the ground. I feel tired and decide to move through the circle and into the woods. I am afraid that I will burn the trees—that the flame I am will set the trees on fire. But all is well, and my flame simply lights up the way. I can see my path. The trees have faces and without smiling or frowning, they watch me and encourage me. I hear them thinking *We see you,* keep going, and they indicate the way. I continue the adventure ever curious.

Facing Your Fears

Facing a fear head on is an effective way of banishing it. Some fears cannot be met in such a fashion, because to manifest them would be impractical or impossible. But if it is a fear concerning something manageable, such as fear of speaking in front of a group, or starting a conversation with a member of the opposite sex, then taking small steps towards that fear is the best and most effective way of moving through it.

Of the fears that you have listed, which ones could you face head on?
What steps can you imagine taking that would allow you to move up to and through each of these fears?
Imagine what it would feel like if you did not have that particular fear. How would your body feel differently?
What would you be able to do if you did not have that fear?

What would you be able to not do if you did not have that fear?
In what way would your life improve if you were to conquer that fear?
In what way might your life be worse if you were to conquer that fear?

Living Beyond Your Fears

Give yourself permission to put aside that fear for the next ten minutes. Know that if you choose to take up that fear again in ten minutes you can. Understand that the world will keep on turning for the next ten minutes even if you are not standing guard over that fear.

Take in a deep breath, allowing your physical and emotional tension to flow out of you with each exhale. As you relax and experience being free of that fear, how would you describe your feelings—both in your body and in your emotions? How is that different from how you normally feel throughout the day?

Imagine yourself in the future when you no longer have this fear. You have confidence, and trust that you are in control of your life and your future. That fear no longer is valid and has no place in your life. What do you notice about that future you? If in that future you had some advice for the present you, what would that be? From the perspective of that future you, if you were to turn around and look back over the time between then and now, what would you notice about the process that allowed you to arrive in that fear-free state?

The Fortress

Imagine a scene where you are standing in a fortress surrounded by the stone walls representing your defense mechanisms against this dreaded fear. Through the barred gate, you can see daylight and freedom from this condition. Only in pushing aside the bars that block your way, and passing through this threshold, will you attain the freedom of the meadows and blue skies that await you outside the fortress. No one else can go through the gate for you. Your freedom is only attained by your willingness to proceed.

You may inch through slowly, or march boldly through. Either way, you will never be the same. Once you have been outside the gates, and have experienced that new lifestyle, even if you choose to return to your guarded fortress, you will have the knowledge of and will have tasted the greater experience.

Only by facing and, ultimately, overcoming the fear, will you have the opportunity to move to the next level of enjoyment of life. Freedom!

CHAPTER FIVE

High Self-Esteem and Unshakable Self-Confidence

Self-esteem is the value that you give to yourself—it is the measurement of the worthiness that you have for yourself as a human being. A healthy self-esteem tells you that you are worthy to be alive, to think for yourself, and have independent goals. It is the love that you have for yourself. Self-esteem is your sense of worthiness, your right to be alive and to be happy.

Later in the chapter you will also learn about self-confidence. Self-esteem differs from self-confidence in that self-confidence is the belief you have about accomplishing something. If you were going to play against Gary Kasparov in a game of chess, you may experience very high self-esteem and very low self-confidence about your possibilities of beating the world chess champion. A person with high self-esteem will try very hard to beat Kasparov, persisting until it becomes impossible to win. A person with low self-esteem will likely give up almost immediately.

> *Self-esteem is a synergy of worthiness and competence.*

When you were born, a small baby coming into this world, there was no question about the value of your life. You fought and struggled to enter this world, you screamed for your needs as a human—food, warmth, comfort, and care—and you cried when it was delayed or denied. You held your life up as the one and only thing of value. You were in the center of your universe. To be the center of your own universe is to be egocentric.

Ego. What is that? You hear so many things about the ego it becomes confusing if you do not stop to sort it all out. Ego comes from the Greek word that means "I". It is funny to hear and read about the ego being a bad thing. It is a matter of semantics, because they are really referring to arrogance. To have an ego is vital. In fact, it is your ego that keeps you alive and well. It is your value for yourself that drives you to acquire the basics for survival. It is that which motivates you to work to get what you want out of life. It is, in fact, that which has inspired you to read this book. If you did not value yourself, why would you want to learn something and go to any effort to improve your life?

So, self-esteem and ego are positive and vital to our lives.

Another concept that has gotten a bad reputation is selfishness. Being called selfish has a connotation that you are doing something wrong. However, almost everyone is selfish. And that is a good thing! Being selfish is the only thing that is going to allow you to achieve your goals. It is the action of preserving your self-esteem. If you value yourself, in other words, you have high self-esteem, and being selfish is how you give yourself honor. By being selfish you make sure that your life is moving along as you have planned it. As you will it. As you desire it to be. No one else will look after your best interests better than you.

You might make mistakes but that is part of the learning process. For that reason it is always a good idea to get advice from people you trust and whose judgment you value. However, the choice of who that person would be is your decision, based on your estimation of their character. So, even asking another person for advice is an act of selfishness. You want the advice to make your life better. Who does that help? You.

When someone calls another person "selfish" in a derogatory fashion, it is generally because that person wants their own way, and the so-called "selfish" person is doing something that will delay or deny them their wishes. If anyone ever wants to make you feel bad by calling you selfish, take a long moment to analyze his or her motivation. What is it that they are trying to accomplish? Why is what you want any more selfish than what they want?

You have to be selfish in order to live an independent, goal-oriented life. To the extent that you give in to the wishes, desires, and demands of others, is the degree to which you are giving away your power to achieve your own dreams and goals.

Now, this is not to say that you can not have friendships and relationships, or that you can not come to agreements on small things. This is not to imply that you have to be stubborn and uncompromising. There is a difference. If it comes to where you will dine tonight and what movie you will see, perhaps that does not make a life-altering difference. Where selfishness is important is when you have a particular goal and someone is trying to distract, delay, or prevent you from achieving it.

An example is if you want to take up painting as a hobby. It is consequential to you and your creative expression. However, the demands of family and work just keep getting in the way. In this case, it is important to prioritize your desire, carving out both time and space in order to materialize your dreams. Can you see that if the spouse or children were to call you "selfish" because you were manifesting your dreams, it would only be because they "selfishly" want you to be attending to their needs before your own?

Your self-esteem is inversely proportionate to your willingness to sacrifice your needs, desires, and dreams for another person or situation.

A Metaphor

My daughter's name is Alice. She is so precious to me, but my heart always ached for her. She was born with one leg shorter than the other and she had such a difficult time even walking. She would sit in school and watch the other children giggle and pass notes. There would be secrets, playing, and special handshakes that she never was let in on. When the bell rang and the teacher dismissed the class for recess, all the other children would run outside and begin to have fun, playing on the equipment and with balls and bikes. But for Alice, walking was so difficult she barely had time to go to the bathroom during the recess period. She would limp and struggle, feeling so unattractive and unhappy. So she would stay indoors with the teacher, helping her clean erasers and blackboards. The teacher, Miss Franklin, was tall and very strict. She was not so very beautiful, but Alice thought she was.

One day when Alice was helping during recess, Miss Franklin sat her down and took hold of both of her hands. She told Alice, "It is not what the exterior is, you want to nurture and allow your interior to grow. Just develop and nourish it." Later Alice would tell me that when her teacher looked at her she felt whole and perfect.

Alice walked to the bathroom where there was the only mirror in the school. When she looked into the mirror, she was able to see just what the teacher could see. That reflection made her valuable and of worth. She was truly happy. I know that she carried that feeling for a long, long time.

Later, whenever people would make fun of Alice, she would always be kind to them, because she knew they must be hurting, too. Many years later Alice, too, became a teacher. She would always take the children that did not feel so good about themselves and bring out the very best in them. It feels so good to be able to help others.

The Building Blocks of Self-Esteem

The primary building blocks of self-esteem are reason and productivity. Reason is your ability to think and to make judgments. It is the recognition that your brain is capable of thinking things out and of coming to your own conclusions. It is the understanding that you are able to set out your goals and devise the path that will get you there.

Productivity is the measurement of what you have accomplished. It is not just punching in the timecard and moving through your day by rote. It is the distance that you have moved along that path towards your proscribed goal. It may be one small step, but that is more significant than all the papers you have filed, dishes you have washed, or errands you have run. If you have taken pen to paper and can only draw stick figures, that is a step toward your dream of painting. That is productivity.

When you can look back and trace the steps that have brought you closer to the actualization of your dreams, then you can determine your productivity. That is where you gain your sense of pride. You will know that you have accomplished something, no matter how small or grand. You will understand, and feel in your heart, that you are a worthy human being.

That is self-esteem.

Raising and Lowering Self-Esteem

Pride is equally vital to your life. Again, it is a word that is often misused to mean the equivalent of arrogance. Pride is the rational assessment of your accomplishments, the honoring of your productivity. To be proud of your accomplishments is natural and healthy. It is the feeling you have, based on the truth of your life.

Arrogance, on the other hand, is an inflated view of what you have accomplished. Arrogance exaggerates stories and often attempts to hide the person's self-doubt and disappointment that they have not done better with their lives.

So when someone calls you selfish, proud, and egotistical, you can smile sweetly and thank them. If you are called arrogant, altruistic, and sacrificing, you will want to examine your life to see if that is true, and what might need to be changed. Perhaps they are wrong. On the other hand, perhaps you need to make adjustments in certain areas.

Besides arrogance, altruism and sacrifice are the destroyers of self-esteem. Altruism and sacrifice are very closely related. They have been touted as virtues throughout history, but you might want to check your sources. Whenever someone tells you it would be good for you to be altruistic or to sacrifice, examine his or her motives. What will they gain by your sacrifice?

Again, we have to be careful in our understanding of altruism and sacrifice and how they operate in our lives. It is not a sacrifice to put off buying that new car because you want to save money to put your children through college. If your value system includes having happy, educated children, then saving for their education is not a sacrifice by any means. If your goals include making this world a better place for you and your children by making your city a safer, happier place to live, then helping hand out blankets and food at a homeless shelter is not altruistic, but an expression of your value system.

Altruism is the act of putting yourself at a disadvantage for the sake of another person. Sacrifice is giving up something of value to you for something of less value. Neither of these acts serve a purpose in raising your self-esteem. They are counterproductive to your value system and to the achievement of your goals—both will drain you of your energy, your resources, and your life. Before long, you will not have any more to give and you will end up on the receiving end, begging and relying on the goodness of others.

Bill Gates is a good example of a selfish, egocentric person. He has done what he wants, built his dream, and gone after his goals relentlessly. His productivity has brought rapid growth in the world's technology. It has made this technology available to the masses, making life easier for millions of people. Furthermore, he has earned billions of dollars that he has chosen to donate to charity. What if Mr. Gates had given up his dreams? What if he had "selflessly" chosen to work for someone else, doing the jobs that he was told to do, not creating any waves? No—it was his brains and ability to think and make judgments (reason), his unwavering drive to create his dreams (productivity), and his belief in himself and desire to make it happen (self-esteem) that has propelled the technology of this world the farthest (and in the shortest length of time) in our history.

In order for you to become enthusiastic about your own goals, it is important to understand what your purpose in life actually is. Many people feel like they are floundering in life, and even think they are not very important, because they have not figured out what it is they really should be doing. Some people know right from the start what they want to do with their lives, and others have a harder time focusing in the right direction.

The following meditation will help you to determine what your purpose in life might be. Feel free to record it so that you can relax, allowing it to guide you through the process. Pause briefly between paragraphs to enhance the effect of this meditation.

The "Do and Be" Room

Sit back in a comfortable place, free from distractions. Allow your eyes to gently close as you begin to pay attention to the rhythm of your breathing. Just breathing, in and out, in and out. Notice any tension that you sense in your body. Tense up the muscle and hold it . . . and then release. Relaxing even further. Breathing into your body, relaxing your muscles . . .

Imagine will a hallway stretching out in front of you. As you begin to move down along the hallway, you begin to notice the texture of the floor covering beneath your feet and the color of the walls. Notice the decorations and the lightness or dimness of this hall. As you continue to move along the hall, you notice that there is one doorway.

This door leads to the "Do and Be" room. This is a room where you can do anything that you want to do, and be anybody you want to be. When you enter this room it will be very much like when you were a small child, and you would play for hours as and in your favorite make-believe roles. Do you remember when you would play and you would completely become the character that you were pretending to be? When you enter this room it will be exactly like that. There will be objects in this room that will provide you with everything you need to accomplish the purpose that is most suitable for you. Now as I count from three to one, you come to stand in front of that door to the "Do and Be" room. Three . . . two . . . one . . . and what do you notice about the door you are standing in front of?

Are you ready to step through the door? When you are ready, go ahead and step through. As you enter the room, what do you notice first? Is it light or dark here? What objects do you begin to notice around you? When you are in the "Do and Be" room you have all the time in the world to explore and enjoy and play. Go ahead and take your time to explore. What else do you notice about this room? What else do you notice about the objects in the room? What do you enjoy doing most when you are in here? What do you learn about yourself as you explore the room?

What have you learned about your purpose? How could you begin to accomplish this in reality? When do you plan to begin? When you have enjoyed the "Do and Be" room fully, and when you are ready to return, you simply have to count from one to three. When you do you will return to the present moment refresh, relaxed, and remembering all that you have learned from this experience. One . . . two . . . three . . . Wide awake and alert, and returned to the present moment.

It is advisable to write down your experience, detailing all that you noticed in the "Do and Be" room. Although some things may not make total sense when you first experience it, more may become clear after some time has passed.

Self-Esteem is Self-Love

If you can not love yourself, how can you possibly love someone else? So many problems in relationships stem from the lack of self-esteem and self-love of the parties involved. Many times people will choose a partner based on a lack or need within themselves. They seek to fulfill that need through the other person.

Not only does that set up a co-dependent relationship, but it further fosters a growing sense of resentment in each of the parties. One can never provide self-esteem for another person. It is something that is within you and can only be nurtured by you.

Let us look at your personal self-esteem. Give some thought to, and answer, the following questions:

How would you rate your self-esteem at present?

In what ways do you love yourself?

In what ways do you feel badly about yourself?

In what situations do you find yourself holding back from going after what you want?

To which people do you give over your power or authority?

What goals would you like to achieve?

What is preventing you from attaining them?

Throughout our lives, we have been given messages from other people that have contributed to our view of ourselves. These messages can be encouraging and supportive, or they can be stunting and abusive. It will be important to discover those messages that you have received, trace them back to their roots, and decide whether they are valid and supportive of your life and goals, or whether they are invalid and destructive towards your life.

Everything that we have ever experienced (heard, tasted, touched, felt, seen, smelled, or thought) is housed in your unconscious mind. Whether or not you can recall any of it, it is still there. All of these experiences continually contribute to our sense of life. Sense of life is our worldview, our perspective, the "colored lenses" through which we view life. Our sense of life tells us whether this is a safe world or not. It contributes to whether we are optimistic or pessimistic. It plays an important part in how we see ourselves in relationship to all that is around us.

The messages, or scripts, which are delivered to us, and forever remain lodged in our unconscious minds, can be insignificant, or can drill away at us, becoming a part of our reality. Like you have heard it said, if you hear something long enough you begin to believe it. So, if you were given a message that made you feel unworthy all during your childhood, you may have come to believe it. Further, you may no even be able to hear all the other messages that would argue to the contrary.

What scripts do you hear playing in your head about yourself? Let us take a look at what recordings you have stored up through the years.

Put a check next to the messages you hear in your head.

Positive Messages

You are so pretty, beautiful.
You are so smart, bright.
You are very clever.
You are so creative.
You are punctual.
You are responsible.
You will be so successful.
You are always so nice, pleasant.
You are so very welcome here.
We love seeing you.
We love having you here.

You do such a good job.
You are so interesting.
You have a bright future.
You always make the right choices.
You should be proud of yourself.
You will go far in life.
Everyone likes you.
You are really wonderful.
You are important to me.
Other _____
Other _____

Negative Messages

You are ugly.
You are stupid.
You are not very clever.
You are always late.
You are so irresponsible.
You will never amount to anything.
You are mean and nasty.
We do not want you around here.
I do not want to see you ever again.
You do sloppy work.
You are dull and boring.
You will end up in the gutter or digging ditches.
You can not think for yourself.
You should be ashamed of yourself.
You have no future.
Nobody likes you.
You do not deserve love.
You would be nothing without me.
Other _____
Other _____

What do you notice about your responses? How many are positive? How many are negative? If there is a preponderance of negative scripts, it would show a need to start working diligently on desensitizing those past experiences and messages.

By desensitizing them, you will take away or alter the power they have in your life. They will no longer effect you in the same manner that they have. In this way, you will be able to leave those experiences and messages behind you, learn what lessons they provided for you, and move into a new sense of life.

The positive messages that you responded to above are favorable influences in your life and will be left in place. The negative statements that you recognized will be the ones that we work on here.

A Tool to Increase Self-Worth

Before we start to work on desensitizing the negative messages, it will be helpful for you to have some positive tools to work with. One that will be helpful for you would be a symbol of your self-love. This will be something that represents a time when you have felt really good about yourself and that you were worthy of love.

You may begin by taking in a deep breath and relaxing in a comfortable location, free of distractions. Now go back to a time in your life when you were really feeling good about yourself. You knew that you were a good person, worthy of life and all that it has to offer—a time when you felt capable of achieving whatever you set your mind to doing.

Perhaps this event was a time during school, or in sports, or at work, or at home. A time when you felt good about who you are. As you think of that time, notice how your body feels. What are you experiencing? What does your energy feel like? As you think about this event and notice the sensations that you are experiencing, imagine that you are holding a symbol that would represent this event and these feelings.

What does your symbol look like? How big is it? What color is it? How do you feel when you hold it?

Still holding your symbol in your hand, remember a recent incident when you were experiencing self-doubt and feeling insecure. How does that event seem different now that you are viewing it with this symbol in your hand? What might have changed had you had that symbol in your hand then? How do you feel differently about that incident now?

Remember that this symbol is for you to visualize and hold any time that you want to experience this heightened sense of worthiness and self-love.

Now, whenever you are ready to open your eyes you simply need to take another deep breath and sense your surroundings. Feel yourself here in the present, in your body, and open your eyes. Now.

Learning About the Roots of Those Scripts

Let us begin to work towards desensitizing your feelings about these statements by examining the nonproductive scripts that prevent you from achieving your dreams. Working one at a time with each of the negative statements that you had marked earlier in this chapter, answer the following questions:

When you hear the statement in your head, whose voice do you hear?
What do your emotions feel like?
If it is anger, is there any other emotion or emotions underneath that anger?
When you feel those emotions, where do you sense those feelings on your body?
If you were to look at that area, what color or shape would that sensation be?
Is there a way that you could change the color or shape in order to make it feel more comfortable? If so, go ahead and do that now. Now how does it feel?
What do you know now that you did not know then about the person who said those things to you?
What is it about that person that would cause them to say such things to you?
How were they feeling about themselves?
How old does that statement make you feel?
If you could sit down and have a conversation with the child that was you at that age, what would he or she like to hear from you that would make him or her feel better?
What wisdom could you share with him or her that would help the child understand why the person is saying those things?
How does that make the younger part of you feel?
Is there anything else that you could say or do to make him or her feel better and not accept the negative messages that the child is hearing? What positive thing about yourself can you tell that younger you that will help the child to feel better about who he or she is and who the child will turn out to be?

Can you show the child your symbol of self-love?

Can you share it with or give it to him or her?

How does having that symbol make the child feel?

How will having that symbol change how the child handles the messages that he or she is hearing?

Is there anything else that you can do for that child at that age to help him or her feel better?

What would you have rather heard instead of the negative messages that were given?

Can you say that new message to the young child that was you?

How does that make the child feel to hear the new, positive message?

Desensitizing Your Responses

Now that we have examined these statements and discovered the basis for why they affect you, let us begin to desensitize your feelings towards them. In this way, you will be able to put these thoughts and feelings behind you and move on freely into your future.

Choose one of the above negative statements that has been affecting your thinking and your feelings. Go back to a time when you heard that message. Play out the entire scene from start to finish. Now play the scene backward to the beginning. Now begin playing out the scene again, this time making the person who said the negative statement look ridiculous by putting a clown nose on their face or a dunce hat on their head. When you have come to the end of the scene, play it all backward to the beginning again. This time, as you go through the scene, make that other person shrink while you grow to be larger. Move through the scene to the finish and then rewind again to the beginning. Now play the scene forward and backward over and over again until you get really bored doing it.

If you repeat those steps until you are thoroughly bored, you should have no noticeable reaction to the statement when you hear it in the future. That script may actually have become comical, depending on how ridiculous you have made the other person look in your scenes. You will now be free of the effects that statement has previously had on you. Repeat these steps with each negative statement until you have achieved desensitization for all of them.

Self-esteem is the basic building block of life. With high self-esteem, your life will be all that you have dreamed of. With self-esteem you will have increased confidence, which will allow you to increase your knowledge and abilities, and, most importantly, give you the freedom to live your own life.

Unshakable Self-Confidence

Earlier in this book you read about the elimination of irrational and unwarranted fears. Unwarranted fear is the door that stops progress toward that which we want in life and it is the door that closes on self-confidence. If you skipped over the chapter about resolving your fears, go back and read it now, because fear and self-confidence do not reside together. They can not dwell in the same mind together because they are opposite states of mind.

Using self-hypnosis and visualization allows you an opportunity to create believable futures in your mind. When you create a future in your mind that you believe you can truly attain, then self-confidence comes as a byproduct of this new frame of mind. Self-confidence is in large part a belief about you. Once you see in your mind's eye the direction you are going and what your future is, then the action you take to live your dream will obviously help you achieve your goals. The certainty of this fact is the birth of self-confidence.

> *Self-confidence is a belief about your ability*
> *to perform in some context.*

In Napoleon Hill's incredible encyclopedia of personal achievement, *The Law of Success,* he compellingly shows that there are six basic fears that stand in the way of you and self-confidence.

The fear of Poverty.
The fear of Old Age.
The fear of Criticism.
The fear of the Loss of Love of Someone.
The fear of Ill Health.
The fear of Death.

Overcoming these fears leads directly to being able to build the foundation of self-confidence. There are many opposites and antonyms of fear. Some of these are confidence, security, love, and trust.

Self-confidence is something that springs, in part, from persistence. In fact, persistence is one of the keys to developing self-confidence. Self-confidence is a commodity that is developed over time. The formula for developing self-confidence at the cognitive level would be as follows.

1) Know what you want in life, specifically. (Clearly define it by writing "it" down!)
2) Actively and persistently pursue that which you want in life.
3) Be aware that thoughts are things and that which you allow to reside in your mind is that which will ultimately be attained.
4) Take action in your life that will lead directly toward attaining that which you are pursuing.
5) Use self-hypnosis as outlined in this chapter to program the unconscious mind with feelings and experiences of self-confidence.
6) Be certain you know what you will do in return for reaching your objective(s).
7) Know that there will be others you will meet in life who are pursuing that which you pursue . . . and that the law of attraction will help them come into your life.
8) Cause others to believe in you by taking massive amounts of action and doing massive amounts of service for others in pursuit of your goals.
9) Watch people's perceptions of you change as you become more charismatic and certain.
10) Accept your new feelings of self-confidence with humility and appreciation.

People who have a high level of self-confidence are not afraid to go out and "do it now." They may have no more skill or competence than anyone else, but going out and doing "it" is no problem because they feel certain they will succeed. They are less afraid of making mistakes and utilize more opportunities to succeed than those who have low self-confidence. Self-confident people, in general, make more mistakes than those who are not self-confident, but they also have far more successbecause of their certainty in themselves.

Confidence and competence should not be confused, of course. Competence means that a person has the ability to do something well. There is an enormous population of competent people who are not self-confident. Some competent people simply worry that they will fail.

Therefore, they spend time trying to become perfect so that they do not make mistakes when they set out on a new project or try to find a new relationship. Perfection is impossible and making very few mistakes can only happen if you use very few opportunities. In order to develop self-confidence, therefore, you want to allow yourself the experience of making a mistake, or even failing once in a while.

There is a certain charismatic quality that exudes from people who are self-confident. You will almost always notice a sense of attraction, an almost magnetic quality toward people who have confidence in themselves. We feel at ease with people who are comfortable with themselves.

On more than one occasion, Elvis Presley was known stop mid-way through the first verse if he felt he or his band was off even a little. It never bothered him to say, "No, we're off key, let's get it right for the audience." The band would start playing again and he would be energized because he was going to do it right. I always thought that was a good slice-of-life lesson because if the person who was the world's most charismatic entertainer could make a mistake and say so in front of 50,000 people, why couldn't I do the same thing? When Presley was on stage his self-confidence was often total. He took many chances in front of thousands. He did not care if he looked bad starting the song over. He was going to do the right thing for the people who were there to see him. That was one part of his charisma.

You can have the same experience. In a sense, we all can be like airplane pilots. We set our course—then we take off. We get off course and we have the opportunity to make adjustments. Certainly, many people do not get back on course, and many people do not set a course in the first place. You do not have to be like most people, though. You can begin to take control of your life and set your course. You can allow yourself to fly off course and then re-set yourself and get back on course, knowing that if you stay focused you will get to where you want to go. It takes a lot of self-confidence, though. You must be able to allow yourself to drift off course and make mistakes. You must allow yourself to be able to correct yourself mid-flight and not try to make everything perfect from the start. There has never been a flight plan where a plane did not go off course in mid-flight. There simply are too many variables to control. Be like a great pilot. Plan well, be safe, be secure, be prepared, and then take-off. Make corrections and adjustments as you fly toward your destination, knowing that you will get there!

A Metaphor

Julie was just a little girl and usually played all alone. She was not that popular and the other kids did not always choose her to play with them. She never knew from day to day whether she would be asked to come over and play or not. Julie enjoyed being by herself, but it sure would have been nice to have had other friends to play with once in a while. Sometimes there were games that Julie wanted to play that required more than one person, but she had become too shy and insecure to ask the others to come over. They might say no, or tease her like they sometimes did. She did not really understand why that happened. But it did not feel very good inside.

One day, she was invited to come over and play with the neighborhood children. They were all sitting in a circle, cross-legged. That was really fun. Everyone was laughing and telling stories. Someone even had cookies for everyone to eat. Julie enjoyed the feeling of being a part of the group. It was fun and it made her feel so good inside.

When it was her turn to tell a story everyone became very interested. Her story was so detailed and colorful. The other children were fascinated by Julie's story, but she did not know exactly why they should be. After all, it was a story that she had pieced together from several books that she had read. She thought they would find her story silly because it was not her original story, but no one seemed to know that. They were all giving her their attention as she grew more and more animated in the telling of her story. When she finished, another child began to tell a story and her thoughts began to wander away. She was thinking back on her experience as the storyteller and was trying to understand something that was beginning to creep into her mind.

She realized that while the other kids were playing together all the time, she had been reading adventurous books, and had been writing her own stories and taking time to contemplate many things. She was already feeling more grown up and mature than her neighborhood pals. She had something inside of her that she did not find in any of them. She was giving that a lot of thought as the other child finished up his story. She looked around her and saw that these young faces began to fade. In their stead, she saw a much different scene. A scene in which she found herself standing up and walking to a door.

As Julie took hold of the doorknob and turned it, she could feel herself growing taller and becoming older. As she walked through that door, she discovered that she perceived herself as an older, more mature person.

In her mind's eye she no longer was in the circle with the other children. She now saw herself entering an auditorium, where many students were coming in and finding their seats. At first, Julie was not sure whether to find a seat or to walk to the podium.

My goodness, she thought. *What will I say to these people? What if they are bored by my words or do not like me?* The more students that entered the hall, the more confused and anxious Julie felt. Then she looked around and made eye contact with just a handful of the students. When she looked at each of them she realized that what she had to say just might affect their lives in a positive way. Then she understood that it did not matter if most of the students found her talk boring, if she could just make a difference in one person's life that day.

Confidently she moved to the podium. A vase filled with flowers had been placed there. She began to speak, from her heart, telling the audience of her knowledge and the wisdom she had gained over the years. Some of their eyes were glazed over, but a few of them were riveted on her in attention. Julie felt so good expressing herself, sharing her feelings and giving of herself to those students.

When she was finished, several of the students approached her with questions and stories of their own. There was laughter and joy.

Circle of Confidence

The "Circle of Confidence" is one of our favorite hypnotic experiences that creates self-confidence quickly.

Imagine that you would like to have dynamic self-confidence in certain situations. For example, the next time you go talk with your boss or go on your sales calls you might want to have self-confidence that makes you virtually unstoppable. The "Circle of Confidence" will help you move toward this powerful experience. Follow the process below and you will experience high-powered self-confidence today!

1. Stand up in such a way that you have at least four feet in front of you and two feet of floor space behind you.
2. As you stand up, close your eyes and return to a time when you felt totally self-confident. Return to one specific event where you had the self-confidence that you would like to have when you are going to need it most. As you think about this experience, imagine that you are back in your body at that time . . . and that you see what

you saw then, hear what you heard ,and feel what you felt. Be there now . . .

3. When you feel totally self-confident, imagine a circle surrounding your feet where you are standing now. The circle can be any color at all . . . what color is it for you?

4. As the feelings of self-confidence begin to fade, step backward one step, out of the circle, and let all of the feelings of self-confidence stay in the circle, waiting for you to step back in.

5. Take a deep breath as you step forward into the circle, bringing in all of the feelings of self-confidence that you had left here and that you can take forward with you out of the circle when you are prepared to go forward.

6. Feel those feelings of self-confidence and notice how you change inside. Notice how your posture changes. Notice how your breathing changes. Notice how you feel.

7. Step backward out of the circle, leaving all of the feelings of self-confidence within the circle . . . as you can only take them forward with you, not backward.

8. Notice the change and the lack of self-confidence that is behind the circle.

9. Take a deep breath as you step forward into the circle. Feel all of the feelings that the circle is there to give to you. Soon you will be able to take them forward with you into specific situations.

10. Think of a trigger to remind you of these feelings. Maybe you see a door handle in front of you . . . and maybe that is the door to your next sales call or your boss's office. From this moment forward when you see a door handle or a doorknob . . . or even a door or entry way, you will see and feel your circle of confidence under you and then you can walk forward through the door with unshakable self-confidence.

11. Now, walk forward, out of the circle, and bring those feelings with you as you open the door that you see within your mind's eye. Good!

Who Do You Know That Has Great Confidence?

We all know someone who we would like to emulate in some way. Whether the person is a celebrity, a friend, or an acquaintance, we all see good qualities in other people. The quality of confidence is one we are drawn to. We all are interested in people who have that sense of comfortable certainty about them. Using a similar tool of hypnosis that we did in the "Circle of Confidence" exercise, we can bring in the characteristics another person holds into our self as well. In some ways, this is like modeling other people. The process works wonderfully well and you can use it anywhere you are.

Confidence Modeling

1. Think of someone you know, or know quite a bit about, that has great confidence. This should be someone you would like to be like in some ways. Close your eyes and think of that person now.
2. See that person in your mind's eye behaving in a confident manner. Notice how they move, how they carry themselves, how their face and eyes look. What is their posture like? Notice how they walk. Notice how they use their hands.
3. Notice how they interact with other people. Notice how they communicate with others. Notice the words they say and the way they talk. What are their vocal intonations like?
4. Imagine that person is standing in front of you now. Imagine that you can take one step forward and walk "into" them and take on all of their qualities of confidence and certainty. Imagine they are like a hologram. They are right there in front of you, just waiting to share their space with you!
5. Imagine that person is one step in front of you and you can feel the confidence emanating from them. You can see, feel, and hear them communicating with certainty and clarity. They are comfortable with everything and everyone around them.
6. When you can actually feel the confidence they exude, take one step forward and let them merge into you, taking on all of their confidence and sense of inner strength.
7. Take another step forward and notice that those feelings now stay with you and allow you to feel even more confident and self assured. You do not just feel self-confident, you ARE self-confident.
8. With this new experience and feeling of self-confidence, look around in your mind's eye and see who there is to communicate with, so you can take advantage of this new found confidence.
9. Notice how people respond to the more confident and more comfortable you.

10. Decide if this is how you would like to be and act from now on. If it is, take one more step forward and feel the feelings and experience of self-confidence permeate every fiber of your being . . . now . . . good.

11. When you open your eyes you can bring these feelings and learnings with you into your everyday experience, knowing that you can always add another person's inner strength into your own. You can let go of this individual's confidence by simply stepping three steps backward and releasing those feelings at will.

12. Now, open your eyes. Take one, two, three steps forward and be as confident as you now are and desire to be from this day forward . . .

The Mountain Metaphor

Close your eyes and take a deep breath in . . . and hold . . . and release . . . take another deep breath in . . . and hold . . . and release . . . good . . .

The mountain has been calling you for years . . . you have been afraid for so long to climb the mountain for so many reasons . . . you have wanted to see the view of everything that is from the peak of the mountain . . . you have wanted to know something other than the meadow . . . which . . . although beautiful . . . and familiar . . . is only the meadow . . . and you have been coming here for years and years and years . . . and once again you see the mountain . . . but you have always been afraid . . . Sure, those that ascend the mountain came back wiser . . . and happier . . . and healthier . . . but it could take a long time to climb the mountain . . . experience the mountain and come back down changed . . . a long time . . .

From the meadow you can see the peak of the mountain . . . the snow around the top . . . and you know that there are overlook points on the mountain that would allow you to see . . . with clarity . . . all that is around you . . . for miles and miles and miles . . . but it is so far up to the overlook points . . . and the meadow is, after all, a beautiful place to come to . . .

You wonder what would happen if you fell and hurt yourself or became exhausted from climbing . . . it could be a very frustrating experience . . . you imagine . . . yet . . . you know that it would change your life . . . but you would feel the pain of the trek . . . the pain and the effort to climb the mountain is enormous . . . the experience is not even certain . . . you may get up there and be fogged in for a day or a week or more before you can experience the view . . . the clarity of vision . . . the insights that you seek . . . so why not stay in the meadow . . . it is pretty here, after all . . .

You look up and the mountain calls. It has been calling you for years . . . but part of you is afraid . . . you would look down and you would feel like you might fall . . . you would probably lose your grip and hurt yourself like you did when you tripped in the meadow the other day . . .

. . . and then you wonder what would happen if, maybe, you simply kept your eyes on the peak and did not look back . . . what would happen if you stayed focused on the peak like a target and simply continued regardless of the elements . . . after all, you know that eventually you would get to the top if you climbed just a little bit every day . . . and even if you slipped and tripped you could always get back up, even in pain and continue on . . . knowing that you would make it . . . just because you decided you would make it . . . and it might be foggy . . . and you might not see anything . . . but then you do not see anything from the meadow . . . there is no clarity here either . . . you can not see all that is from here . . . so staying here . . . in the meadow . . . is no different from climbing the mountain and being fogged in . . .

You decide you will do it . . . you will keep your eyes focused on the peak . . . you will climb the mountain carefully and with the certainty that you will reach the top . . . and that everyone at some point in their life must make the trek out . . . to see what is "up there."

You collect your backpack and all of the tools and utensils you will need for the adventure . . . and you begin your climb . . .

As you suspected, the backpack is heavier than you are used to and you find it is difficult to negotiate the narrow trails that have been made virtually invisible by their lack of use. Yet, a growing part of you inside knows that you can climb this mountain if you stay focused.

Your map shows that this trip will take several days . . . maybe more . . . but as you climb . . . you realize that this is what life is about. You begin to believe in yourself. You sense that you have what it takes to not only climb this mountain but the ability to maybe make it an adventure.

The first night comes and it rains hard at the lower elevation. Your little pup tent provides some relief from the rain but not much from the cold . . . that goes through your body. You begin to wonder what you were thinking. It certainly is not raining back in the meadow and it certainly is not raining back in the quaint little home you packed up in last night . . . yet . . . the adventurous part of you decides it is time to move on . . . up . . .

It is time to venture upward again . . . the rain pouring down on you . . . and you slide and slip through the mud and wet grass heading in a mostly upward direction . . . until you fall on your back . . . and backpack

. . . the rain pouring in your face . . . and you feel a sudden soreness . . . and for some reason you laugh. You begin to see that it is almost as if some-one laid this experience out for you as a kind of game and your difficulty level had been raised up . . . and when you think of it that way you really laugh out loud and get up . . . not even bothering to scrape the mud off of your back . . . and you hurt and you climb . . .

Part of you wonders if life is like a game . . . with rules and bound-aries and random events that make you slip . . . to build character . . . and strength and problem-solving skills . . . and then you wonder . . . how would you win . . . if it were . . .

. . . all day you think of life as a game as you climb higher and higher . . . the rain stops and you appreciate that . . . and the trail flattens for a stretch and you appreciate that to . . . if life was a game you could only win if you did everything you could with whatever you had . . . like that old story of the talents you had heard when you were a child. Use your tal-ents and you are rewarded. Let them stay unused and you lose . . . The story said that everyone is given a different number or type of talents . . . it certainly is not fair . . . but the winners are those that take their talents and use them . . .

You know that there are some things you are good at and some things that you can learn so you can be good at other things . . . and these things are all things you are certain can help you make it . . . to the top of the mountain or to win a game . . .

The climb is going well by the final day . . . you feel as if you have learned that one thing it true—if you believe in yourself then you can do almost anything . . . including climbing this mountain . . . If you stay focused on the peak you will get there . . . it is part of the game. You get there . . . if you are willing to play the game . . . falling, tripping, getting wet and muddy, being sore and tired, straining muscles, and feeling like a novice at every turn. You realize that if you are willing to do that you will win the game . . .

That's it, you think . . . if you know it is a game you can go forward and play . . . if you can see the peak and follow your map, you will get there. It is not going to be easy . . . because anyone can do something that is easy and the rewards for easy are essentially nothing. The rewards for believing in yourself and taking on challenges though . . . they . . . are . . . you turn a corner and there is the final trail . . . not even a trail . . . but the final steps to the peak of the mountain . . . you look out and you see what is the most breathtaking view you have seen in your life. Extraordinary.

From up here you realize that you can see everything. You can see what seems to be forever in all directions. In one direction you look out and you see answers to problems you have not even experienced yet. As you stand . . . looking out . . . you realize that you are here alone . . . only a small number of people come to the top of the mountain and see what you are seeing. Very few people ever gain the insights you are experiencing now . . . seeing how you have done what others fear and that is why you see life from this vantage point . . .

Remember when you climbed up the mountain . . . how you slipped in the mud . . . you were cold in the rain . . . and you may have wondered what you were doing . . . now you begin to feel the sense of accomplishment and you begin to feel it grow . . . knowing that because you refused to quit . . . you succeeded at what others would have quit long ago . . . and because you refused to quit . . . you began to believe that you could get to the peak and look out . . . for as far as the eye could see . . . and now you know that you can bring all of these learnings and experiences with you into the present and the future . . . with you . . . every day . . . always remembering that if you have your goal in mind . . . and keep moving toward your goal . . . that . . . you will reach your goals . . . and that you will become more certain and confident each day that you can do most anything you set your mind to . . . and that helps you feel good inside . . . ready to face life each day . . .

. . . And now you decide to stay here at the peak for a day to learn all there is to learn here . . . for in the morning you will begin your trek back down the mountain with the realization that anytime you want to come back to the mountain you may not have to climb it in the future, for you have now been here and you may be able to simply come back at your bidding by closing your eyes and seeing and feeling and hearing yourself in this space that gives you unshakable self-confidence and the inner strength to persist until you succeed . . .

And now . . . it is time to return to the present with the feelings and learnings that you have acquired on the mountain . . . becoming more aware of all that is around you . . . all the sounds around you and when you hear or see the word one you will be wide aware and refreshed . . . three, becoming more aware of your surroundings, two, hearing all the sounds around you and one . . . wide aware and refreshed . . . eyes open . . . good . . .

CHAPTER SIX

Making Better Decisions . . . Faster

Life is filled with decisions. Every moment of the day we are faced with some choice we have to make. Some are major decisions that will change the course of our lives, while others are minor choices that appear to be rather insignificant.

The fact is, all decisions change everything about the future. Perhaps you stand instead of sit, choose one outfit over another, and drive home in the usual pattern or choose an alternate route. At each moment, we are selecting from an infinite variety of choices.

It is as though at each moment of the day we are standing at the center of a circle that represents our life. We could turn and head in any direction—three hundred and sixty degrees of a circle. Our choices are infinite. However, within that infinity is a group of choices that are actually possibilities. And, within that group of possibilities, is an even smaller group of probabilities. Among the probabilities is a choice that we will actually make, which will move our lives forward along a particular path, in a particular direction, and at a particular speed.

If we think too hard about it, we would become completely paralyzed by the concept. So for the most part, we have trained ourselves to adhere to certain patterns, habits, or rituals, to get us through our everyday duties. If you do not consider yourself to be a habitual person, try moving through your morning ritual in a completely different order, consciously choosing each activity. It is a total nuisance. It generally takes longer and there are steps that may be forgotten or omitted. Part of the stress of traveling or moving lies in the fact that these routines are disrupted.

For this reason, we leave much of the mundane part of life in the care of our habituated unconscious. However, what about the rest of the day's activities? What do we do when a crisis arises—or when new situations, in our ever-changing world, are thrown at us to deal with?

Some of you have a knack for thinking on your feet, making rapid decisions, and deftly handling the results that ensue. Others suffer from "analysis paralysis," finding life's choices to be profound, weighty, and laden with consequences that may be difficult. Some of you jump off the cliff, knowing that you will figure out a way to sprout wings on the way down, while others will spend a lifetime calculating wind draft patterns and never get off the ground.

Either way, a path has been chosen. A decision has been made. Whether you take control and pick a direction and speed, or stand perfectly still letting others or the environment control your experience, a choice has been made.

"To be or not to be" . . . Shakespeare revealed to us the most fundamental question of humanity. To be, to exist, in a conscious present moment, or to not. To choose life and purpose, or to stand in stagnation and oblivion.

A Value System is Fundamental

One of the basic steps in decision-making is to have a value system in place. What is important to you? Who is important to you, and in what order? Every decision, choice, and action should support your value system.

Now you may say you do not really have a value system. The truth is everyone does. It is evidenced by your actions—no matter what a person says is important to them, what they do will reveal the truth. The Bible tells us, "You shall know them by their fruits."

For example, you might say that your child is the most important thing in the world. But, if you never find time to spend with him, the truth is that whatever else you are doing with your time, that is actually more important. So you may find you have a dual value system, which, in the strictest sense of the phrase, would indicate hypocrisy. You would not want that, so you should work on the exercise below in order to align your words with your actions.

Decision-making becomes a great deal easier once you have your values clearly organized and stated. Let us see where you stand today in your value system. As you make your list, be sure that you are basing your answers on your own thoughts and feelings, and not on what others urge, demand of, or suggest to you.

Your Personal Values

List your ideal values. These would be what you think and say, or the right order of value of the activities, people, and things in your life. List them in order with the first one being the most important to you:

Now list your actual values. These are what your values are according to your actions and the amount of time, thought, and energy spent on each activity, person, or thing in your life. List them in order with the first one being the one you put the most energy and time into:

For example, a value list might look like this:

Ideal Values:	**Actual Values:**
My husband, Cliff	My job (I do not have time for any one/anything else)
My son Steve	Education (I am not going to stop learning for anything)
My daughter Susie	My mother (I have to please her even when it hurts my family)
My mother	My children (I'll side with them over my husband any day)
My job	My best friend (I spend more time with her than with my children)
My car	My husband (I love him but we just cannot communicate)
Education	My car

The example may have been extreme, but I think you will get the idea.

Evaluating Your Lists

What discrepancies do you find between your two lists?
What do you notice about your value system that you had not realized before?
What can you do to rectify any discrepancies in your lists?
How will you change your actions based on what you learned by doing this exercise?

Philosophy and Your Sense of Life

As was discussed earlier, our brains are divided into the cortex (rational, logical) side and the limbic (emotional, feeling) side. We can define those two in yet another way. The rational side can be equated with your philosophy. The emotional side corresponds to your sense of life. Your philosophy is a mind-set that you have reasoned out based on your observations, education, and ideas. Your sense of life is your reactions to events based on your emotional nature, your childhood environment, and how you were affected by your circumstances.

Your sense of life is formed early in life. As an infant, you began determining whether the world was a safe and congenial place to be. Perhaps you found it terrifying and without comfort, nurturing, and support. Whether you were born with a silver spoon in your mouth, or without food in your mouth, will shape your perceptions of the world and tint the colored glasses through which you view it.

It is our sense of life that prompts us to say things like:
  "All men are savages."
  "Life sucks."
  "Girls are silly and unreliable."
  "I am never lucky."
  "The whole world is against me."
  "Things never turn out right."
  "I'll always land on my feet."
  "Of course I'll get that job."
  "A little setback shouldn't get you so down—things will be better tomorrow."

Notice how some people's colored glasses are dingy and dark, while others' are bright and shiny? Neither may be accurate. They are simply different perspectives brought on by different mind-sets developed during the formative years.

Fears are developed in the sense of life, along with insecurities, self-doubt, and other negative perspectives. So are the optimistic views attributed to the sense of life, along with the Pollyanna idealism. These perspectives can reflect reality, but most often they do not. There is always an emotional component to the sense of life that tints reality to a hue that is congruent with its expectations of life.

The rational part, the philosophy that a person develops, begins to form in preadolescence when the child begins to act on what they know to be right and wrong, and not just on their emotions. They may want to steal that piece of candy, but they do not because they have come to understand that it would be wrong. The stronger and more balanced that the philosophy has become determines how rationally the adult will be able to make their decisions.

Shall I do What I Want or What I Know is Right?

We all struggle with the conflict between our sense of life and our philosophy. It is natural and a part of our everyday lives. However, the goal is to work on ourselves so that we bring the gap between these two closer and closer together.

An example of such a struggle is my (M.L.) own enjoyment of driving different, nice cars. One year, in fact, I went through four nice cars. Most anyone should be able to figure out that that was not a rational thing to do! Now granted, there were some excuses. A recalled engine and an accident contributed to the statistics. But still, I was enjoying the change of vehicles and was getting caught up in the diversity to the point that I was about to buy yet another car—unnecessary this time. My emotions were telling me it was fun to have a new car with new toys, a change of pace and view. It was feeding my ego and my comforts. However, reality, reason, and a financial statement brought me back in line with what was really important in my life and a more reasonable approach to my finances. It was my rational mind, not my sense of life, that made the right choice to forego yet another new car.

Philosophy and sense of life can be like two differently tempered horses hitched to the same cart. You, the driver, have to take hold of the reins and keep them both in line. If you were to let go, whichever is stronger will take over and the cart will go off in that direction—perhaps dangerously so.

Finding a Balance

Both the rational and the emotional sides are important. The emotional side wants to play and have fun, and have all its nurturing needs met. The rational side wants to grow up and be responsible, do what is moral, and make life more orderly. If you lean in either direction too far, you may run into problems with your finances or your health or any other aspect of your life. As always, balance and moderation are important.

However, when it comes to making decisions, the final determiner should be your rational side. Only when your sense of life is lined up very closely with your rational philosophy can you rely on it to make the correct choice. Otherwise, you run the risk of choosing out of whim, fancy, idealism, rashness, or all sorts of other catalysts that could lead you astray in your life. Your mind, and therefore your reasoning capability, is your only tool for ultimate decision making.

I find it amusing when people tell others to follow their hearts. Do you remember the old saying, "If it feels good, do it"? If a person is in perfect balance, that might be all well and good. However, if their emotions are out of balance, and even worse, of an evil nature, that advice can be quite dangerous. After all, people who commit hate crimes and other atrocities are often "going with their feelings." Young girls have unwanted pregnancies because they were listening to their hearts when they should have been paying attention to their heads.

> *Decisions should be made rationally and not emotionally.*

Until your "Ideal" list and your "Value" list are totally in sync, you run the risk of your emotions not giving you the best feedback when making decisions.

A Metaphor

I am at the bottom of a long, dark stairway. I am in a medieval dungeon and all around me are instruments of torture. I am on the wheel, going round and round in circles. It seems that I am always doing it for someone else. I want to be like the bird in the cage that gets let loose to fly out the window. I leave the wheel and move to the cage. The cage door swings open and I am free to fly. But I have been a domestic bird all my life and I might not know what to do if I were free to fly. I am used to being fed, and being given a birdbath and a clean cage. I always complained about being in the cage, but now that I am free to fly, I hesitate, worried that I am not ready to fly free. What will I do? How will I take care of myself? Where will I go?

And yet, out there I won't be bound to a small space where I would live and die. I won't be on the wheel, going round and round, the same thing everyday. I have wanted to be free to fly, and yet now where will I go? What will happen?

I take flight, knowing that I could come back to the cage if I wanted to. At first, I notice all the directions that I could fly if I wanted to. There are seemingly too many choices. There are so many turns and swoops that I can make, taking my time going here and there. There are few restrictions on what I can do. It almost makes it more difficult to choose. Yet it is so grand to be able to choose. I fly up to the velvet dark sky, flying past the sparkling stars and the twinkling city lights. I always liked the idea of flying in the dark. There are so many mysteries to solve . . . or to let exist.

I am no ordinary bird. I am a falcon. I have ultimate freedom, being a bird of prey. I have nothing to fear. I am fast and I am beautiful. I owe allegiance to my master because he feeds me and cares for me. However, he lets me loose to fly, and when I fly I am my own master. I can fly wherever I want to. I only return because it pleases me. It is like being in two different worlds. I come back to my master because it gives me a sense of centered-ness and balance. I enjoy the familiarity, love, and appreciation I experience with him. It is such an honor that someone loves me so deeply that they keep me and take care of me just to let me fly. And when I fly, it is not for them, it is for the joy it gives me. It is like addressing the universe. I can carry my message to the world, whether far away or close by. It gives me inspiration. I am liberated.

Decisions Support Your Goals

Once you line up your two lists, and you come to an agreement with yourself as to what is truly important to you, you will find that making decisions will become easier. When faced with a choice, you can ask yourself, "Does this support or distract from what is most important to me?"

Having a clear set of values—a value system—is only truly understood and easily adhered to when you understand your purpose in life. Having values implies a goal. If you are wandering around with no place to go, it becomes rather irrelevant where you are at a given time, how long it took you to get there and what happened along the way. However, when you have a specific goal, a purpose, and a desire to achieve it, it will be invaluable to you to have your priorities straight. That is exactly what a value system is—a defined set of priorities.

When you make a decision to do something or get into a certain relationship, you can always measure it against your priority list. You might ask yourself, "Does this activity or person support and further my goals?" If the answer is yes, then it would be appropriate to continue with that activity or friendship. If the answer is no, it would be counterproductive to continue. Doing so would only delay or prevent you from achieving your goal.

> *Decisions should be made in the context of your*
> *goals and life purpose.*

So we need to determine what our goals are. To discover this, you need to ask yourself some questions.

What is it you would like to achieve?

What would you like to accomplish before the end of your life?

Where do you see yourself in six months?

In one year?

In two years?

In five years?

Imagine sitting in your rocking chair at the end of your life. Would you be glad with what you had done with your life?

What would you regret having done?

What would you be glad that you avoided?

What would you regret having not done?

What have you learned about yourself by having answered these questions?

Does having answered these questions change the value list you previously made?

What are you willing to do to begin moving towards those goals?

What decisions will you make, now that you more fully understand your goals?

Once your goals and priorities are thoroughly understood, decision making becomes easier and easier. Each and every activity, thought, and relationship needs to support and move you closer to achieving those goals.

Yours do not have to be lofty goals, or goals to be rich and famous. They can be simple, wholesome, basic needs. Many people want to have a safe home and a family. They want to help others heal or make a difference in their children's lives.

Here is an example of how your value list can aid you in the future. Perhaps buying a house is very high on your priority list. One day you go into a store and see an expensive piece of jewelry you really want to buy. Having rationally determined that the house has more value, it is easier to control your urge and put that money into a savings account earmarked for real estate.

Self-Hypnosis for Decision-Making

An effective self-hypnosis method for decision-making involves a very simple procedure.

> Sit in a quiet location away from distractions. Take a deep breath and close your eyes. As you begin to relax, think of the decision, conflict, or dilemma that you wish to resolve. Divide the decision into the two fundamental parts, placing one side of the decision in one hand and the other side in the other hand.
>
> Using our jewelry-buying dilemma as an example, you would put that part of you that wants to buy the jewelry in one hand, say your right hand. In the left hand you would put the part of you who disagrees with that choice.
>
> Now fully get into the part of you who wants to buy the jewelry, allowing no room for any other part of you. Give that part the opportunity to speak, to express its opinions, and fully explore its desires and reasons in favor of buying the jewelry. When it has fully expressed itself, leave that part, and fully get into that part of you that rejects the decision to buy jewelry. Allow it to put forth its opinions, objections, and wisdom.
>
> When it is finished, go back to the right hand again, allowing it to fully respond. Go back and forth until one side prevails with reason, fully aligned with your values and your bigger life purpose. At that point, the other side should acquiesce and come to an agreement with the favored side.

Once one side of the decision becomes the favored path it is important to ask if there is any part of you that still has a problem with the decision. Even though it may feel like the conflict is settled between these two sides, there still may be other factors that contribute to further turmoil in settling on a final decision.

Simply ask yourself to "sense" whether you are still feeling at odds with coming to this conclusion. If so, repeat the same procedure as above, with the opposing sides now comprising the part of you who made that decision and that part that is uncomfortable with it. Continue this process until all of you feels satisfied that you are making the right decision.

Meditation

Think of an impending decision that you would like to bring to a conclusion.

Sitting in a comfortable position, in an area free of distractions, allow yourself to relax and close your eyes. Quiet your mind as you begin to notice the rhythm of your breathing . . . slow down . . . relax. Fully relax as though you have put a blanket of relaxation over you where you sit or lie. Any tension is simply absorbed by the blanket as it lays across you.

Imagine, if you will, that you are walking down a path. You may create a path that looks like anything you wish. What do you notice about your path? What do you notice about the scenery around you as you walk along?

Before long, you come to a fork in the path. The path may divide sharply, veering off in widely differing directions. Or the path may gently divide. Only you will know.

And as you approach this fork in the road, what do you notice about the two paths? What is different about the way each of them looks . . . and feels? You may have the opportunity to travel down both of these paths, or you may only be able to travel on one. Which one will you choose to follow first?

As you begin to walk down that path, what do you notice that is different about this path? How does the scenery change? How does it feel to be on this path? Continue to walk further until you come upon something different or unusual. What do you notice?

Continue on this path until you reach the far end, or have gone as far as you need to in order to know where this path will lead you. What do you know about the final destination? Are you happy to have traveled along this path? Did this path take you to a place where you wanted to be? Is there anything else that you would like to notice about this path or this destination?

Now, allow your mind to take you back to the fork in the path. What do you notice when you look at that fork now? What do you notice about the path you have not taken?

Begin to walk along the second path now. What do you begin to notice? How do you feel? How is it different from the other path?

Continue along this path until you come upon something different or unusual. What do you notice? Continue on this path until you reach the final destination, or have gone as far as you need to in order to know where this path will lead you. What do you know about the final destination? Are you happy to have traveled along this path? Did this path take you to a place where you wanted to be? Is there anything else that you would like to notice about this path or this destination?

Again, allow your mind to take you back to where the fork is in the path. Knowing now where these two paths lead, which one leads you to the more desirable destination? Which path would you choose to follow?

If these two paths represented two choices that you have in your life, what would each of the paths signify? What does the first path you took represent? What does the second path you took represent? What have you learned about these choices by having experienced these two paths? How will this experience influence how you make your choice?

When you have discovered everything that you would like to know about your two choices, and these two paths, you may easily return to the present moment by simply counting from one to three. So take your time and learn all there is to learn. And then, when you are ready, count yourself awake. When you say the word three you will open your eyes and feel refreshed and wide aware.

Feeling Pressured?

Another factor that has to be considered is whether a decision needs to be made at all. Sometimes we find ourselves in situations where we have convinced ourselves of the urgency of making a decision. For instance, a friend of mine and I (M.L.) had decided to buy a piece of property together. We spent weeks looking at properties and then my friend decided to invest in an apartment building on his own. I continued to look for a condo to buy, expending a lot of energy, time, and effort. Then it suddenly occurred to me that there was no real urgency in finding a condo to buy. I liked where I was living and was perfectly happy to stay there for even a year longer until the right deal came along. As soon as I realized that, I eased myself from the pressure that I had placed upon myself, and released myself from the need to make a decision.

There are also times when others lead us to believe that we have to make a decision when in reality we do not. I had a client come to me (M.L.) for counsel concerning whether they should marry a particular person. They were feeling pressured and thought they needed to respond quickly. They were in turmoil because they were not sure they were ready to make a commitment and they were still somewhat interested in a couple of other people that they had dated. So, after some conversation and soul searching, my client realized that they were feeling pressured to make a decision, but that a decision did not really need to be made at that time. They decided that they could allow themselves to take time to consider it more closely and gather more information before coming to a conclusion.

Thus, if you feel pressured to make a decision or feel stuck between choices, remember that there may also be the choice to not make a decision at all.

Pause and Take a Breath

It may be wise to allow yourself to pause, take a deep breath, and consider the reason why a decision has to be made at all. Examples of times when we may think we have to make a decision right away, under pressure, may include the decision to get married, to have children, or to buy a house. The pressure for these decisions may come from our internal perceptions, or they may have initiated from another person, such as your potential spouse, your parents, a realtor, or your financial advisor. Allow yourself the wisdom to realize that sometimes when someone is pressuring you for a decision, it is because they will benefit from your choice. Take a good look at what they have to gain from your decision, and particularly look at what you have to gain or lose.

By pausing and determining the source of your pressure to make a decision, you may conclude that there is no need to make a decision at the present time. If that is true, and you choose to delay the decision, you may have to use one of a variety of techniques to enforce your decision to delay making a decision.

If that pressure was internal, you will want to use a meditation or self-hypnosis technique to shift your energy away from the urge or compulsion to make a decision. In other words, you may have had your heart set on buying a new car. You have been hunting around for the car and test driving models that you are starting to really like. You have been imagining yourself in that new car and getting very excited. Then, just before you finalize the deal, you realize that you can not afford to upgrade to that car this year after all. You have to decide to not buy the car. It will be important for you to redirect that energy into something that will make your decision not to buy the car more palatable.

Even though you chose not to buy the car, which was your desire, we will assume that you made the decision in favor of a higher value on your list. For instance, you may have decided that it made more sense to pay off old debts. So you would want to tailor your meditation to include your personalized details of your decision, including how very good you will feel to achieve the new goal instead of the old one.

%eImagine if you will, driving down a road very fast, seeing the scenery flying past you as you race towards a city that promises great entertainment and fun. You really are looking forward to arriving there and it feels like you can not get there soon enough. Then, suddenly, you see a sign along the road for a turn off to another city. You had not really planned to go to that other city, nor will it seem as exciting. However, once you read the name of the city you realize that there is a much better reason for you to turn off and go there. That it will be more worthwhile and rewarding in the long run if you bypass your original destination, turning your car, your energy, and your thoughts to the new city. And, as you do that, you have a sense of calm and assurance that you are doing the right thing. As you approach this new city, you begin to notice how much better you feel.

Life here is more secure and it is good to know that you made the right choice. Take a moment to observe how you feel now that you have arrived in this new city. Notice the friendly faces and the ease with which you are able to move about. Feeling good about yourself—calm and at peace.

You can also create a short meditation wherein you simply visualize yourself redirecting your energy towards your new goals, disconnecting from your previous ties to wanting to buy that car.

If the decision-making pressure was from another person, you will have to be confident that you wish to delay, or not make, a decision, and then be prepared to defend that position.

For instance, if your girlfriend wants you to make a decision about a marriage date and you are not ready to commit, you may have to prepare to defend yourself to her and her girlfriends, family members, and whoever else she has gotten "on her side". So when she says "Well, are we getting married or not," and you say, "I am not ready to take that step," you will want to be ready to maintain that stance.

First, you will need to make a list of the reasons defending your stance. It is important that it is clear in your mind, so that you can easily and succinctly convey to the other party your position on the matter. It is also very helpful if you are certain, within yourself, that you are right. Even if that means you are right "for you." Then you will want to convey your position to the other party in a manner that will be agreeable to them.

Remember earlier in the book when we discussed the castle wall? Convincing another person of your position may be similar to putting ideas through that type of barrier. Therefore, couching your words in concepts and in a manner that is acceptable to the other party will be most effective.

You could tell your girlfriend, "I am not interested in making a commitment to you at this time." Or you could tell her, "Because I know that it is important to you to finish college, maybe you will agree that getting married right now might undermine your goals. Perhaps it will be better for us to discuss this when you graduate."

Which of those sentences gives you the impression that it would be received more readily? Certainly the one that will be more acceptable will be the one that includes the reasons why the other party will benefit from your position. And, of course, we use words like "because" and "maybe" and "might" to open up that barrier wall.

Whether your choice is to delay or not make a decision at this time, or to make a decision, knowing that you will have to defend yourself, you may want some extra tools handy. Often we make choices for our own best interests, and they are not favored by other people in our lives. It is important that we have the tools and the determination to stand by our decisions and choices. That can be rather difficult if those who disagree with you have power over you, or know how to apply the right pressure to persuade you to their side.

Empowering Your Decision

The following is an effective empowerment tool that you can use whenever you need a boost of courage and confidence.

Sit back in a comfortable position. Closing your eyes, take a deep breath and hold it . . . as you release your breath, allow the tension in your body to melt away. Taking another deep breath and holding it . . . as you release, imagine that any stress in your thoughts just float away.

Allow your mind to drift back in time to an event in your life when you made a decision that turned out well. A time when you knew that you made a choice that determined the outcome of a situation. Remember that event in detail now. As you remember that event, notice how you feel. How do you hold your body? How do you hold your head? What does your energy feel like? What else do you notice? Do you feel like you could do anything you wanted in this moment? Do you feel as though you could accomplish any goal that you set for yourself?

As you fully experience these feelings, let your imagination create a symbol that you could hold in your hands that would represent that very feeling. Perhaps it is a star, or a sun, or another symbol. It is your symbol and only you will know exactly what that is.

Now, as you hold that symbol in your hand, how does that make you feel? Carrying that symbol with you, go back to another situation in your past when you faced a situation when you could have benefited from having more courage and confidence in your decision making abilities. Relive that event again in your mind, this time moving through it with the symbol in your hand.

How does holding that symbol change how you feel about that event? How would that have made it different? What else do you notice this time as you are remembering that event?

Now go into the future, to an event that you anticipate will happen, when you will need extra courage and confidence in making a decision. As you imagine this future event, be sure to carry your personal empowerment symbol with you. What do you notice now about that event? How do you feel about the way that you are able to handle it now? What do you notice that is different about the way you imagine it, now compared to the way you previously imagined it?

Continue to imagine going through that event several more times until you notice that you feel bored or nonchalant about it. Until you feel completely secure in your ability to make a proper decision and stand by it.

When you are ready to return to the present moment, remember that you will be able to access your empowerment symbol anytime you imagine it to be in your hand. Whenever you imagine holding it, you will regain these same strong feelings of empowerment. And now, returning to the present moment as I count from one to three.

One . . . becoming aware of these surroundings. Two . . . coming up to awareness. And three . . . wide aware and returned to the present moment. Refreshed, alert, and confident.

Whether you use your empowerment tool for bolstering your confidence in facing those who would question your decision, or to give yourself the determination to stick to a decision you made for your own betterment, you should notice a substantial change in the ease of maintaining that decision.

If you find that you have made the right choice, but have trouble sticking to it even in the face of reason, then refer to the chapters on procrastination and smoking cessation where the "Swish" is discussed. There may be a stimulus that elicits a particular response from you unconsciously.

Perhaps you have made a decision not to commit to a marriage date with your girlfriend, but when you are confronted by her, and see her tears, or hear her side, you buckle under and give in. People close to us oftentimes know exactly how to press our buttons and take advantage of our weaknesses. Following the steps for the "Swish" will help you determine what buttons might get pushed, and how to respond with new behavior that will allow you to achieve the goals that you seek.

It is Your Choice!

We will always have decisions to make. From morning until night, we are making choices that will alter the rest of our lives. We can choose a course that will enhance our lives and lead to happiness, or we may make a decision that we will forever regret. Our lives and futures are in our hands.

We will all make mistakes, and hopefully we will learn from them and move on. The more we practice good decision-making skills, the better our chances of making choices that will bring us happiness, health and prosperity.

CHAPTER SEVEN

Attracting Special People
Into Your Life

There is a metaphysical principle, which I (K.H.) sometimes call a "law," and that is the "law of attraction." The law of attraction is a simple law that states that like attracts like. You can understand the law of attraction from either a physical or metaphysical perspective. From the metaphysical perspective, one would say that individuals with "like energies" will attract each other. From a physical perspective, one would say that we tend to attract those people into our lives that we are looking for to fulfill needs or desires. The reticular system of our brain then begins filtering people out of our life, only leaving "in" those people who can qualify to meet our needs. Whether you look at the law of attraction from a physical or metaphysical process is not important. What is important is that it works.

A couple of years ago I knew I needed to attract someone into my life to be my business partner. I realized long ago that I have certain skills that are among the best in the world. I speak dynamically. I have a quick mind and a big heart. I also know I am deficient as a businessperson in many areas. I am aware that, in business, partnerships are much more likely to yield long-term benefits than solo artists. There are exceptions but, generally speaking, teamwork is ideal because when one person has a bad day, the other person can pick things up.

I prefer working with women, but I probably would have settled for a man. Certain aspects of this person, however, were not going to be up for grabs. This person would have to have the equal of my very high level of energy, someone who could keep pace with me on many levels, especially intellectually. She would have experience, talents, skills, and abilities that

I do not have, so that I could feel like I was gaining as much from the relationship as I was giving to it. The person would have to be a superb promoter, marketer, and public speaker. I put that "energy" out "there" a couple of years ago. This person would have to be able to work like a workaholic, and also help me enjoy life as well. The request was submitted to the universe and I went about my business. Along the way I ran into a few people who came close to filling the bill, but things just did not quite "click." Usually the people I brought into my life filled the entire bill, except that of being a good marketer and self-promoter. There was no room for negotiation on marketing and promotional skills. I am a good promoter and it is a value I place highly in business. Marketing is hard work and I needed a partner, not someone I would have to pull along to keep up.

One day in May of 1999, I was the keynote and featured speaker at a convention in Seattle. I was introduced by Richard Brodie, the inventor of Microsoft Word, and the author of one of my favorite books, *The Virus of the Mind.* I was really looking forward to the presentation I was about to give, but frankly, I had been waiting for some time to meet Richard and I just wanted to go out with him after the evening's activities were over.

After my presentation, Richard came up from the back of the room, and I signed a number of autographs while he patiently waited for me to finish. One of the people who came up for an autograph that night was Mary Lee LaBay. She was dressed attractively enough, but I really was focused on getting Richard to take me out. Mary Lee and I had made eye contact twice during the presentation I had just given. She sat in the front row because her friend had asked her to, not because she wanted to . . . and, as fate would have it, it was a good thing.

I would later learn that it was then that she wanted me to be her teacher of advanced hypnosis and her mentor. She had predestined this in her mind, and then Richard and I were out the door. I did not know what was about to hit me, but she did!

She came back the next day to listen to me give yet another presentation about hypnosis. She was dressed for the banquet that would shortly follow my presentation for the conventioneers. After I was done talking, she invited me to come and have a drink with her and her girlfriend in the hotel bar. I did not accept, but did show up later at the bar, en route to the banquet. She impressed me with her easy going conversational style, obvious intelligence, and elegance in how she handled herself. She was thinking mentor/teacher, and I was just happy to meet someone that was fun to talk to for the evening.

I arrived at the banquet a bit late and there was a vacant seat at Mary Lee's table. I sat down next to her and was immediately engaged in talking by a gentleman who was ready to share his entire life story with the rest of the table. Mary Lee knew her opportunity to pursue me as a mentor was fading. I shared with the table that I was leaving in four hours to take a flight back to my family in Minneapolis. Inside I was praying for a bit of time distortion . . . *dear God, please let time pass faster,* I thought . . .

Mary Lee asked me during a break in the monologue, "So, what have you seen of Seattle?"

"The inside of this hotel," I said, with a mentally numbed expression.

"How would you like to go to see the sights of Seattle?" she whispered in my ear.

"I have to leave in a few hours for the airport," I said, significantly disappointed.

"Let's go," she said, "I'll take you to the Space Needle and a whirlwind tour around the city."

"The Space Needle?" I was tempted.

"C'mon, you can't go back to Minneapolis saying the only thing you saw was the inside of the Best Western hotel."

"OK. Let's go to the Space Needle."

We excused ourselves and raced to her car.

We went to the Space Needle at the speed of a potential traffic ticket. Frankly, it was a seemingly ridiculous trek. I had to leave in three hours and . . . then she got her chance.

"I want you to be my teacher. I am already very good in this business, but I want to be where you are."

I was impressed by this woman. I was particularly impressed by her ability to be spontaneous and assertive. She had me cornered in the passenger seat of her Buick Regal at 80 miles per hour. Well, what could I say? She started telling me about her education and her experience in the business, and, somewhere on top of the Space Needle, looking out over an incredible city view, she said, "Well?"

"Sure, I'll mentor you, but I am not sure that you need all that much mentoring. I think you are already in the top 1/10 of 1% of hypnotherapists in the country."

I then told her that I was looking for a business partner. I was looking for someone who was remarkably like her. I wanted to work with someone who was fun and assertive, hardworking and relentless in promotion and marketing. She was excited by the possibility of linking up with someone who was in my position and I was excited about the possibility of linking up with someone who had her background and experience.

Two hours and five stops in the city later, she dropped me off at the airport. She had taken me to dancing water fountains, the gazebo in town, over two floating bridges, and a tour of downtown, all in two hours. I felt like a 17-year-old the way the night flew at the speed of light. She pulled up to the drop off curb at the airport and, one hug and two good-byes later, the partnership had been proposed and it appeared as if it would last.

Comparing notes months later, we both found that we had put out our metaphysical feelers by using the power of our mind to find someone to work with—someone who could take us to the next level, someone whose energy level would help us expand and not drain our own reserves. Then she spotted me, was relentless, spontaneous, assertive, broke the rules of decorum, and closed the deal . . . in three hours. Not bad.

This process of bringing special people into your life works well for love relationships as well. Consider the scope of love. Loving relationships are only one aspect of love. There is also the love of humankind, animals, the cosmos, God, and the self. All of these areas of love include some similar concepts and some themes that are quite different. Without further ado, let us look at loving relationships.

When you "fall in love" with someone, you often are blinded to many of that person's faults or negative behaviors. True and lasting love has an important distinction. The people involved in a true and lasting love relationship eventually discover and uncover their mate's less than excellent points and love them regardless of the flaws.

In this chapter, we will start at the beginning. If you currently are unmarried or are "unspoken for" and wish to be married or spoken for, the balance of this chapter will show you how to get from now to then. If you are currently spoken for or married, this article will show you how to have a true and lasting love relationship. If you are having some minor challenges in your present relationship, the balance of this chapter will show you how to turn the problems into propulsion systems to even stronger bonds of love and happiness.

Who are You Looking For?

Many people, when beginning their pursuit of a life partner, simply look "out there" and wonder why the person of their dreams is not there. Because you are looking for a life partner, an important decision will be made when you find this person. You will commit to a lifetime bond of marriage. With that in mind, you need to consider what you have to offer a partner, and what you truly want your partner to offer you. You want to know who you are looking for before you go looking.

There will, no doubt, be many people that will meet your description of who you are looking for. You are simply going to be taking note of general ideas about an important someone. All of these ideas are subject to change. Similarly, you will be willing to make some personal alterations, if necessary, to create a happy love relationship.

At first, this may seem to be in conflict with the philosophy of acceptance without judgment. It is not. If you are not a well-kept person and you meet someone who sincerely cares for you, but is having mixed feelings about you due to cleanliness, it would seem reasonable to improve upon an area that can only benefit your environment and yourself.

What your strengths and weaknesses are, as a potential partner, will largely determine your success or failure in developing this lifelong relationship. In the exercises below, you will discover what makes you attractive to others as a life partner and what you are looking for in a life partner.

What the Partner Will "Get"

In the spaces below fill in what your partner will be excited about getting in you. In other words, when this special person marries you, what are you offering that person? List your most positive spiritual, emotional, mental, and physical attributes. Everything counts.

1) _____

2) _____

3) _____

4) _____

5) _____

6) _____

7) _____

8) _____

9) _____

10) _____

What inherent problems do you have that you may bring into a relationship? (Are you in debt? Are you a member of a religion that forbids marriage outside the faith? Are you obese? Are you unhealthy?)

1) _____

2) _____

3) _____

4) _____

5) _____

6) _____

7) _____

8) _____

9) _____

10) _____

For each of the ten liabilities you listed above, write down whether or not that liability can be changed. If it is impossible to change something that is an inherent problem about you, write the word "impossible" in the space corresponding to the number above.

1) _____

2) _____

3) _____

4) _____

5) _____

6) _____

7) _____

8) _____

9) _____

10) _____

What You Want in a Life Partner

In the spaces below, note the things you *must* have in a life partner. These can be lifestyle choices, mental characteristics, physical attributes, spiritual focus, or anything you feel is a "must." You will know something is a must by answering this question:

If the person had everything else I wanted in a life partner except _____, would I be happy with this person?

If the answer is no, then you have a *must* or *must not* trait that you are looking for. The *must* traits can severely limit your discovery of excellent possible life partners, so think carefully about each one you note. (Some *"musts"* might include being a certain religion, having a certain income level, not being a person with a history of abusive behavior, etc.)

1) _____

2) _____

3) _____

4) _____

5) _____

6) _____

7) _____

8) _____

9) _____

10) _____

Now that you know what you definitely do *not* want, consider what you would like your life partner to offer you. This can include physical attributes, mental capabilities, financial acumen, emotional stability, spiritual focus, or anything else you believe you would find extremely attractive in a potential life partner.

1) _____

2) _____

3) _____

4) _____

5) _____

6) _____

7) _____

8) _____

9) _____

10) _____

You now have a good start at being able to identify what you want in another person and what your contribution to the partnership will be. Once the relationship has begun on a permanent basis, you have the ability to create long lasting love and happiness. Most marriages are not of this variety, and the balance of this chapter is dedicated to building a magnificent marriage.

Bonds of Marriage

If you are married, the "bonds of marriage" may sound like a prison, or it may sound like a special kind of "oneness." As a designer, you obviously want to have the most loving and intimate marriage you can imagine. Half of all marriages end in divorce. Of the remaining half, the majority of marriages are not "happy" marriages. This seems to lead us to the conclusion that marriage needs a little more thoughtfulness to be what we want it to be. Marriages that work have partners that work for the success, happiness, and love of the marriage.

How can we "work on a marriage?"

A marriage is not like a car. A car is something that can break down and be fixed, given the right parts. A marriage though, is a dynamic interaction between two people. Changing one part of this system will definitely help the marriage improve. Changing both parts will propel the marriage toward long-term happiness and love.

Most people who do not have excellent marriages discover that the marriage is not succeeding for at least one of two key reasons.

1) The partner unconsciously sought a mate who in many positive ways reminded them of their opposite sex parent. At least one partner married someone who, in important ways, reminded their unconscious mind of one or both of their parents. You've probably heard, "He married his mother." "She married her father." The fact that you may have married someone like one of your parents does not mean the marriage is doomed. It does mean that you need to be aware of the inherent problems with this kind of relationship.

Surprisingly, engaging in a relationship that is similar, in many facets, to that of your relationship with your opposite sex parent is very common. This is one time when truth is stranger than fiction in the majority of cases of mediocre or unhappy marriages.

2) At least one partner married someone who reminded their unconscious mind of their opposite sex parent in aspects that were very
negative in nature.

Both of these unconscious "searching" experiences create powerful
romantic bonds when the two people "home in" on each other. In essence,
they are "completing their childhood" in some fashion. One, and probably
both, individuals needed to link up with the security of the familiar relationships that they had in childhood. Whether the person had a parent who
was caring and loving or abusive is irrelevant. The point is, the unconscious mind of at least one of the persons sought out his/her parent in order
to complete his/her childhood and complete any unfinished business.

Successful Marriage Elicitation

Once you are in a relationship, you should elicit the responses to these
questions from your partner (at least annually) to be certain you both are
focused on what it is going to take to have a successful relationship.

What about our marriage do you love the most?
What is the next best thing about our marriage?
What is the next best thing about our marriage?
What could I do to make our marriage even better?
What else?
What do you believe you should learn about me to improve our marriage?
What do you think I should learn about you to improve our marriage?
What are two things I do that annoy you?
What are two things you do that you think annoy me?
How happy are you with our sex life?
What can I do to make our sex life more intoxicating?
What would you be willing to do to make our sex life more intoxicating?
When we argue from now on, should we agree to kiss and make up
    before the argument gets out of hand?
What will our "cue" be for that to happen?
What do you do around the house that you think I do not appreciate?
What do you do at work that you think I do not appreciate?
What do I do that you probably do not appreciate as much as you could?
What do you want to know about my past that I have not told you?
What do you want me to know about your past that you have not told me?

When should I be jealous?

When do you think you should be jealous?

How can we go from having a really good marriage to having a fantastic marriage?

All of these questions allow us to discover more about our partner in a couple of hours than we may have discovered in past years. Questions are an under-used piece of communication in our culture. Beginning to gently ask questions will put you on the track to improved communication.

Learning what is important to your partner and being certain your partner understands what you need and want makes it much easier to have a good marriage. It takes away the guesswork that may have been there previously.

Write one question here that you need to ask your spouse or loved one.

_____

Questions help the unconscious mind focus on what is important. These questions are guaranteed to help the unconscious mind move in the direction of happiness and contentment in your relationships.

. . . Close your eyes and take a deep breath in, and hold and slowly release . . . now take another deep breath in and hold . . . and slowly release . . . good . . . now pay attention to your breathing as you allow your mind to clear and bring up the experience that will shortly change your life in wonderful ways you may not have dreamed possible . . .

Allow yourself to go out into the future and imagine yourself with that certain someone . . . someone special . . . someone who you may not have yet met . . . and you are having a wonderful time . . . and part of you wonders why this took so long to manifest . . . and part of you is so happy just to be in the moment with this special person . . . now . . .

And as you look at this person . . . what do you see . . . do they look happy to be with you . . . to be in your presence . . . to be with you . . . and as you feel the energy this person sends to you . . . what does it feel like inside . . . now . . . and how does that make you feel . . .

Now . . . allow yourself to go and do something that is even more enjoyable and wonderful with this person . . . allow yourself to find yourself in a time that is even more happy and more enticing than this moment . . . and go there . . . now . . . that's right . . . good . . .

And now you become aware of how this person communicates with you . . . the things they say . . . the tone of voice . . . the words they use . . . as you listen to what they say . . . and you seem to like it very much . . . now . . . and notice how that makes you feel inside . . . now . . .

And now . . . you find yourself closer to this person than you had been before and maybe you feel their touch, the warmth of their skin, the breath that they exhale . . . and you feel a sense of connection as you may not have before . . . and notice how that makes you feel inside . . . now . . .

And now . . . allow yourself to be grateful for the patience you had in finding this person to share these moments with . . . realizing that by being patient . . . you were able to find someone who shares happiness and joy with you . . . someone who makes you feel so good inside . . . and be thankful that you did not rush into other experiences in the past . . . because this is what the universe had in store for you and notice how that makes you feel inside . . . now . . .

Good . . . now . . . allow yourself to bring all of these realizations and experiences with you back to the present, having had a taste of what the future will be like, and the feelings it gives you inside to know that the law of attraction will work in your favor . . . now . . .

And when I say the number *one* I want you to be wide aware, refreshed and ready to put your energy out there into the universe . . . three, you become aware of the sounds around you . . . two, you become oriented to the present time . . . and one, you are wide aware and refreshed.

CHAPTER EIGHT

Look Attractive Longer and Feel Better Forever!

We can not turn back the hands of time but we certainly can find effective ways of minimizing the effects it has on our bodies, our energy levels, and our attitudes. In this chapter, we will discover methods of increasing our energy levels and maintaining a youthful appearance without surgery or drugs. You will learn how reducing stress, proper nutrition, exercise, and having a positive attitude will enhance your vitality and lengthen your life.

When we were children, we were anxious to look older and grow taller. We were rewarded for gaining in age by having birthday parties with lots of presents. All the important people around us (grandparents, parents, teachers, etc.) would praise us for getting big and being so "grown up." Our unconscious minds, and more than likely our conscious minds, were translating those words into a message that sounded more like "it is good to get older." Older people get respect, older people are listened to, older people have autonomy and get to do anything they want. It is *very* good to get older.

However, soon enough we become twenty-one and all the rewards are behind us. We can drive, we can make our own decisions, we can drink alcohol. We can be responsible for our bills, our mistakes, and our decisions. Suddenly getting older no longer serves much of a purpose. We begin to understand that, but our unconscious minds are still playing the old recording.

It is not to say that getting older is all bad. There is a lot to be said about it actually. As my (M.L.) mother has so wisely pointed out to me, there is only one alternative to getting older—death! So, we want to be around long enough to age. We just want to do it gracefully and with vitality.

We gain a great deal of wisdom with our years. There is knowledge, maturity, and experience that older people generally would not be willing to trade for anything. But there comes a time in most people's lives when they start looking back at their youth with wistful sighs as they join in the chorus stating "Youth is wasted on the young."

It is not only the quantity of the years, but the quality. As we live out our years, we are given the opportunity to gain experience, develop character, and learn our lessons. Yet, those years would be more enjoyable and fruitful if our faces were to retain a more youthful appearance and our bodies were more fit.

"Ah, to have my thin youthful body back." "If only I could regain my energy and flexibility." "How did these wrinkles replace my flawless smooth skin?"

If you have begun to make these statements, then you may find the following information to be useful in slowing the aging process.

Theories about Aging

According to an article in the Life Extension Magazine dated March 1998 (The Roots of Aging, by Marilyn Bitomsky), one of the most favored theories about aging is the Free Radical theory. It maintains that aging is due to the cumulative damage caused by oxidative free radicals. Supporters of this theory are generally in favor of the use of food supplements, particularly antioxidants such as Vitamin C, Vitamin E, melatonin, beta-carotene and foods containing phytochemicals and fiber. It should go without saying that a healthy, balanced and varied diet is necessary to provide the body with the building materials it needs.

There is further research being done on aging and longevity headed up by the Geron Corporation of Menlo Park, California, along with the University of Texas Southwestern Medical Center at Dallas. According to a press release from Geron dated January 13, 1998 and a subsequent paper published in Science magazine dated January 16, 1998, their research is showing that the aging process is linked to the deterioration of the DNA strands in certain cells of our bodies. The end portions of the DNA strands are called telomeres, and these shorten as the cell divides. As the strand becomes shorter, it signals the cell to cease dividing.

According to the research done by Geron and their colleagues, there is an enzyme called telomerase which, when activated, functions as the key to turning off the shortening of the telomeres. If this is proven to be the case in humans, and is eventually made available to the general public, the indications would be far-reaching.

As we know, from the time of conception and throughout our lives, our cells are dividing. Each time they divide they must replicate the genetic information contained in the DNA, much like making a photocopy. The more closely they replicate themselves, the more intact our cells remain. During the copying process anywhere from 50-200 nucleotides are dropped off the ends of the DNA strands. When enough of the strand is reduced, and the integrity of the DNA compromised, the cell ceases to function correctly and ultimately dies.

Although telomerase is not available for public use, the continuing research in this area promises a bright future for generations to come. And although we don't have the use of this type of enzyme available to us now, we can certainly contribute to our own longevity as well as maintain healthier bodies into our later years, through the attentive maintenance of our nutrition and exercise programs, giving our bodies the building blocks for regeneration that are presently available to us.

Stress Takes Its Toll

Another important step in maintaining a youthful appearance is to have a youthful attitude. If you walk around with the weight of the world on your shoulders and a scowl on your face, it will not be long before you are bent and wrinkled. In fact, stress is one of the factors in aging that we can take control of, even if we can not entirely eliminate it.

Let's take a look at how stress factors into the aging process.

There are several sources of our daily stress. Environmentally, we have noise, pollution, crime, traffic, and weather conditions. Furthermore, we are taxed by the processes of growth, menses, and menopause. Our bodies suffer from accidents, illnesses, poor eating habits, lack of exercise, and disturbances in our sleep patterns.

Our stress levels rise with responsibilities at home and at work, with deadlines, conflicts, and financial concerns. A death, divorce, or a move from home can create tremendous pressures. Equally as strenuous are our worries, fears, and emotional disturbances.

When the body senses stress, the brain sends a series of signals through the hypothalamus to the sympathetic nervous system, which in turns registers it as a warning to prepare for a flight or fight response. If the stimulus does not go away, but rather, continues to send stress signals to the brain, the body will continue to secrete adrenaline, epinephrine, and nor-epinephrine into the system.

In our modern world, this is quite normal. Although we can, for the most part, control our perceptions and reactions to stress in our lives, we cannot generally hit someone with our fist, change the traffic patterns, or control the weather. Most people learn to "control" their emotions and turn the stress inward. This, in turn, creates tremendous wear and tear on the body.

When the fight or flight response is maintained for a length of time in the body, the systems begin to shut down. Digestion, reproduction, growth, and tissue repair are slowed, and there is inhibition in the immune and inflammatory systems. Over time, severe and permanent damage can be done to the body including chronic disease and early death. Among the leading stress-related diseases are heart conditions, high blood pressure, chronic fatigue, diabetes, osteoporosis, and failure of the reproductive organs.

> *Stress and distress predisposes people to illnesses of all kinds.*

Imagine if your body was an automobile. You bought it new and every-thing was running just great. Then you decided to only change the oil once in a while, way beyond the scheduled service dates. You also chose to use the cheapest quality oils and gasoline. Sometimes you would even put flu-ids in the tank that would cause the car to not run at all or could potentially seriously harm the other parts. The tires wore thin and there were more and more dents and rust, but you never really paid attention to that. How long do you think your car would continue to perform well for you?

We treat our bodies in a similar fashion. We feed it fast food and processed foods that have little nutrition and lots of dubious ingredients. We fail to cleanse the systems regularly. We would rather give it drugs, tobacco, or alcohol than to fix what really hurts. We allow our bodies to get overweight and soft, and we do not always fix things as they fall apart. Then we wonder why we are looking so aged and out of shape.

Work Out That Stress

There is no doubt that the alleviation of stress will play an important role in maintaining a youthful appearance and a healthy, vital body. The best way to expend all the energy we are building up due to stress is to get enough exercise each and every day. By letting the body exhaust itself, it feels it has completed the cycle that triggered the fight or flight response.

Furthermore, you can identify what is creating the stress in your life and focus your attention on "working it out" during your work out. I (M.L.) used to practice kung fu and kickboxing. It was helpful for my psyche and my body to imagine my target as the object of my stress. The result was that my performance was more energetic and focused, and my mind felt resolved of the negative emotions that had previously been there.

If you are running, imagine yourself running away from your stresses, leaving them behind. If you are lifting weights, imagine lifting the weight of your stress (your job, your bills, etc.) up off of you. If you choose to play a sport such as tennis, golf, or baseball, you can imagine the object of your stress to be residing in that ball as you smack it away. You know that person or problem is not in that ball, but your unconscious mind is easily fooled. You will experience a wonderful relief.

An added benefit to working out is that you will gain muscle tone. One of the first signs of aging is sagging skin and flabby muscles. Tightening the muscles will improve your posture, provide you with more energy, and increase your metabolism. It will be easier to maintain your proper weight and you will feel better in your clothes. The better you feel about your appearance and the more energy you have, the more likely it is that you will engage in social activities and be involved in life. This in turn will lead to a more positive attitude and more youthful outlook.

Attitude is Everything

In studies done in Europe in the 1970s, it was determined that people who scored highest on a test of positive attitude were 30 times more likely to be alive more than 20 years later than those who scored the lowest. Many health organizations are also now recognizing that attitude and emotional wellbeing are more important to survival of serious illness than any other factor.

Let's see how positive your attitude is. Take a moment to take this short quiz. Answer "yes" or "no" to the following questions:

I have one or more goals that I am working on.
I maintain my boundaries when others try to slow me down.
I get out of situations that undermine progress with my goals.

I take care of my own needs before helping others with theirs.
I can easily express my emotions.
When I am hurt or angry I let people know.
I am able to find various ways of making my days pleasurable.
I find my daily activities to be satisfying.
I do not mind if people observe me singing and dancing.
I look forward to going to my work.
I find my work interesting and pleasantly challenging.
I enjoy regular exercise or engage in sports.
I feel a strong spiritual connection regardless of my religious beliefs.
I frequently enjoy a movie, a sensuous bath, or a beauty treatment.
I am never too busy working to take time for myself or my family.
I enjoy getting out in nature.
I enjoy frequent contact with a few close friends.
I feel good about myself.
I want to live a long and fruitful life.
I feel I can influence others.
I have high hopes for my future.
I am confident in facing my difficulties.
I continuously look for way to change self-sabotaging behavior.
I ask friends for help when I am depressed.
I like talking about my successes as well as my mistakes.
I do not feel guilty when I am not to blame.
If I make a mistake, I am quick to change my ways.
I feel I am in control of my life.
I know that my attitudes and emotions affect my health.
I allow myself a period of relaxation every day.

If most of your answers were "yes," you are on the right track. If you had a preponderance of "no" answers, you will find that reading further will be of great assistance in changing your life for the better.

Self-Sabotage

From the nature of the statements in the evaluation above, you have probably figured out some of the issues that contribute to aging. Among the leading offenders are self-sabotaging behaviors, not having a strong support group around you, and not taking good care of your body, mind, and spirit.

Self-sabotaging behaviors are activities you engage in that undermine the goals that you have set for yourself. If you are trying to lose weight, but allow yourself unhealthy, fattening foods, you are sabotaging yourself. If you want to achieve a certain goal, such as taking dance lessons, yet you let the needs and schedules of others get in your way, you are only letting yourself down. Not only does that hinder your growth and advancement, it sets you up for a multitude of additional negative experiences. Eventually you will become resentful, guilty, frustrated, and perhaps even ill because of the built-up stress around this issue. And, as we know, stress is a major contributor to aging.

A Strong Support System

Having a strong support group around you is vitally important to the reduction of stress and the furtherance of a long and happy life. A support group may consist of friends, family, professional colleagues, neighbors, and even pets. Studies show that the cuddling and stroking of pets actually contributes greatly to the comfort and contentment of the elderly, and increases the chances of survival and recovery of patients who have been seriously ill or are recuperating from major surgery.

We do not want to wait until the end of our lives to begin collecting a support group. The signs of aging begin early and that is when we want to begin making the changes in our lives that will slow the process down.

Family can be a strong support system, when the family unit is intact and healthy. Family can also be the most destructive aspect of a person's life. It is wise to take a long look at the structure and environment of your family and determine to what degree they are supportive, and also how and in what areas are they harmful. Often there are so many varied dynamics occurring in the family that it is a mix of positive and negative influences in a person's life.

Friends can be the best support groups for you because you can pick and choose your friends based on similarities of thoughts, goals, interests, activities, and temperament. Choose your friends wisely and then nurture them carefully. It is not unusual to discover that our friends are closer to us, and know more about us, than our own blood relatives.

Supportive friends can help make you well again!

Support groups serve such an important role in our health and wellbeing because they alleviate many of our burdens. We have people with whom to share our joys and our sorrows, to lend us a helping hand, and to give us a different, perhaps a wiser, point of view when we are about to wander astray. They bring color and variety into our lives. People and relationships bring us our lessons from which we can grow and change, becoming even better in our own lives.

Name the people or pets that form your support group:

How often do you spend time with each of them?
In what ways do they enhance your life?
In what ways do you enhance their lives?

The Spiritual Connection

There are many factors that we can not control in the aging process. However, we can take care of our bodies, our minds, and our spirits. It seems so silly that we would not take care of the very things that make us who we are, yet, for most people, that is the last thing we do. We allow our bodies to get out of shape, we push our stress levels to the limits in pursuit of wealth or relationships, and we do not pay attention to the signals that our bodies are giving us that things are breaking down. We have discussed the importance of diet and exercise and also of a positive mental outlook. How can we take care of our spirit?

A spiritual practice is something that is very personal. Only you will know what is right for you. However, meditation, prayer, and a sense of a personal connection to a higher source will give the peace of mind, serenity, and hope that supports a positive attitude.

Many people claim that they do not know how to meditate. However, it does not have to be as difficult as they make it seem. Meditation can simply be quiet time that you spend while working in the garden or taking a walk. It is a time to allow your thoughts to settle down and your body to be relaxed. You can do your meditation by sitting cross-legged on the floor and focusing your mind on a tone, a singular thought, or a mantra. Or you can chant or dance like whirling dervishes. Again, it is a personal choice.

A relaxing meditation can be achieved by simply following a progressive relaxation trance induction, then allowing the mind to focus on one topic that you choose. An example of a progressive relaxation induction follows. You may choose to record this and listen to it while you meditate.

Sit or lie in a comfortable position in a location free of distractions. Take a nice big breath . . . hold it . . . and then release it. Take another breath . . . hold it . . . and release it. Begin to relax your toes and your feet . . . your ankles and your calves. Relax your knees, your thighs, and your legs. Relaxing your legs completely . . . releasing . . . and relaxing.

Relax your stomach . . . your chest and your breathing. Perhaps you notice your breath as it finds its own natural pace. Relax your back . . . your shoulders . . . your arms, your hands, and your fingers. Completely relaxed—that's right—feeling so good to be doing something so good for you.

And I wonder if you can imagine a ball of light at your feet . . . glistening and shining . . . and radiating. And as it moves up along your body, it gathers up the perceptions and sensations . . . leaving behind a completely relaxed body. As it continues to move up along your body, across your legs and your lap . . . continuing up across your torso . . .

Your energy feeling so balanced . . . your body so relaxed . . . now the ball of light travels across your throat and right up into the center of your forehead . . . energizing your consciousness, focusing your thoughts . . . opening the doorway to your higher consciousness . . . your connection to a higher source. And, as you continue to feel the energy there at your forehead, the connections become stronger and stronger . . . feeling so relaxed . . . so at peace . . . so connected.

Now, allowing yourself to remain in this state of meditation for as long as you choose, whenever you desire to return to wakefulness, you will simply count from one to three. When you count from one to three, you will gently and promptly return your awareness to this room and to this present moment.

After you have practiced this a few times you will be able to do it easily without listening to a recording. Some people experience a sense of lightness, while others may describe it as feeling heavy. Some people experience a heightened awareness of all that is going on around them, while others do not sense their surroundings at all. Again, it is a matter of a personal experience. I wonder what you will experience.

Some Stress is Beneficial

Let's talk further about stress. We know that we live in a stressful world. It is easy to feel stress from a multitude of directions—money problems, people's personalities, environmental pollution, deadlines, traffic, family issues, and so much more.

The truth is some stress is useful. A little bit of stress makes us work harder and achieve more. Some people prefer to work under a certain amount of stress in order to pump the adrenaline to get the job done. Competing in business or on the playing field requires a certain amount of desirable stress. Even falling in love creates stress—but, oh, such a pleasurable one!

The Cause of Your Stress

We are most concerned about the detrimental stress in our lives. Let's find out what causes your stress. How would you answer the following questions?

What tension are you experiencing right now?
What muscles do you feel tight or aching?
If you were to concentrate on that area of tension you are experiencing, how would you describe the sensation?
If that sensation had a shape and a color, what would it look like?
If you could communicate telepathically with that shape, what message would it have for you?
If you do not seem to get a message, guess what that part of you would want to say to you.
Does it have anything else to say?
What could you do differently that would allow that part to relax and the tension to go away?
Would you be willing to do whatever that is?

The preceding exercise can be repeated as often as needed, and with each tension that you feel on your body.

Name That Stress

It will also be helpful for you to write a list of all the areas of your life in which you feel stress. Be sure to include family, home, property, relatives, work, people at work, duties and responsibilities, activities, social obligations, expectations, etc. This list would include everything that makes you feel uncomfortable, irritable, angry, sad, pressured, and so forth.

When you have completed your list, look for common threads and patterns.
What do you notice about the items on your list?
How many of these items could be removed from your list?
How many of them could be delegated to someone else?
Which ones would change if you simply did something differently?
What are you willing to do to reduce your stress?
When are you willing to begin reducing your stress?

A Metaphor

I am walking along a path with a wicker basket on my back. It is weighted with items that I am carrying for the others that are walking with me. Whenever they do not feel like carrying something, they just put it in my basket. At first it was easy. I was fresh and energetic and it did not seem like much to add to my basket. But so many people have joined us on this path. My basket is so full, and, as I look, around I notice that the baskets of the other people are not nearly so full. They are marching along not getting tired or pretending to be tired when they are not. They have given me many of their things to carry.

I have asked them to take back some of their things, but they are not interested. They are accustomed to me carrying their things. They like it that way. But I notice that my steps are getting slower, I can not move as fast. My legs are feeling weak and my back is hunched under the weight of my burden. Soon I am falling behind the others. I see their backsides as they are walking on up ahead, merry and lighthearted, while I falter and grow weak.

I sit down under a tree along the path and rest while they continue to move on. I begin to take the items out of my basket one by one. I examine them and turn them over in my hand. I lay each item aside. They lay all around me like flowers I have cultivated in my garden. I stand up and swing my half-full basket across my back. It feels lighter. It will be so much easier to carry. I begin to walk to catch up with my companions. They turn, with scowls on their faces when they see I have left their items behind. They scurry off to gather them up, angry that I have put down their burdens.

I find my gait is strong, faster. I feel light and my back is beginning to straighten. Some of those people continue to walk with me, and some stay behind struggling with their burdens. But it is just fine. New people walk along with us, and some even offer to carry some of the items in my basket. I move faster and fast, lighter and lighter, as I approach my destination.

Alternate Therapies

There are a number of cosmetic things we can do to reduce the signs of aging. It is important to take good care of your skin, using sunscreens, cleansers, and moisturizers. There are treatments that can be enjoyed at a spa or beauty salon, such as exfoliation, vegetable peels, facials, and steaming.

Even having your stylist update your hairdo can work wonders in changing the appearance of your age. It can be great fun to experiment with a little change. Wearing a radical hairstyle obviously too young for your years will actually increase the appearance of your age. Spiked purple hair on a 40-year-old does nothing to turn back the hands of time. And please, if you have a bald spot, do not think you are fooling anyone by covering it with a long strand of hair that lays sideways. Clip it short and deal with it gracefully. After all, many women are attracted to balding men, and most others would be less concerned about the balding than the awkwardly placed strand of hair that inevitably gets blown askew in the wind.

Consider enhancing the color of your hair. As we get older our natural hair color can fade, and streaks of silver can begin to infiltrate our precious locks. Highlighting, enriching the color, and covering the gray can all work wonders in adding youth to your appearance. It is advisable to consult a hair color specialist who can assist you in choosing the right color and maintaining the health of your hair.

Women have an advantage of wearing makeup that can enhance their beauty and conceal flaws and minor signs of aging. Cosmetic companies at the major department stores offer free makeovers, that are fun and educational, about the latest techniques and products available. There are even independent distributors with companies such as Mary Kay and Avon that will come to your home to demonstrate products and techniques.

Avoid overindulging in alcohol, tobacco, or drugs. All of these items tax the body and contribute to early aging. You can do your own research here. Find several people of the same age. Compare those who have smoked, or consumed drugs or alcohol for a long period of time with those who have been free from, or are moderate in, their intake of such products. What do you notice about the texture of their skin? What do you notice about the coloring? Which people look younger and have more vitality?

The clothes that you wear can add or subtract years to your appearance. Wearing frumpy, outdated clothes can make even a young person look older and worn out. As you get older, your appearance is enhanced with lighter colors around your face. However, wearing clothes that are too trendy or juvenile will only make you look older by contrast.

Treat yourself to a shopping trip to a specialty boutique or luxury department store. Allow the salespeople to choose suitable clothing for you. They work in this field and should be alert to fashion trends, proper fit, and flattering styles for your body type and coloring. Even if you do not buy anything from them that day, you will have gained a great deal of knowledge. You will have had the opportunity to see yourself in a different light and, hopefully, enjoyed an entertaining adventure!

Enjoy Your Playtime

Remember to play more often. Allow the inner child in you to come out and express him- or herself. Perhaps there was a youthful part of you who got left behind when you started taking on adult responsibilities. There was less and less time for play as the obligations to family, education, finances, and society made more and more demands on you. Oftentimes we have even thought of our playtime as part of our obligations.

Have you ever caught yourself saying any of the following?

"I *have* to go get some exercise."
"I really *should* go outside and enjoy the good weather."
"I guess I had *better* schedule in a workout."

I (M.L.) have not been overly athletic in my life, but in my younger years I had a lot of energy to ride a bicycle, ski, roller skate, hike, and dance. When my children were young we lived in Europe and our primary transportation was on bicycles or on foot. My energy levels were great, my metabolism ran high, and my muscle tone was enviable.

However, after the kids got older and I started getting involved in my career, things began to change. There was less time to play, and I started using the car instead of walking or riding a bike. There was always one more pressing thing to take care of before I could take a break to relax and have fun. The result was that my body got softer, my metabolism slowed, it became easier for me to gain weight, and my muscles began to ache and feel stressed more often. I kept telling myself that I would just *have* to get out and start exercising.

I thoroughly enjoy rollerblading, and I take every opportunity to get out there to do it. With our rains in the great northwest we have to take advantage of any dry day we get. But my body also needs weight-resistance training. And, although I enjoy it, I can not say that my enthusiasm levels are the same for weight lifting as it is for rollerblading. So each time I would go to workout, jog, or walk, I would have to convince myself to do it, and schedule it in like an appointment.

Recently I started working out with a trainer. One day I decided that I would rather return to my earlier attitude of looking forward to my playtime instead of finding excuses why I couldn't have one. After all, I was only denying myself the benefits of having fun. My reasoning was that if I was going to go to the effort to get some exercise, I might as well allow myself to enjoy it, too. My attitude was not the only thing that had an immediate change. As soon as I decided that I was going to have the same outlook as when I was in elementary school, the idea of getting out of work seemed more appealing.

Time for Recess

Do you remember when you were in school and recess was the highlight of the day? You would sit through class and get your work done as quickly as possible just to get to the next recess period. Your mind was focused on having fun and running around, stretching your body and testing yourself in feats of skill. You still were able to learn and to accomplish all your other work. The difference was that your mind was focused on relaxing and playing. Your body responded to its physical needs of moving and working off excess energy.

To finish my earlier story, I began to look at my day from this juvenile perspective. I would concentrate on the opportunities for fun, relaxation, and movement, and just make sure my work all got done around that schedule. It was amazing how much more fun it was to workout. I even had more energy and drive to do it better, fueled on my enthusiasm for the activity. It was encouraging to learn that all my other work could still get done, too.

Let's take a break here for an attitude adjustment! You can record this onto a tape to play, or read through it once and guide yourself through the steps.

> Sit back, take a deep breath, and allow your eyes to gently close. I wonder if you can imagine a cloud at your feet, white and misty. As it begins to float up across your body, you begin to release any tension as though a cloud of relaxation is covering you like a blanket. As you continue to relax under this

cloud, become aware of any tension that you may sense in any part of your body. Honor that part, take a deep breath and breathe into that part, releasing the tension. Feel it flow out of you as it is absorbed in the cloud blanket.

Continue doing that with each tense part until you feel completely relaxed. Then begin to take notice of the muscles that are even smaller, that may still be holding tension. Those muscles might be around your eyes, your mouth, your forehead—perhaps in your neck, your stomach, or your back. Go ahead now and release even these muscles. Allow your muscles to become soft and to spread like the mist of the cloud that envelopes your body. Isn't it surprising how many muscles are tense that you are not even aware of?

Let your mind drift back to a time when you were a child. You were playing and you were enjoying yourself. The world just seemed to slip away. There was nothing more important to you at that moment than just the fun that you were having. Your mind is focused and your body feels so good and so youthful. Perhaps you run and tumble, and hide, or climb up onto something. You just keep going until you are exhausted and it feels so good. Take your time and really enjoy how it feels to be having so much fun.

How does your body feel? What is it that you really enjoy doing?

After a while it is time to go do your chores. You have things to take care of, but it is alright because it will not be long before you can come back and play again. You can look forward to coming back to play again really soon. It is easy to remember that you forgot how much you like to play, relax, and move your body. It feels so good.

In a moment, you will be coming back to the present moment. And when you do so you will have the opportunity to choose, for you, what you would like to do and how you would like to feel. You may want to feel this good more often, and maybe not. It is up to you.

As I count from one to three you will come back to full wakefulness, fully alert and refreshed . . . and ready to go play! One . . . two . . . coming up . . . three . . . fully aware in the present moment.

This meditation can be repeated as often as needed to retrain your conscious and your unconscious mind to your renewed youthfulness.

Think Young—Stay Young

Now just do not forget that you have remembered to get involved with activities that make you feel young. Socialize with people who think young and act young, and get enthusiastic for the life that you are living!

CHAPTER NINE

Ten Steps to Weight Loss through Hypnosis

In Minnesota, I (K.H.) have helped thousands of people lose weight by constructing their own weight loss program using a simple combination of self-hypnosis, calorie charting, and daily activity. In fact, we have devised a formula to predict how many pounds a person will lose each week based upon two, and only two, behaviors. One simple thing we ask our students to do is to write down the number of calories they are about to consume and then total them daily in a journal. The other change is that we ask people to listen to one tape of our three-tape audiocassette program, each day, until they attain the weight they desire. After they have created their own weight loss tape, (which you will learn how to do in this chapter) they integrate that tape with the other tapes. Then they are to listen daily to one of their tapes, rotating them so they receive the full benefit from all the tapes.

The Weight Loss Formula?

Add the number of days of charting calories as noted above to the number of days listening to our three-tape self-hypnosis program. Remember that counting calories at the end of the day or after food has been consumed does not work and does not count toward the formula. You will come up with a number between 0 and 14. Take this total and divide by the number from the chart below that matches your current weight.

6   < 120 pounds
5   121-170 pounds
4   171-230 pounds
3   231 > pounds

Example: You weigh 150 pounds, listen to your audiocassette tapes four days this week and chart your calories before eating seven days. You can predict your weight loss to be (4+7) / 5 = 2.2 pounds. With over 1,200 students in our study we can accurately predict weight loss to within less than a pound with the vast majority of people.

What are The Catches?

There are several.

First, you must not consume less than 1,200 calories per day. It isn't healthy.

Second, your attention to determining the number of calories before you eat is also intended to bring awareness to the vast amount of food you unconsciously eat. Therefore, we want you to cut your total daily calorie intake by 20 percent. You find this number by eating the way you have been eating for four days. Then find the average number of calories you consume per day. You set your target at 20 percent less than this number.

Third, if you are a woman, do not expect to achieve weight loss during your menstrual cycle.

Finally, do not lose weight too quickly. One to three pounds of weight per week is about right to achieve long-term weight loss. If you lose more than this, you might be more likely to experience weight gain again later.

The Ten Steps

People have been fighting the battle of the bulge for many years. You can probably win the battle if you utilize self-hypnosis properly. To our knowledge no one has ever designed a weight loss program that is virtually permanent in nature, that can be used by the majority of people in all cultures, with all kinds of diets. There are ten steps involved in losing weight with hypnosis. After we highlight the steps we will go into greater detail about this easy-to-use program. Read each of the ten steps carefully.

1) Understand why we gain weight and why most weight loss plans fail.
2) Understand how the mind acts on suggestions and hypnotic commands.
3) Discover the places, times, and emotions that are involved in your personal weight gain experience.

4) Create specific outcomes based on your experiences in step 3 for your future.
5) Link your outcomes to hypnotic language patterns that will bypass the anti-suggestive barrier of the mind.
6) Create a script using the newly created hypnotic suggestions for weight loss.
7) Record them onto an audiotape so that you can listen to them daily.
8) Each day, set aside a time specifically for self-hypnosis and relaxation that will allow you time for yourself.
9) Each day use the calorie charting system (see the chart at the end of this chapter) discussed above and record your progress daily.
10) Record your weight once each week to measure your results.

Why We Gain Weight—Why Most Weight Loss Plans Fail

You gain weight when you burn fewer calories than you consume. The math is simple, and, over the long term, there are no exceptions to the rule. During certain days the body may retain water, making it appear that you are gaining weight that is fatty in nature when you are not. Over any given period of time, when you are eating at least some food, the body may store fat and reduce the metabolism so less fuel is burned. These are typically times of great stress and distress. As a rule, it is very difficult to lose weight when we are "stressed out."

Hypnosis is so effective because, when done properly, it addresses the root of the adverse effects in our life, and metaphorically helps us reprogram our brains.

When you were an infant, you were taught to associate numerous stimuli or causes with a result that was food or eating. As an infant, sometimes you cried and cried without having the ability to express what you really wanted or needed. Your needs, of course, were simple. You wanted love, were hungry, were uncomfortable, or had some other need. When you were sad you cried and typically you were given a bottle and held. This quieted you down and your parent(s) assumed you were hungry. Maybe you were! On the other hand, maybe you just wanted to be cuddled by your mother or father. The food was not always necessary but you were given food anyway.

In other infant experiences, you may have been uncomfortable or afraid of something in your environment. You would cry for your loved one to pick you up and they often did. Unfortunately, it generally followed that your caregiver also fed you, when you simply needed to be picked up and held.

As an infant, eating became linked with being sad, crying, being comforted, loved, being afraid, being insecure, needing to go to the bathroom, and just about every other experience you can think of! It's no wonder that people eat when they feel insecure or experience emotions both positive and negative. For the first few years of life, we learned that no matter what our experience, food was supposed to be the answer. Today in the United States, 55 percent of all adults are overweight. Part of the reason we are such a fat society is because of our early environmental conditioning with those who loved us and just wanted us to be comfortable.

Therefore, we must unplug all the old learned patterns of when we eat and why we eat. There is a time and a place for food and eating. Eating food should be a pleasurable experience, but it should not be the answer to all of life's problems and emotions. When it is the answer, we become fat and unhealthy. Later in this chapter you will learn specifically which causes of overeating are likely to have impacted you so greatly.

Most weight loss plans fail because they do not address the mind as it really functions. The mind will work to protect the individual from harm and help the body to experience as much pleasure as possible. Depending on how each person has learned to avoid pain and experience pleasure, the individual will act upon unconscious desires and needs—instead of doing what the conscious mind would apparently prefer it to do. Affirmations do not work in losing weight unless the individual is lucky enough to have no unconscious issues relating to weight. Therefore, we must work with the unconscious mind in developing a weight loss program. We must find out the specific causes for weight gain and address each issue separately.

How Your Mind Will Accept Suggestions

The mind acts on suggestions (from you or others) as long as the suggestions are in line with the beliefs of the unconscious mind. The mind is, in part, made up of internal representations and pictures from which we draw our beliefs and attitudes. When we see long-term pictures of ourselves as fat and unattractive we are likely to move in that direction in our real life. When we see ourselves as ultimately becoming thinner and more attractive, we are more likely to move in that direction. It is very important to change the pictures, sounds, and feelings that we experience inside. In this way, we can make new mental movies of who we are becoming and what we will be like.

However, if you make a self-hypnosis tape that has numerous suggestions that do not match your current patterns of thinking, the unconscious mind will simply ignore them. In order to rewrite the patterns of your mind we must give ourselves more than simple suggestions. We must address specific negative patterns and beliefs, and then rewrite new patterns in place of the old ones. Then we can offer suggestions to move toward the weight we want to be at!

What Caused You to Gain Weight?

Everyone has several reasons or causes for gaining weight. Genetics can surely play a role in our normal body weight. Your metabolism is very important in exactly how many calories are burned every day. It is not easy to control these elements within the mind-body connection. However, there are other more significant reasons why you gain weight that can be controlled and changed. Many people eat in order to unconsciously fill emotional needs. Some people eat because of habitual patterns they fall into.

> *Most people eat, in part, because they unconsciously*
> *need to reward themselves.*

When you were a child, you were rewarded with a dessert or a snack *if* you ate all of the food on your plate. Your mom said, "If you eat all of your potatoes, then you can have some cookies." You may also remember that when you were a child you would be rewarded with ice cream or cookies when you had done something that was good. "If you are good, we'll get pizza tonight."

There are worse things than eating ice cream or cookies, but if you continue to link achievement, or good behavior, to rewarding yourself with food, you will never break the cycle of gaining weight. The cycle was installed during infancy and has been habitual ever since. Breaking the cycle begins with understanding the when, where, and why we are overweight.

Where do you eat food? Typically, food is best eaten at the dinner table. It's a good habit to get into. If you associate eating food with sitting at the dinner table you probably will eat less food. Most of us do eat a great deal of food at the dinner table, but we also have other places we eat food that probably are not helping us reduce our food intake.

Here is how we begin the process of unplugging old patterns of eating and replacing them with new ones.

Where do you eat?

Which of these questions do you answer "Yes" to and which do you want to change?

Do you eat while you watch television?
Do you eat while you are driving your automobile?
Do you eat more when you have business lunches or dinners than you do when you eat at home?
Do you eat more food when invited to a friend's than when you are home?
Do you eat in bed?
Where else do you eat that you know you would be better off not eating?
Where else do you eat that you would prefer not to eat?

Which of the following "emotional reasons" seem to apply to you? Your emotional experience prior to, during, and after eating is also very important. If you find that you eat when you feel sad or lonely, you may be able to create a new behavior by doing something else other than eating when you are sad or lonely. If you find that you feel guilty after eating, you may find that you can address that issue with hypnosis (or hypnotherapy) as well.

Do you eat when you feel unappreciated?
Do you eat when you are sad?
Do you eat when you are happy?
Do you find yourself eating when you are lonely?
Do you eat when you are anxious?
Do you eat when you are depressed?
Do you eat when you are calm?
Do you eat when you are fearful or afraid?
Do you eat when your self-esteem is suffering?
When you are done eating, do you feel guilty or ashamed?
At what other times do you eat that you would prefer not to?

Solving the Weight Loss Puzzle

Here is the real solution to losing weight effectively and permanently. Please do not simply read past this section, but carefully and thoughtfully consider what you are about to do. It will change your life. The best strategy for unplugging old behaviors is to replace them with a new behavior. It is very important, in fact critical, that you now answer the following question carefully:

In each of the cases above where you had a "yes" answer, what specifically would you rather do than eat food?
a)
b)
c)
d)
e)
f)

Now you have specific experiences that you want to change and specific experiences you want to have instead.

Perhaps you responded "yes" to eating on your way home from work and you have decided that you would like to change that. Now, imagine that you would rather drink water instead of eating on your way home from work. That is one change that we will make in hypnosis.

Imagine another "yes" response was that you tend to eat when you are depressed. Now, suppose you would rather walk around the block when you are depressed—this is another behavior we will change in hypnosis.

See how easy it is? We simply identify when, where, and why we eat, then create new responses to those stimuli! Of course, if you simply decided to make these changes you would go back to your old ways in a few days or weeks. However, if you create a self-hypnosis audiocassette program that will allow you to listen to these suggestions daily, you will likely experience long-term success because of the "layering" effect that happens with suggestions. "Layering," in this case, simply means that you hear repetitive suggestions while in trance that the mind wants to act on.

You should know that the mind does not want to act on all suggestions. That is why affirmations typically do not work. You can not simply say, "I weigh 110 pounds," and expect to shortly weigh 110 pounds, when you really weigh twice that! The unconscious mind will not tolerate you lying to it. Therefore, you must communicate with your unconscious mind in the same way you communicate with a young child. You must talk to yourself artfully and truthfully. This is not as easy as you might think!

The unconscious mind knows when you are not being truthful. You can not fool yourself, but you can make suggestions palatable to the way your unconscious mind accepts or rejects communication.

Remember that earlier in the book we talked about how important words like "because" and "don't" are in communicating with the unconscious mind? Let's take look at how we can use those specific words in making the transition between old and new behaviors. Then we will look at other words and phrases that will help you make suggestions that are acceptable to the unconscious mind.

The word "because" gives the mind the cause-effect relationships between stimulus response it always seeks out.

"It's important that you are good because Daddy will be home soon."

That really is not why a child should be good, but it is a cause-effect statement linked with the word "because" and, therefore, the mind typically acts on the suggestion. (Of course, the implied punishment is correlated to the effectiveness of the statement, too!) As we are learning more about how the mind works, we know that we want to avoid threats of punishment in our communication. We can, however, continue to use the word "because" due to its enormous power over our behavior.

Notice that these sentences are not necessarily grammatically well formed, nor are they always logical! The unconscious mind does not think in terms of logic, but rather in emotions. It also thinks in terms of cause and effect, whether true or not! Here are a few examples of how you can do this when you begin using your own self-hypnosis tapes.

Formulating Suggestions Utilizing the Word "Because"

"I find that I walk when I am nervous because eating no longer makes me feel better."

"Each day I eat better because I will soon weigh less."

"Eventually I will eat at the table and not in bed because I will look better."

"Each meal I eat, I will find myself leaving half the food on the plate because I am no longer a slave to the plate."

"When I get hungry, I will drink a glass of water first because I know that sometimes I feel hungry when I really only need water."

"I will eat less at each meal because I can see myself fitting into the next size smaller jeans very soon!"

"I will lose weight because it is an important that I do."

"I will eat more proteins and fats because too many carbohydrates seem to add weight to my body."

"I will take a walk everyday because it will make me feel great inside and look great on the outside!"

Formulating Suggestions Using the Word "Don't"

The word "don't" is nearly as powerful in trance as the word "because," but for different reasons. Earlier in this book, we discussed that the word "don't" is a directive. It directs you to imagine or think something that you might not have considered otherwise. "Don't" is also effective because when we were young we decided to want to do that which we were told not to do!

"Don't think of dollar bills." (A part of you says, "I will if I want to . . . " and indeed you do!)

"Don't turn the light off." (Click—the light is turned off by the child.)

"Don't go into the street when you go outside." (The child goes outside . . . and into the street.)

You get the idea. We rebelled early on by either doing what we were told to "don't" do or we wanted to do that which we were not supposed to do. Once the unconscious mind decides it wants to do something, it acts in a remarkable target-finding fashion. The unconscious mind does not like to be told what to do. It responds to many commands in a rebellious fashion. It often does the opposite of what it's told to do. Therefore, when you construct your suggestions for yourself, remember that you are not just formulating these suggestions for your rational self, but also for the little child within that acts from rebellion!

Here is how we will use the word "don't" in structuring suggestions for weight loss.

"Don't feel obligated to lose weight." (The unconscious mind says, "I will if I want to!")

"Don't feel like you should push half the plate of food away when you are done eating." (The plate gets pushed away with half left.)

"Don't feel too good inside when you eat less and exercise more." ("I will if I want to!")

"Don't feel obligated to eat more food that is nutritious and less that is going to make you fat." ("I will if I want to!")

How do you use the word "don't?" The easiest way is to attach it to the word "feel," along with the description of what you would rather experience. Typically, if you can respond, "I will if I want to!" and that response propels you to a good behavior, you have used the word "don't" properly!

Formulating Suggestions Using the Word "Now"

"Now" is one of the most powerful words in the English language. Remember when this conversation took place . . .

> "Mom can I stay up late to watch my favorite TV show?"
> "No, honey, get on up to bed."
> "But please, Mom, can't I just stay up late this one night?"
> "Honey, I said, get up to bed."
> "But please, M . . . "
> "NOW!"

Pitter patter pitter patter . . . up the child goes to bed . . . no further words are exchanged as the child knows what comes after "now!"

In hypnosis, we love the word "now" because we know that people take action on whatever is attached to this gently spoken "suggestion." We use the word "now" at the beginning, middle, or end of sentences, and once again, we are not as interested in being grammatically correct as we are in the proper use of the word to create change in the mind of the individual. Here are some examples of how to use the word "now" in your self-hypnosis cassette tapes you will soon design.

> "Now . . . when you feel hungry you find that taking a deep breath in and holding, then releasing allows your hunger to diminish . . . "
> "When you see food you will often feel compelled to take a walk . . . now . . . "
> "Now, what is it that would have to happen for you to begin losing weight now?"
> "Now, when you see your television you will bring any food on the coffee table back to the refrigerator."

"Now, when you feel sad or alone you will find yourself picking up a
book and reading instead of what you used to do . . . "
"Now, allow yourself to pass by fast food restaurants on the way home
. . . "
"Wouldn't it be wonderful if you began eating less each day, now?"

Formulating Suggestions with the Word "Imagine"

"Imagine Yourself in a Mercury Now"

It worked, didn't it? How long has Mercury been utilizing this incredibly powerful hypnotic phrase to create market share? Yes, "imagine" is a
magnificent word that helps you bypass the anti-suggestive barrier of the
mind quickly and easily because whatever follows "imagine" does not
have to be acted upon. In other words, there is no apparent authoritative
command implied when the word "imagine" is heard. The opposite is, of
course, true. Whatever comes after "imagine" just slides right on into the
unconscious mind because the word opens the mind's door so easily. The
word seems to say, *you don't have to do what I now am saying, just imagine it.* But, what it really does is implant the suggestion into the unconscious mind without critique. Then the unconscious mind immediately
goes to work at finding and pursuing whatever it is told to imagine!

Therefore, the suggestions you formulate in replacing old eating behaviors with new positive behaviors will likely be acted upon by the unconscious mind without further thought. Here are some examples in changing
those old eating patterns into productive habits using the word "imagine."

"Imagine that when you reach into the cookie jar for six cookies you
now drop five out of your hand and slowly eat the one . . . "
"Imagine that when you experience anxiety you now write a letter in
place of putting food in your hands . . . "
"Imagine what you look like in the mirror after you have been on your
weight loss program for six months . . . now."
"Imagine what it's like to be able to fit into a pair of pants one size
smaller than you are now wearing and imagine how good that
makes you feel inside when you realize you have made this major
accomplishment!"
"Imagine how much lighter you will feel when you have lost nine
pounds, which is the same as what one gallon of milk weighs . . .

just imagine taking the gallon of milk out of your body and setting it aside . . . forever . . . now . . . "

Isn't it incredible how just a word or two in the right place with the right vocal intonation can change how we think and what we do? There are more ways to use the power of words and phrases in your self-hypnosis program to change your life. Here are some phrases using a number of different hypnotic language patterns and words that are useful for almost everyone's self-hypnosis when trying to lose weight.

"Each day you find it easier to write down calories before you actually eat your food."
"Pushing half away can actually allow you to feel happier but don't feel as if you must!"
"Don't feel as if you have to lose weight too quickly."
"You might find that seeing yourself in pants two sizes smaller in two months is easy to imagine."

Do you see how easy this is? Now it is time for you to begin making your own self-hypnosis cassette tape. Go back and find all of the behaviors you want to change and write them out on a sheet of paper. Then write down all of the behaviors you would like to experience instead. When you have done this, begin writing suggestions using hypnotic language and words that will help your mind accept the suggestions for the new behaviors in a fashion that is quick and easy. At the beginning of your audio tape, use the induction below to begin your tape. Finally, record these suggestions onto an audiocassette and listen to it daily. The length of the tape is not important, but the quality of the suggestions is!

Inducing Trance for Weight Loss

When you make your audiocassette, you want to use a short but powerful induction before you make your suggestions. This induction is adapted from an old induction created by a hypnotist named Dave Elman. We think you will find using this induction very helpful in changing your weight effortlessly and permanently. Notice where the word "Suggestions" is below. It is at that point that you should state all of your suggestions. Then tape the conclusion word for word as you see it below. You will soon be on your way to a thinner and more attractive you!

Your Script for Your Self-Hypnosis Tape for Weight Loss

Now . . . take a long deep breath and hold it for a few seconds. As you exhale this breath, allow your eyes to close and let go of the surface tension in your body. Just let your body relax as much as possible . . . now . . .

. . . Now . . . place your awareness on your eye muscles and relax the muscles around your eyes to the point where your eyelids just will not work. When you are sure that they're so relaxed . . . that as long as you hold the relaxation, they just won't work . . . hold onto that relaxation and test them to make sure the eyelids stay closed and don't work . . . good . . .

. . . Now . . . this relaxation you have in your eyes is the same quality of relaxation that I want you to have throughout your whole body. So, just let this quality of relaxation flow through your whole body from the top of your head to the tips of your toes . . .

. . . Now, you can deepen this relaxation much more. In a moment, I am going to have you open and close your eyes. When you close your eyes that is your signal to let this feeling of relaxation become twice as deep. All you have to do is want it to happen and you can make it happen very easily. Okay, now, open your eyes . . . now close your eyes and feel that relaxation flowing through your entire body, taking you much deeper. Use your wonderful imagination and imagine your whole body is covered and wrapped in a warm blanket of relaxation.

(pause)

. . . Now, we can deepen this relaxation much more. In a moment, I am going to have you open and close your eyes one more time. Again, when you close your eyes, double the relaxation you now have. Make it become twice as deep. Okay, now once more, open your eyes . . . close your eyes and double your relaxation . . . good. Let every muscle in your body become so relaxed that as long as you hold on to this quality of relaxation, every muscle of your body will not work.

. . . In a moment, I am going to have you open and close your eyes one more time. Again, when you close your eyes, double your relaxation you now have. Make it become twice as deep. Okay, now, once more, open your eyes . . . close your eyes and double your relaxation . . . good. Let every muscle in your body become so relaxed that as long as you hold on to this quality of relaxation, every muscle of your body will not work.

Now, in a moment, I am going to have you lift your right index finger.

Just allow yourself to experience that index finger raising up . . . up . . . up . . . good . . . that's right . . . all by itself . . . and when I say release it, you will notice that it just plops down and you'll allow yourself to go much deeper. Ready? . . . Good . . . and . . . release it . . . twice as deep. Very good.

Now this is a wonderful state of relaxation. Each time you experience this state of relaxation you will be more relaxed and comfortable within yourself.

Now, I want you to know that there are two ways a person can relax. You can relax physically and you can relax mentally. You have already proved that you can relax physically, now let me show how to relax mentally. In a moment, I'll ask you to begin slowly saying the alphabet backward, out loud, starting with Z.

Now, here's the secret to mental relaxation, with each letter you say, double your mental relaxation. With each letter you say, let your mind become twice as relaxed. Now if you do this, by the time you reach the letter V, or maybe even sooner, your mind will have become so relaxed, you will have actually relaxed all the rest of the letters that would have come after V, right out of your mind, there just won't be any more letters. Now, you have to do this, I can not do it for you. Those letters will leave if you will them away. Now start with the idea that you will make that happen and you can easily dispel them from your mind.

Speak into the tape recorder: Now, say the first letter, Z and double your mental relaxation.

You in trance: Z

Speak into the tape recorder: Now double that mental relaxation, let those letters already start to fade.

You in Trance: Y

Speak into the tape recorder: Double your mental relaxation. Start to make those letters leave. They'll go if you will allow them to fade . . . away.

You in trance: X

Speak into the tape recorder: Now, they'll be faded away like chalk being erased from a chalk board . . . Good. Faded. Good. Now relax, feel comfortable and be calm.

Your "Suggestions" go here.

Speak into the tape recorder: Now I want you to become more aware of the sounds that you hear around you and slowly bring your attention back to the sounds and the people in this room. Allow yourself to comfortably feel the air temperature and know that I am here and when I say the word one you can open your eyes and feel wide awake and refreshed. Five . . . four . . . becoming more alert and aware . . . three . . . two . . . and now wide awake and refreshed . . . when you want to open your eyes let them open and feel great.

Your self-hypnosis tape for weight loss is now complete and you are ready to listen to it once per day for the next couple of months. You will soon feel better and look great as you allow yourself this time each day, reprogramming your mind with the suggestions of the behaviors you always wanted but never knew you could have!

Charting Your Progress: Day by Day

The chart below is something you will want to copy and hold on to for as long as you want to keep your weight off. Each day write the date in the date column. Then write how many calories you consumed today. We suggest you keep a notepad with you all day so you can write how many calories you consume immediately before you put the actual food into your mouth. This makes eating a conscious function. In other words, you now become aware of all the food you will eat, and you decide in advance what and how much it will be. All you record on your note is the number of calories you will consume before eating.

In the column that says "Tape?" you simply write "yes" or "no." The question thatthis answers is, "Did you listen to your self-hypnosis tape today?" Listening to your tape before bedtime, or even while in bed, is just fine, and, yes it is okay if you fall asleep during your tape! The column that says "activity" is for you to answer "yes" or "no" to. This answers the question, "Did you participate in moderate exercise for 25 minutes or more today?" We have found that walking for 25 minutes each day qualifies for a "yes" answer.

Record your weight once each week and your measurements once each week. Weigh yourself three times on your scale and always use the heaviest of the three weigh-ins. We suggest you purchase a digital scale as they tend to be more accurate than the analog/needle scales.

Keeping track of your daily weight loss program takes approximately two minutes per day. It is this very simple ritual that will play such a big role in your daily progress toward success. In 90 days you will find this progress chart to be a daily reward for your changed behavior. You will also see this record as one of the major causes for how much better you will feel every day! Using self-hypnosis to lose weight is truly easy and you will be eternally grateful that you took the time to invest in yourself!

Here is an example of a man who charted his calories every day for four days, then cut back his calorie intake by 20 percent. This person listened to his tape six days in the week. We would expect about 2-3 pounds lost and that is what he experienced. "W" indicates waistline (at the belly button). "H" indicates hips at their widest point.

Date	Calories	Tape?	Activity	Weight	Measurements
11/1	1,800	Y	Y	178	W/36 H/36
11/2	1,675	Y	N		
11/3	1,750	N	N		
11/4	1,850	Y	Y		
11/5	1,500	Y	Y		
11/6	1,450	Y	Y		
11/7	1,600	Y	N		
11/8	1,500	Y	N	176	

Weight loss is something that you can do and something that you can maintain, if you will only take the time for yourself to make it happen! Here is a script that you can incorporate into your own self-hypnosis tapes or use it all by itself to help you achieve the success you desire.

Draw a deep breath into your lungs and release . . . good . . . now . . . draw another deep breath into your lungs . . . and hold . . . and slowly release . . . good . . . now for a moment pay attention to your breathing and how it feels when you breathe deeply into the deepest parts of your lungs . . . good . . . that's right . . . now . . . one more deep . . . in . . . good . . . breath . . . and gently release . . . good . . . and feeling in control of your self and you feel good about that . . . as you begin to notice that you have been paying attention to your breathing . . .

Imagine . . . now . . . as you close your eyes . . . gently and comfortably, that you are . . . looking at a plate of food that has been prepared for you. It looks . . . oh, so good and . . . you are tempted to eat all of the food on the plate and you think that would be good . . . and then you realize that . . . now you are going to make a change in how you have been eating . . . good . . . because this is the starting point . . .

Imagine that you begin to eat the food on the plate . . . eating slowly

. . . and when a quarter of the food is eaten . . . you begin to feel that full feeling in your stomach . . . because you do . . . and now you feel that you can eat a little more and feel good . . . and you do . . . and you eat a little more food until about one half of the food is left on the plate . . .

And you think about what you were told when you were a child . . . remember? . . . "you must eat all of your food because there are people starving somewhere else" . . . and you smile inside when you realize that whether you eat the food or not . . . it does not change that truth does it? . . . that's right . . . it seemed to make sense when you were a child . . . but now you realize that it's all right to leave half of the food on your plate and it reminds you of a time when you were a child . . . and much thinner than you are now . . . when you left food on your plate . . . or didn't want to eat it all . . . and you may have gotten scolded . . . remember . . .

And you realize that now you can begin to take back control of your own decisions about eating and that you don't have to answer to anyone but yourself . . . and that makes you feel good inside . . . to begin to regain the control in your life that you had lost for so many years . . . and it feels good . . .

And now you look at someone in your mind's eye and you see them eating food and they are overweight . . . and they eat all of the food on their plate . . . and they look like they always finish all of the food on their plate and you know that is what you have been doing for so long . . .

And now . . . you see someone thinner . . . more attractive . . . who has life and vibrancy. . . and is fun to be with and now . . . you realize that as you watch them eat . . . they leave half of their food on their plate and then get up and walk away . . . they enjoyed their food but felt good . . . and full . . . and satisfied inside . . . to know it is all right to walk away having eaten half of the food on the plate . . . and you know that is what you will do . . . from this moment forward . . .

And you feel . . . back in control of your life . . . and free . . . and it does feel good . . . to be back in control means that you can choose not to eat the sugars that you once did . . . because sometimes that can make you feel better inside . . . sometimes . . . the cravings that you felt were part of what may have taken you out of control . . . now you feel better . . . as you eat less . . . you feel more full . . . and you feel healthier . . . and that makes you feel better . . . and when you do feel hungry there are some things you can do . . . now . . . to make you feel full inside . . .

You begin to breathe deeply when you find yourself craving food . . . a deep breath in and then slowly out . . . and then a deep breath in and out

. . . and then slowly out . . . and that curbs the hunger . . . and when you need more assistance you find a nice cool glass of water . . . pure water . . . that you can drink in . . . and feel comforted inside . . . feeling better than you have in years . . . and you feel good inside . . . water . . . water . . . water . . .

. . . and sometimes when you feel hungry . . . you will find that taking a walk or becoming active will help you feel better inside . . . just by walking . . . and feeling in control . . . and it feels good . . . to be active again . . . to move . . . and be fluid . . . like water . . . back to how you were when you were younger and you were thinner . . . and free . . . and you feel so good inside . . .

Remember when you were young and you used to play outside and being outside could be fun . . . and sometimes it was easy to lose track of time being outside . . . having fun . . . playing . . . running around . . . enjoying yourself . . . while you were active . . . remember that now . . . and imagine being in those shoes . . . again . . . now . . . and see how you feel inside . . . and hear yourself . . . tell yourself . . . that you can have fun . . . and look better . . . and feel better . . . now . . . because you deserve it! . . . and . . .

As each day passes . . . you find yourself . . . looking better . . . feeling better . . . enjoying life more . . . being in control . . . living with a passion . . . and happy . . . feeling proud of the progress you make each day . . . as you chart your progress . . . every day . . .

And now . . . as you orient yourself back to the present . . . you bring all of the things that you have learned . . . in this experience . . . back with you to the present . . . and you know that you are making progress inside . . . because you already feel better inside . . .

You become aware of the sounds around you, you feel fresh and ready to take on the world and be alive . . . orienting yourself to today and the room you are in and when you hear the word one *you can open your eyes, feeling wide aware and refreshed . . . three, two . . . and* one.

Record this script into a tape recorder then listen to it daily or as part of the audiocassettes that you will design or purchase for your weight loss program. By reinforcing the suggestions you make for yourself you will find yourself experiencing weight loss with almost no effort on your part. The simplicity of the program is the key to its effectiveness. Reprogram your mind, relax, chart your progress every day and watch yourself become thinner than you dreamed possible. Be patient and don't lose weight too quickly. Losing weight at the rate of 1-3 pounds per week will enhance the likelihood that you will keep it off, permanently!

CHAPTER TEN

Putting the Cigarette Out

What is a Habit?

Humans are habitual by nature. Our habits are what allow us to do many things in a routine fashion, leaving our conscious minds to think of new and different things. We brush our teeth, shower, and get dressed, pretty much by habit. Think about all the regular activities that you participate in during a day, and see how many of them you have turned into habits. These daily routines become automatic. So many of our habits are a matter of convenience and are positive attributes of our lives.

Our habits are formed by the training we receive. When we were young children, our parents helped us to form habits either by demonstrating certain behaviors that we emulated, or by having us perform certain routine activities. By following suit, we were rewarded or were able to avoid punishment. So, not only have our unconscious minds been taught that habits and routines create convenience and expedience, but that punishments and rewards follow certain behaviors. These punishments and rewards can be delivered physically, mentally, or emotionally. Early on in life we began to seek patterns of behavior that gave us the results that we wanted.

We can also train ourselves to have distasteful, unhealthy habits. Yes, we train ourselves to have these habits, too. For most people it is not natural to begin drinking alcohol or coffee, or to take that first puff off a cigarette. Do you remember the first time you had a cigarette? The experience most people have is one of choking, coughing, difficulty breathing, a burning throat, and being disgusted by the taste left in their mouth.

Now, you may ask yourself why would anyone go to such lengths just to acquire a habit that, in the end, is not going to benefit their health or life? Well, there was some type of reward or result that was desired for the smoker in order for them to try so hard to have the habit. Those rewards, as well as several other factors, are what we have to determine in order to begin the process of quitting such a habit.

In this chapter you will learn:
* What motivated you to begin smoking
* What motivates you to continue smoking
* How to resolve the conflict inside you between the part of you that wants to continue smoking and the part that wants to quit
* The difference between physical and mental/emotional addictions
* Factors that prevent you from quitting and how to negate them
* Encouraging health statistics
* Why we sabotage ourselves and how to prevent that
* How to alter your stimulus response
* Meditation, visualization and breathing techniques
* How to remain a non-smoker
* Good news for those who quit

Why, Indeed, Did You Begin Smoking?

The answer to that question may appear to be obvious at the onset. It may have been peer pressure, or a dare, or to feel grown up like mommy and daddy. It could be a number of reasons. But, what we want to really know is, what was the true purpose of smoking? What are the underlying causes? What is truly being satisfied with each puff of the cigarette?

When we find those answers, we can begin to satisfy that need in other, healthier ways. By doing that the smoker can truly begin the healing process and cease smoking once and for all.

Smoking By the Numbers

Before we learn to discover those hidden motivators for smoking, let's take a look at some of the statistics about smoking.

Each day, an average of 3,000 Americans become regular smokers. Of these people, 1,000 will die early from a smoking-related cause. According to the Center for Disease Control, each year tobacco smoking kills more people than AIDS, alcohol, drug abuse, car crashes, murder, suicide, and fires combined.

And yet, even with those statistics available to the public, people young and old continue to buy and consume tobacco products. We must seriously ask ourselves why.

In various eras throughout history, smoking has been touted as fashionable. You were considered part of the "in crowd" if you, too, were seen with a cigarette in your hands or hanging between your lips.

Of course, the tobacco industry has annually poured billions of dollars into advertising and promotional products. But, is advertising anything other than hypnosis and persuasion? If they can implant suggestions and persuade our unconscious and conscious minds to act in a certain fashion, why can't similar methods be employed to counteract those very messages?

There are other reasons why people start to smoke. One of the most important keys for success in smoking cessation will be to determine the exact underlying reason why you, personally, have taken up smoking, and continue to participate in this habit.

Getting to the Root

The reason why a person smokes is completely an individual matter. Beyond peer pressure, beyond the advertising gimmicks and enticements, there lies a very personal issue. In my (M.L.) practice, I have heard reasons such as the following:

It gives me an excuse to take a break at work.

The smoke cloud around me keeps people away.

It's the only thing I can control in my life.

There is an empty place in my throat that wants to let out a scream of frustration and the smoke fills that space and keeps me quiet.

There can be many other reasons why people begin smoking. Let's discover what that root cause is for you.

The Root Cause of Your Smoking

Read through this exercise before doing it.

Sit back in a comfortable location, free of distractions. Take a deep breath and allow your body to relax in the manner that you know is best for you.

As you close your eyes, allow your mind to take you back to your very first experience of smoking a cigarette. Relive that experience starting at a moment just before you took that first puff. Move slowly through that event, remembering how you felt physically, what was going through your mind, and what emotions you were experiencing. Continue to the end of that event. Then go over the same scenario two more times, remembering more and more with each passage.

When you have finished, answer the following questions:
How old were you when you smoked your first cigarette?
Where were you?
What else were you doing at the time?
What emotional state were you in just prior to smoking your first cigarette?
What mental state were you in?
Who were your friends?
Who were you with when you smoked your first cigarette?
Were any of your family members smokers?
What was your physical reaction to smoking?
What was your emotional reaction to smoking?
What was your mental reaction to smoking?
What were your needs at the time?
Did they appear to be satisfied by smoking?
What rewards did you perceive that you attained by smoking?
Who were you proud to share your experience with?
Who were you ashamed to share it with, or felt you had to hide it from?
What have you learned about yourself from having experienced this exercise?

You may have to repeat this exercise a few times before you get the profound "ah-ha" experience. And yet, some people will have these revelations right away. Just remember that the underlying motivation to start smoking is generally not the obvious one you would expect, such as peer pressure or because your parents did it. It is usually something deeper such as: you don't know how to ask for what you want, it prevents you from speaking your mind, or you aren't fulfilling your life dream.

Why Continue?

So once you have determined the initiating cause of smoking, you want to determine the true reasons why you continue to smoke, even though you already understand that your body is being harmed.

Since you are reading this there seems to be a part of you that really would like to stop smoking. We know that there is a part of you that also wants to continue smoking or you would simply have quit. It is, therefore, obvious that there is an internal argument going on. The simplest way of settling an internal argument is to completely separate each part out from the other part so they are not jumbled and confused inside of you.

Have paper and pen handy as you do the following exercise.

Begin by relaxing again. Sit back and take a breath. That's right, just plain old fresh air, in the lungs and out.

Now, allow the two parts of you that have differing views of this smoking issue to separate. Collect on one hand the part of you that wants to continue smoking, and collect on the other hand the part of you that wants to quit smoking. See them as distinctly separate, as though they were two separate people with opposing opinions.

Allow yourself to "get into" the energy of the part of you that wants you to continue smoking. Without any input or interruptions from the other part of you, begin to write down all of that part's arguments, thoughts, feelings, fears, and concerns. Let it express itself without any filters or judgments until it has said everything it wants to.

Then leave that side and move over to the other side, into the part that wants you to quit smoking. Allow yourself to fully be "in" that part. Have that part express itself completely, in writing, in the same manner as before. No interruptions, no judgments.

When they have each expressed their points of view, go back to the part that wants you to continue smoking. Allow it to respond to the arguments it heard from the other side. Write them down. Let it continue until it has said all it wants to say. Then allow the side that wants you to quit give its rebuttal until it has completely expressed itself. Continue back and forth until they have each completely expressed their point of view, or one side has given in to the reasoning of the other side.

If the side that wants to quit has convinced the other side, then you will be able to proceed with giving up the smoking habit with little or no conflict. If the side that wants to continue smoking still holds out, more work will have to be done on the unconscious motivations. In that case, proceed to the next step.

No part of you should ultimately want you to engage in any activity or habit that is injurious to your well being. When that is the case, something even deeper has to be revealed. We will address that issue in just a moment.

Effects of Nicotine Withdrawal

Before we proceed to the next step, I want to discuss some of the ramifications that you may experience as you withdraw from nicotine. Nicotine is a chemical with strong addictive properties. One of the reasons why smoking cessation is so challenging is because the body becomes accustomed to a certain amount of the chemical. When that is no longer supplied, it reacts. The more nicotine it is accustomed to, the stronger the potential reaction.

There are two levels of addiction occurring when a person smokes. There is the physical addiction, and the emotional/mental addiction. In hypnosis, we address the emotional/mental aspects first to ease the transition to being a non-smoker. Once the emotions and mind are aligned with making the change, the physical reactions can be dealt with in a stronger, more congruent, fashion.

Let's talk about the possible physical repercussions of quitting smoking. With withdrawal you may experience any of the following symptoms:

Sweating, rapid pulse, increased hand tremor, insomnia, nausea, vomiting, physical agitation, anxiety, and transient visual, tactile, and/or auditory hallucinations. There have even been reported cases of grand mal seizures from nicotine deprivation.

The more nicotine your body is accustomed to, the stronger the reaction may be when it is taken away.

Research has shown that nicotine is a stimulant that contributes to the alleviation of depression. If depression is suspected, you may want to consult your doctor. Perhaps an alternative anti-depressant would reduce the need for cigarettes.

However, there is encouraging news. According to the FIND (Foundation for Innovations in Nicotine Dependence), your body has a tremendous capacity to heal itself and rapidly responds to the elimination of nicotine in the system. According to their findings, the following changes begin to occur in your body:

- Twenty minutes after your last cigarette, your blood pressure begins to drop to normal and the temperature of your hands and feet increases to normal.

- Eight hours after your last cigarette the carbon monoxide levels in your blood drops to normal and the oxygen level increases to normal.
- After twenty-four hours from your last cigarette, your chances of a heart attack are reduced.
- After forty-eight hours, your nerve endings start to regenerate. In two weeks to three months, your circulation improves and lung function increases up to 30 percent.
- In one to nine months, coughing, sinus congestion, fatigue, and shortness of breath fade away. Cilia regenerate in the lungs, increasing their ability to handle mucus, clean the lungs, and reduce infection.

As you can see, the benefits of giving up the smoking habit can be rapid and significant. By maintaining your sights on the benefits, perhaps you can keep yourself motivated to move through the difficult stages.

The Next Step

What continues to motivate you to smoke? In the face of all the knowledge that is available about the detrimental health effects of smoking, why would there be a part of you that continues to want you to smoke?

It is highly likely that the reasons that inspired you to start smoking are not the ones that keep you smoking now. Perhaps your original reason was to act grown up. You are grown up now and probably want to look younger! Maybe your original reason was to be rebellious. Who or what are you rebelling against now? Could it be your own better judgment?

It is time we examined why you are continuing to smoke, even in the face of so many reasons to quit. You want to quit, and your loved ones want you to quit, so why do you continue to resist putting that habit behind you?

Let's do another exercise. Go ahead and relax again in a comfortable place. This time, as you close your eyes, remember the last time you had a cigarette. Go over the event in detail from just before you lit up to right after you snuffed it out.

When you have finished, answer the following questions:
What triggered the idea to have a cigarette? (A location, a person, an activity, a mood, etc.)
What thoughts were going through your mind as you lit up?
What emotional state were you in?

What were you trying to gain?

What were you trying to avoid?

What physical sensations did you notice as you took a puff?

What other changes did you notice in your body, emotions, mind?

What occurred while you were smoking the cigarette?

What did you notice as you put out the cigarette?

What were your thoughts, emotions and physical sensations as you put out the cigarette?

What have you learned by having gone through this exercise?

When you have finished answering these questions, go through the same exercise again. This time think back to your first cigarette today. Then answer the above questions again.

When you have finished this time, go through again. This time think about your last cigarette yesterday. Answer the previous questions again, and then proceed to the next set of questions.

In what way are all these episodes similar?

In what way are all these episodes different?

What new information has come into your awareness?

How is smoking satisfying a present day need?

In what other way could that need be satisfied?

What need did you think that the smoking habit was satisfying, but now you realize that it really isn't?

Is there anything you can do right now to change your behavior so that your needs are being satisfied without the use of tobacco?

Think carefully about these possibilities, as any corrections you make in these areas will greatly increase your ability to quit smoking permanently and with more ease.

Take a Deep Breath

The next step is a breathing exercise.

Simply sit or stand tall and erect. Take in a deep breath of air, filling your lungs to capacity. Hold your breath for just five seconds and then exhale. Repeat this ten times, taking in ten full, deep breaths of air. When you exhale, be sure to push out all the air in your lungs. As you take in each breath, feel the fresh, clean air coming into your lungs and moving through your body. Imagine the molecules of air surrounding every cell of your body, cleansing it and helping it to regenerate. As you exhale, imagine the air carrying away any unhealthy debris. This exercise should leave you feeling refreshed and invigorated.

The preceding breathing exercise should also reduce your desire for a cigarette. For the maximum benefit, it should be repeated each and every time that you feel the urge to reach for a cigarette.

It is additionally helpful to meditate, visualizing yourself in a serene environment, surrounded by a clean natural setting.

Take a Five-Minute Vacation

Sit back comfortably in your chair. Take in a nice, long breath . . . and as you exhale . . . allow your eyes to gently close. Relaxing your body completely . . . relaxing your mind. The busy-ness of the day can simply be put on hold for the next five minutes so that you can relax and regain your energy. Any noises that you hear around you will simply fade into the background, reminding you to go even deeper inside . . . deeper into relaxation.

Continue to breathe . . . perhaps you are noticing the rhythm of your breath as it finds its own natural pace . . . inhale . . . exhale . . .

Imagine that you are taking a walk in a beautiful park carrying a pack on your back. There are flowers and birds and a scattering of tall shade trees. You are following a path that meanders through the beautiful green lawns. Before long, you come upon a small lake, not much bigger than a pond. There is an arched wooden footbridge that crosses from the shore where you are standing over to a small island. That island looks so inviting. There is a willow tree in the center that gives shade to most of the small island. There are ducks swimming around the perimeter and you think you even see a swan. It would be so enchanting to go to that island and enjoy its serenity.

You decide to put down your backpack on the shore—and then you begin to cross the bridge. It is so quaint and charming. And there is also something rather mysterious about it. You discover that with each step you take across the bridge you feel more and more distant from the shore and its activities . . . so much lighter and carefree.

Once you arrive on the island, you are free to walk around, exploring and enjoying the quiet solitude. You find that there is an altered sense of

time here. You are able to enjoy this island for as long as you desire . . .
relaxing . . . peaceful . . .

Continue to relax for as long as you would like to stay in this place.
You know that there will always be a part of you that remains there on that
peaceful little island. You are welcome to come back and visit anytime you
desire. And when you decide to return to the shore and back to your daily
life, you will simply walk back across the bridge and count from one to
three. One . . . aware of this room . . . two . . . coming up . . . three . . . wide
awake and energized. You may open your eyes.

Becoming a Non-Smoker

In what ways will you benefit by becoming a non-smoker?

What will you most look forward to being able to do once you are a
non-smoker?

If someone you loved very dearly was a smoker, what advice would
you give them?

In what ways do you love yourself even more than any of those people?

If you don't quit smoking, who do you think will do it for you?

What stops you from becoming a non-smoker right now?

What could you gain that is even more important than that by becoming a non-smoker?

And if you were to gain that, what could you do or have that is even
more important?

If you were to imagine, now, that you had already gained this last thing
that you named, something so important to you, something that
would enrich your life, wouldn't it seem right to just be a non-smoker, and have that now?

Record the following script, speaking slowly. It is important to go into
a deep hypnotic trance when using suggestive therapy. Do not worry
about whether you think that you are going into a deep trance or not. You
are usually deeper than you think. Also using the tape as you fall asleep
will be very beneficial.

Sitting or lying comfortably in a place free of distractions, allow your
eyes to gently close. Turn your thoughts inward as you begin to notice the
sensations in your body. Perhaps you begin to notice the temperature of the
air against your face . . . or the light pressure of your clothes against your

skin. Do you notice the difference in sensation between your right foot and your left? Perhaps you notice your heartbeat and the way your pulse feels as the blood flows through your body. Relaxing . . . as you notice the places where your body touches the chair or bed.

Allowing your body to relax even deeper, as you begin to relax your toes and your feet .. . . relax your ankles and calves. Letting go now of your knees and your thighs. Breathing and releasing . . . breathing and releasing. Relax your stomach . . . and your chest . . . and your breathing. Once again noticing the rhythm of your breath as it finds its own natural pace. Inhale . . . exhale . . . inhale . . . exhale . . . That's right . . . very good . . .

Now relax your back. Relax your shoulders, your arms, your hands and your fingers. Feeling so good to be so relaxed . . . so comfortable . . . feels so good.

Now I'm going to ask you to relax even deeper as I count from ten to one. I can't do this for you . . . only you can really let go and relax. Ten . . . relaxing even deeper. Nine . . . doubling your relaxation. Eight . . . that's right . . . feeling so good to go even deeper. Seven . . . going way down. Six . . . deeper and deeper. Very good. Now five . . . even deeper. Four . . . double that relaxation. This feels so good . . . so warm . . . rhree . . . even deeper . . . two . . . that's right . . . you know what to do . . . and one . . . so deep . . . so relaxed.

At this level, you will be able to understand many things about yourself. You will know what is best for you. But I wonder if you will remember to forget . . . or forget to remember . . . that you were ever a smoker. It seems so far away . . . like it was someone else . . .

Because right now it feels so good to breathe in and out . . . to allow fresh air into your lungs. To give your body what it wants. You want fresh air. Clean air . . . in your body.

And you know that you love yourself and that you are ready to feel so much better. And you are willing to forget to smoke because you don't want to remember. Because you know that you have a choice. And I wonder if you are a non-smoker now or will be when you stand up again. Because you can always choose to be a non-smoker.

Imagine how good it feels to feel good about yourself. And you do feel good about yourself because you are a non-smoker. And you may forget that you ever remembered that it may have ever been different.

And I wonder what's it's like, and if you already know, to feel so proud of yourself. To see the smiles on the faces of your loved ones, so happy that you are healthy. And it feels so good just to breathe in deeply . . . breathing in . . . and breathing out . . . clean fresh air . . . so deep . . .

so fresh . . . Knowing that every time you breathe in fresh air you are a non-smoker. Every breath reminding you that you are satisfied.

And perhaps you can access . . . the comfort . . . revealed by the purpose . . . that co-creates confidence . . . While transforming . . . the love . . . that leads . . . to completion . . . and harmony . . . in a reality . . . where . . . passion . . . observes . . . the answers . . . and the intention . . . surrounding . . . logic . . . where there is experience . . . and curiosity . . . within . . . the depth . . . that allows you to imagine . . . the touch . . . that changes . . . the paradox . . . running through knowledge . . . and solutions . . . where the meaning . . . is embraced by commitment . . . and the intention . . . contained in silence . . . around consciousness . . .

And in a moment you will be returning to wakefulness, refreshed and relaxed . . . one . . . two . . . three, coming up . . . four . . . aware of this time and space . . . and five . . . wide awake and alert and returned to the present moment.

Being a Non-Smoker

Now that you have become a non-smoker, you will be called on to maintain that stance. There will be tests. There always are. There will be a time when you will go out with friends and someone will be smoking in front of you. Or perhaps you will be driving, or waiting for a train, and recall a time when, by habit, you would take out a cigarette and light up. However, that was old behavior. Just like there was a time when you drank from a baby bottle, and then learned to drink from a cup. There would be no reason to go back to drinking from the baby bottle. You have learned new, more appropriate, and useful behavior. You are gaining what you really want.

However, as we talked about in the beginning, we are creatures of habit. Habits are emotionally, mentally, and physically based. Once we have eliminated the emotional and mental causes for the smoking habit, and even made it through the nicotine withdrawals, there still remains a pattern of behavior called stimulus/response. Like Pavlov's dogs that salivated whenever they heard a bell, there will be signals that your brain responds to that will trigger the mechanical pattern of reaching for and lighting up a cigarette.

Smoking cessation requires the elimination of emotional, physical, and stimulus/response habits.

There are simple techniques for redirecting those patterns. The simplest and most effective is a Neuro-Linguistic Programming (NLP) technique called the "Swish." (You used the Swish pattern in the chapter about procrastination.) Simply stated, it repatterns your brain to respond differently than you previously would have to the same stimulus.

For instance, if someone walks directly up to you and holds out their hand for a handshake, chances are you will put your hand out there before you even realize that you have done that. There are certain patterns of behavior that are so automatic that we are engaged in them before we are aware that it is happening. Reaching for a cigarette, for smokers, can be this same type of pattern. So it is important that this final key is turned in your unconscious mind so that you find yourself responding differently next time you are in that same circumstance.

The stimulus that triggers smoking for you will be a very personal one. It is important that we discover what that is for you. For this reason, a generic script or suggestion will not be nearly as powerful and successful as one that is tailored just for you.

Before you start to actually do the next exercise, it will be important for you to answer a few questions. Take your time and be as honest and accurate as possible. If you find that the exercise does not completely take away your automatic response, it may be that there are additional triggers to your smoking behavior that you are not fully aware of. Just know that as soon as you become aware of those behaviors you will be able to do this exercise again and achieve even greater success.

Think carefully and thoroughly as you answer the following questions:
In what circumstances do you typically find yourself unconsciously reaching for a cigarette?
What details do you notice about those circumstances?
What is a commonality about those events?
Is the trigger something that you feel, see, smell, hear, think, taste, or touch?
How would you like to respond instead of lighting up a cigarette?
Can you imagine yourself responding in that new way?

Okay, we are ready to proceed.
This exercise is similar to the Swish. You can do it as described in the earlier chapter with a large screen and a small screen, or you can do it in this alternate way.

Sit back in a comfortable position, in a quiet area free from distractions. With your eyes closed, imagine you are holding a picture of yourself in a circumstance that is just prior to the activation of the stimulus that creates your old behavioral response. Hold that picture in your right hand. In your left hand, imagine holding a picture of yourself responding with the new behavior that you desire. So, there you are, holding two pictures. The stimulus in the right hand, and the new desired response in the left hand.

Now, look at the picture in your right hand and allow the action to move forward to the moment that the stimulus actually occurs. As it does, allow the picture to turn to black and white, fading, like an old photograph. The picture shrinks until it disappears in a dot. Immediately, focus on the picture in your left hand—the photo of your new desired behavioral response. See that picture grow larger, more colorful and bright. Allow it to become lifesize so that you can step into that picture. Feel yourself in this new you, acting in this new way. Notice what you see, feel, and smell. When you have completed this new response, take a deep breath and hold it for several seconds. Then open and close your eyes.

Now repeat the entire procedure again, this time much faster. Doing the exercise as fast as possible is the key. Your unconscious mind learns very rapidly. You want to teach it to respond in the new manner naturally, quickly and seamlessly.

Continue to repeat this entire procedure again and again until you become extremely bored with it and find yourself yawning.

When you have completed this exercise, we need to make an "environmental" check. In other words, we need to check to see if the work is, in fact, complete. There are many reasons why it may not be complete. Perhaps the exercise was not repeated a sufficient number of times. It also could be that there are additional stimuli that trigger a smoking response that have not been "swished" away. If that is the case, the Swish needs to be performed on each of those stimuli as well.

So let's try our environmental check.

Allow your eyes to close and begin to imagine yourself moving into the future. See and feel yourself in a situation that would have previously triggered your old behavioral response. What do you notice yourself doing in this new future? How do you respond? How do you feel? What else do you notice?

If the work is complete, you should notice that you now have the new, healthy, desirable responses and that to act any other way would feel unnatural or awkward. If you still experience the urge to smoke, you will want to go back through the questions that helped you to identify the stimuli that you have been responding to. Perhaps there are more triggers than previously suspected. If you still cannot seem to determine the cause that leads you to unconsciously reach for a cigarette, wait until the next time you actually do reach for one. At that moment, take the time to determine what is going on in your environment, your thoughts, senses, or emotions that may be a catalyst for this behavior. Once that is discovered, go through the steps of the Swish once again.

You will find that if you experience these different exercises and meditations with an openness and willingness, your ability to quit smoking quickly and easily is greatly enhanced. It could occur immediately, or it could take a bit of diligent effort and discipline. Even so, there could be a time in the future when you will have one more cigarette. It could be in three months from now, or it could be in three years. And that's natural and a part of the process. At that time, you will realize that you do not enjoy it. You will know that you really are a non-smoker, and that the healing and changes are taking place.

CHAPTER ELEVEN

Pain Relief through Self-Hypnosis

Author's note: Chris McAtee, a Certified Instructor of Hypnotherapy, is one of America's leading experts on relieving pain with hypnosis. He has been kind enough to share with us his strategies and techniques for reducing pain with self-hypnosis. The remainder of this chapter is straight from the expert. Welcome, Chris McAtee!

Without a doubt, every one of us experiences physical pain in our lives, whether we are great or small, young or old, rich or poor. Not only do we all experience pain, but we each perceive it in a personal, subjective manner. In other words, any two people with the same source of pain may report very different reactions to the same stimulation. Some people might say that the person who experiences less pain has a higher tolerance or threshold for the sensations.

The subjective nature of pain has confounded the healers of the day, from the faith healers and shaman of the past to the medical practitioners and physicians of our modern world. While a person should never ignore their pain, pain does not have to decrease the quality of our lives or be the focal point of our attention each day. Self-hypnosis can be a very powerful tool in achieving the relief, that you deserve, from pain.

Why must we experience pain at all? Pain definitely has a purpose, and it is a very important one at that. Take, for example, the rare medical condition of the person who feels no physical sensations whatsoever, pleasant or painful. They never learn to remove their hand from water that is too hot for their skin nor from water that is too cold. Our experience of pain can save us from life-threatening burns or hypothermia and in these cases it is obvious that pain is of great benefit to us. However, for our purposes, let's examine the more common, everyday examples of pain that many of us have. Then we will see why it is important for us to experience pain before we learn how to reduce and occasionally eliminate it.

Pain As a Signal

Pain is the mind's way of telling us that we need to take care of ourselves.

Headaches, for example, may be a sign of any number of problems that we must be aware of, from excessive eye strain to TMJ problems, to a tumor that may need immediate diagnosis and attention. Aches and pains in the body that seem difficult to locate precisely are definite signs that we should seek a full diagnostic checkup from a physician.

These signals that we receive in the cortex of our brain as pain from the physical location in our body are messages for us to take action to correct the cause of the signal, be it disease or injury. This is the purpose of our pain, even though we often continue to feel it long after it has outlived its usefulness. This is where self-hypnosis becomes a great tool to reduce the unpleasant sensations we no longer need or want. Please remember that self-hypnosis is very powerful and you may very well be able to mask these sensations.

> *It is important that we always consult a physician before taking any action to reduce the pain or self-diagnosing its cause.*

Redefining Success: How Much Relief is Enough?

Self-hypnosis has helped thousands of people overcome their pain. There is a very real possibility that you too will find great relief from your discomfort with the power of your own mind. However, just as medicine carries no promise of a cure, hypnosis is not a panacea for all of our ills. You may have become accustomed to the disclaimer that comes along with the various pills, drugs, and potions of the day: "Results may vary." While this is true for any healing modality, hypnosis has the distinct benefit of being helpful more often, while having no list of possible negative side effects. This may be one reason why you should consider using hypnosis as an adjunct to any medications or therapies you currently find helpful.

So, just what kind of results should you expect from self-hypnosis? When will you know you have succeeded in reducing your pain and discomfort? Many people think of their pain in terms that are very black and white. Either they are currently experiencing discomfort or they are not. The truth is that we experience pain subjectively, in degrees. Pain can hurt a little bit, or it can hurt quite intensely. It is even possible to notice the messages your body sends to your brain without being bothered by them at all! We'll learn how to do that shortly, but first let's look at what degree of change you might experience in your discomfort and how much relief that would bring.

> Think of a physical activity you engage in regularly that includes a bothersome amount of pain. For some people this may be just getting out of bed. For others it may be playing your favorite sport or working in the garden. Once you have this activity in mind, close your eyes and think of the areas of your body where you experience this discomfort, then give the pain a rating of 0 to 10, with 10 being the strongest and 0 the weakest.
>
> Go ahead and do this now . . .
>
> All right, now that your eyes are open and you have a number we can examine what kind of change would be satisfactory for you.
>
> Suppose that the level of pain reported was an 8. That is pretty strong. Now, if you were able to reduce the level of pain with self-hypnosis from 8 to 6, that would be a 25 percent decrease in the amount of pain. How much more would you enjoy that experience with such a decrease? What if self-hypnosis reduced it 50 percent, from an 8 to a 4? How much easier is it for you to enjoy the experience? Close your eyes again and imagine the same physical activity as before with a 50 percent decrease in the level of discomfort and notice exactly what is different about the experience. Go ahead and do this now . . .

All right, now that your eyes are open and you have thought about the difference that a 50 percent change would bring, how much easier do you think your life would be with this kind of a change? Would you consider that much improvement in your discomfort a success? Most people would, and it's easier to achieve than you might think! The more you work with self-hypnosis and try out different techniques, the more you will be able to master your ability to alter the experience of pain. You may eventually forget about your pain entirely for longer and longer stretches of time with practice. In order to master your pain, however, it will help greatly to learn about it in detail. Learn how to "take it apart" and really understand it so you can better know how to approach and manage it with self-hypnosis.

Know Your Pain: The Components of Your Pain Experience

The more we examine the experience of pain in people, the more complex it becomes. Perhaps you have never thought of your pain beyond the fact that "it hurts." It is worth pointing out that when a physician or family member tells a person that their pain is "all in their head," it often seems they want to invalidate the person's experience. No matter what someone may have told you, if you feel your pain, then by all means your experience is true and real for you.

Regardless of origin, however, there are a number of components that contribute to our overall experience of pain. Oftentimes, separating and examining them can help us to begin feeling better before we even apply the techniques that follow. Let's start by looking at what they are:

- The expectation of pain
- The physical experience of pain
- The mental/emotional experience of pain
- The duration of pain
- The language of pain
- The secondary gains of pain
- The common themes of chronic pain

As we cover each of these seven components, you may find it useful to grab a pen and paper to keep notes with. This will be very useful later in understanding your pain better and designing your approach to hypnotic pain control.

The Expectation of Pain

Ask any friend who was spanked as a child and they will tell you that most of the fear and crying occurred well *before* the actual punishment itself. The threat of punishment in school or at home was often enough to discourage the behavior from continuing. The same applies for the pain we receive from illness and injury. Some people who suffer from migraines can tell you of the "aura" that precedes another occurrence of the incapacitating headaches. The visual and sensory effects of the aura are not painful, although the feelings of anticipation and fear that go along with it signal the beginning of what seems like an inevitable process. Those with chronic pain also experience these signals and feelings as they awake each day. It is common to hear from the long-term sufferer that each day begins with an evaluation of the level of pain they expect to bear. As a result, we increase the amount of time that we needlessly take notice of our pain and the associated feelings. However, knowing the signals your mind and body give you can help them to become less of a warning and more of a reminder to once again take care of yourself.

Take a moment now to write down any feelings or sensations that you normally have before the actual experience of pain. What physical sensations do you have? How long after these sensations does the pain begin? What is your normal reaction to these warning signs?

Are there any other emotional events that typically precede the pain, such as stress at work or contact with certain people? As you uncover the patterns that emerge you can learn which strategies you have been using that have not been working, and start taking steps to change them.

The Physical Experience of Pain

The physical experience of pain can be described in quite a number of different ways. While those with pain are able to tell you when they are hurting, they do not often examine exactly how it is that they are hurting. The broad category of "pain" can be experienced as a single sensation or many at once. Even when it is felt as one consistent sensation, there may be various aspects of that feeling that are experienced simultaneously. Paying attention to each of these aspects, and knowing what they are, can be very helpful in deciding where to start in easing your pain.

As you look at the following list of questions concerning the common physical descriptions of pain, write down those that you experience yourself. Be sure to write down any others that may come to mind that are not included here, keeping in mind that you may not be able to answer some questions as specifically as the rest.

In what area of your body do you feel the pain?
How far throughout the area does the pain extend? Where does it seem to end? Can you draw a picture of the shape of the area?

Does the pain feel hot? Warm? Cold? Does it ever change degrees?
Does the pain feel sharp or dull?
Does the pain feel like cutting, stabbing, or grinding? Can you think of
    a physical object that would cause that feeling?
Does the pain seem to be pulsing or throbbing?
Is the pain strong and consistent or does it vary in intensity?

As you look at each of the descriptions of your pain, ask yourself
which ones seem to bother you the most. If you could reduce only these
aspects of the pain you experience, how much better would you feel about
your situation overall?

Now that you have a better understanding of how your pain is felt, let's
find out how much you feel it. A good way to approach this is to use a pain
scale. Using a pain scale can be very easy and useful in judging the degree
of pain you feel. Begin by imagining a gauge or mechanical control for the
level of pain. This might be a volume knob, a thermostat, a tuner, a ther-
mometer, or a sliding toggle. Use your imagination. You may have already
used one of these ideas when you rated your level of pain during a physical activity earlier in this chapter. As before, let this scale be numbered
from 0 to 10, with ten being the strongest sensation possible.

When you have this scale in mind, think of the amount of pain that you
feel the majority of the time. Close your eyes and notice what point on the
scale your average amount of pain is at. When you have written this down
as your average pain, close your eyes again and think of the strongest
intensity you feel in a typical week. After you have written down your
strongest pain, close your eyes one last time and think of the least amount
of pain you might feel in a typical week. Feel free to think of this time of
relative relief for a little while longer if you like. Whenever you are ready,
you may open your eyes and write down the number on the scale for your
least amount of pain.

Now that you have these three numbers, look a your range of experience. Is there a large difference between your high and low? Do you ever
experience a "0" during the week? If so, what are you usually doing when
you experience a 0? As you think about each of the different aspects of
your pain can you assign different values to each one? Is the burning a 4
and the cutting a 7? Think of each of these individually as you look at
your list and give them individual ratings on your pain scale, if possible.

You are now beginning to understand your discomfort much better. In
order to help you gauge your pain more accurately, you may find it very

useful to keep a pain journal for one or two weeks. In your pain journal you may include the times during the day when you overtly notice your pain, what you are doing at the time, and what rating it receives on the pain scale. Be sure to notice any patterns that present themselves here. Once again, they can point to areas that you may want to focus your attention on to change, giving you more clues as to which techniques of self-hypnosis may be the most helpful.

The Mental and Emotional Experience of Pain

The mental and emotional experience of pain can be summarized in one word: suffering. If you experience fear, anxiety, or depression due to your pain, then be assured that you are not alone. A large number of people with pain have one or more of these feelings associated with it. The basic difference between physical pain and suffering can be expressed simply as the difference between how much pain you feel and how much it actually bothers you to feel it. Making this distinction can change your whole view of what pain means to you.

You can rate your suffering on the pain scale just as you do with your physical pain. It is interesting to note the disparity in their values. Some people may report a rating of 10 for their physical pain while giving their suffering a rating of 3 or 4. Other people may report a rating as low as 3 for their physical pain while expressing suffering upwards of an 8 on the pain scale. When keeping your pain journal, it would prove useful to include a rating of your suffering along with the other factors included in your entries. Those who reduce their level of suffering find that living with the physical sensations of pain is no longer a barrier to a productive life. This sometime relates to the topics covered below on the common themes of chronic pain.

The Duration of Pain

The duration of your pain is a simple but very important aspect to determine. Begin by asking yourself if the sensations are chronic or intermittent. In other words, do you feel pain all of the time or does it come and go? If the pain is chronic, how strong is it on average? If the pain is intermittent, does it occur every day? When it does occur, how long do you usually feel it? A migraine headache may incapacitate a person anywhere from three hours to three days at a time. These attacks can happen once a week, once a month, or even further apart. The same kinds of variations can occur in many different types of pain. Write down in your notes the average duration of your pain. The average strength of chronic pain can be reduced just as the average duration of intermittent pain can be shortened using self-hypnosis. More strategies for relief are becoming available to you.

The Language of Pain

The language we use in relation to our pain can be surprisingly relevant to the way we experience it. "Pain" is one of the most "painted" words in the English language. The mere utterance of the word in casual conversation will remind the sufferer of their plight within moments. Those without pain will still cringe upon hearing descriptions of painful feelings or situations from others. When the doctor tells you that the next procedure you undergo will "probably be a little painful," you tend to tense up in anticipation, thus making the actual experience worse than it needs to be. All of these negative reactions come from hearing the word "pain." One way to begin changing your personal experience is to start changing your language. You can begin by using the words "uncomfortable" and "discomfort" more often in place of "pain." These words are just-as-valid descriptions of the experience and do not elicit as many of the less desirable reactions we tend to have upon hearing the word.

In addition to changing our verbal descriptions of the discomfort, it can be very enlightening to take note of a phenomenon known as organ language. Do you frequently use any of the following phrases or ones like them to describe situations in your life that you dislike?

"I just can't *handle* it!"
"Just thinking about it makes my *head* hurt."
"It's a pain in the *neck/rear* to me."
"That person is just a *headache*."
"I can't *stomach* the situation at all."
"The whole problem is on my *shoulders*."
"I can't *stand* to be this way."
"That person broke my *heart*."

As you look at the emphasized word in each phrase, you may begin to see the organ language involved. These phrases are also typically uttered or thought of in an emotional moment, bypassing your anti-suggestive barrier, and act as easily accepted direct suggestions to your unconscious mind. The frequent repetition of these types of phrases in thought, or verbally, tends to create and reinforce the actual physical manifestation of the symptoms the emphasized words indicate. Many cases of back pain, headaches, pain in the joints and limbs, and various areas of the entire body are exacerbated by organ language, as well as occasionally finding their cause there. If you find yourself using organ language, write down what it is you say to yourself and think of different ways that you might be able to express those ideas. Once more, we may find clues in areas of our lives that pain is being used to draw our attention to for change and healing.

The Secondary Gains of Pain

The idea of secondary gains may be a new one for many people. The basic idea behind secondary gain is that every illness we experience also creates some positive effects. These positive effects are often experienced as social and financial incentives. These may be hard to accept at first, but they are very real and more common than most people know. When a secondary gain is strong enough, it can even prevent someone from having all of the relief or healing they desire despite their great desire to get better. The three most common secondary gains are listed below:

Financial compensation for pain—Do you receive disability or insurance reimbursements for a continued debilitating illness? How would you feel if the payments stopped?

Attention/Affection—Do you receive more caring or attention from family and loved ones due to your physical or emotional condition? Do you enjoy receiving it or fear losing it?

No need to work—Does your physical condition give you a much needed break from an occupation that you dislike or find very stressful? Does it give you more time with your family?

Be as honest with yourself as possible when answering these questions. They may lead to very important issues for you to deal with as you find healing and relief from your discomfort. Although you will be learning techniques that may sidestep these issues, it is advisable to work with a reputable hypnotherapist in these areas for the maximum benefit and long term change.

The Common Themes of Chronic Pain

The final aspect of pain that we will examine are the personality traits commonly found in chronic sufferers. These traits indicate certain general beliefs about ourselves that place limits and conditions on our lives and relationships. When we internalize these concepts they can manifest as pain and illness. They can worsen existing problems and occasionally cause them. Bringing them to consciousness and using other techniques described in this book to release or change them can bring great relief to your pain and suffering.

If you can identify with one of the following four themes, then you can begin to unravel their connections to your discomfort.

Repressed Hostility—When we hold on to anger and rage it often does our self more harm than those that we hold it for. We are the only ones being hurt by these feelings when we internalize them. Anger is observed in a high percentage of those with pain.

Feelings of Guilt—When a person is found guilty in a court of law they receive punishment and imprisonment. When we have ongoing feelings of guilt we may punish ourselves with physical pain and imprison ourselves emotionally. Forgiveness of ourselves and others can create great improvement in our feelings of personal wellness and physical health.

Perfectionism—Traits such as extreme neatness, self-criticism, low self-esteem, and a sense of inadequacy are the negative side of perfectionism. We can sometimes feel deserving of our pain for falling short in areas of our lives in which we hold high standards. Reprioritizing our needs and setting goals that empower our lives can lessen our suffering.

A Need to Be Good—When we seek approval from society and others we can sometimes feel as if it is too difficult to live up to their expectations. This can contribute to the challenges that come with perfectionism and guilt. Recognizing this theme in your life can open up wonderful doors for positive change and healing.

When you look at your notes from each of the prior sections you should begin to gain some new insights into the discomfort that you have been experiencing. Many of the clients I see find that as they recognize these aspects of their pain, the insight gives them greater hope that they can tackle the challenge of improving their situation. I would suggest that you keep a pain journal for one to two weeks before you begin using the following techniques. The better you understand your pain, the better your chances of developing effective strategies for dealing with it.

Self-Hypnosis and Mindbody Techniques: For the Relief of Pain

Many different approaches to reducing your discomfort are offered here. You are encouraged to try as many different ones as possible and use those that work best for you personally. Self-hypnosis is a skill that can be improved with practice. These techniques are no exception. Feel free to be creative and use these ideas as springboards to develop your own customized strategies. Keep working until you succeed and take note of the smallest improvements. Anything you can do to alleviate your discomfort is a sign that you are gaining greater control of it and should be noted as a positive accomplishment. Remember that every great achievement is a combination of small steps. A sample script is included after these techniques for general relaxation and the easing of discomfort.

Opening Up to Pain/Focus of Attention Induction

Focus on your pain and use your concentration on it as a hypnotic induction. You may use the earlier section on the physical characteristics of pain as a starting point for areas to direct your attention to. Open yourself up to each of the different feelings you notice. Simply allow yourself to feel it fully for a few seconds. When we normally pay attention to pain, our muscles in that area tense up. As the muscles tense up, the pain increases and we pay more attention to the area. We create a vicious circle of tension and pain. If your pain makes relaxation techniques difficult to follow then opening up to the pain and taking it apart minutely can help you to achieve a deeper trance. Once the tension is released in this manner, the discomfort can be viewed much more objectively and pave the way for using other techniques.

Anchoring Positive Past Experiences

While in self-hypnosis, think back to a time when you were engaged in a physical activity that you enjoyed when you were without your current discomfort. Notice every detail of the situation. Pay attention to the good feelings in your body, the way it moves, your rate and depth of breathing, and the sights and sounds that surround you in this experience. When you are fully immersed in the memory and the sensations are at their strongest, establish a post-hypnotic cue to feel these sensations again when you want relief. You can use a physical cue such as pressing one of your fingers to your thumb, closing your eyes and imagining the scene briefly, or make up your own. You may also think of a current activity that relieves your pain such as a massage, a bath, a hobby, or being in a peaceful place, and bring back those positive sensations by activating the memories of relief you associate with them.

Re-creating Effects of Pain Relievers

If you have ever had effective anesthesia or other pain relievers then you can re-stimulate the areas of your mind that these medications activated. If you have had a general anesthetic at the doctor or dentist's office then think of that experience while in trance. Take your time as you think about the different qualities of how it felt and how fast or slow it spread through the area. Give your self plenty of time to work with it. If you can create just a little bit of the effect once, you can create more with practice. Try moving the sensation into different parts of your body. This works rather well with dental discomfort and post surgical pains.

Sensory Substitution

Look in your pain journal at the verbal descriptions of your various pain experiences. You can learn to substitute more pleasing sensations for those you currently have. Imagine changing them into feelings of cold, tingling, itching, warmth, vibrations, numbness, heaviness, lightness, or pressure. You might imagine covering the area of discomfort with a soothing, healing liquid or lotion. One important benefit to this approach is that you are still aware of the sensations but they do not bother you as much. They are not entirely pleasant but they are much more tolerable. This can help to bypass some secondary gains and reduce suffering, while maintaining your awareness of any important signals that your body may be giving you relating to your physical condition.

Metaphor for Mechanical Controls

Think about the type of gauge you use when you imagine your pain scale and rate your sensations. You can use your gauge as a mechanical control to experiment with increasing and decreasing your level of discomfort. Begin by imagining your gauge in trance and turning it up just one notch for a few seconds. Notice how easy it is to feel that small increase. When you can feel that change, bring the gauge back to its normal setting. Notice what a relief it is to be back at your normal level. Now bring your gauge down one notch below the normal level and leave it there for a minute or two. Bring the gauge back up to the normal level and then go back down two notches. Practice moving it up and down, working gradually over time as you slowly decrease the sensations. Take your time and have patience. You can imagine your controls as turning down the temperature, volume, or intensity.

Guided Imagery

You can imagine going to a different place of your own creation while in trance. You should choose a setting that feels safe and comfortable for you, and surround yourself with any sights, sounds, and feelings that remind you of relaxation or healing. You can find a number of examples to use throughout this book. While you are there, you can imagine a comfortable chair for you to sit down in. You can then imagine your discomfort as a color and let it drain out of your body and into the earth below you, like opening a spigot on a water line. Imagine yourself being filled with white light. A variation of this is included at the end of this section.

Displacement

This technique is excellent for localized pain. Once you have a good idea of the general area of discomfort, then take plenty of time to play with your own versions of this. The steps are as follows:

a) Imagine the general shape and area of the discomfort. Focus on this until you have it.

b) Once you have the shape, give your discomfort a color. Red and black are the most commonly reported, but you may have a different one.

c) Imagine slowly changing the color of your discomfort to more soothing or healing colors. You can go from red to orange to yellow to white, draining the color from it. You may end up at whatever color you find most pleasing. Black can start by changing to brown, then on to beige to cream to pink to white. Play with the order you find most natural. Always continue until the color can change no more.

d) Once the color of the discomfort has been changed, you can begin to change the size of the area that it covers. You may imagine it shrinking into the center of itself. You can also picture it as a piece of paper slowly burning inward from the edges. Do whatever it takes to minimize the area to something more manageable.

e) When the area of the discomfort has been made as small as possible, you can imagine moving it to a different part of your body where it will be less noticeable or bothersome. Some people like to place it in the tip of one of their fingers. Others take this idea further and imagine it entering the fingernail where it causes no sensation whatsoever.

Conclusion

Remember, any decrease of the sensations of discomfort or suffering is a positive gain and a sign of success. Your initial gains may be small or surprisingly effective. Whatever you learn can be practiced and improved. As you become more elaborate in your approaches, you can focus on the different, specific aspects of your discomfort one piece at a time. Continue to keep your pain journal as you try these approaches and use your pain scale to measure changes over both the short and long term. Change does not always happen overnight. Persist until you succeed and you will soon be pleasantly surprised at the results. Many people have returned to work, changed or reduced their medications, and found totally new directions in life as a result of mastering these techniques.

Always make sure to check with your physician before using these techniques and you will be able to proceed safely. You may use the following script as a starting point for your self-hypnosis programs for pain relief. Enjoy your path to positive change and relief!

The Healing White Light

Allow yourself to get comfortable and relax while you pay attention to the rhythm of your breathing. Gently close your eyes and breathe deeply as you begin to relax. Just let any other sounds you hear help and guide you to become relaxed, deeper and deeper, as you begin to imagine yourself in a beautiful outdoor setting. Imagine a clear day with the sun shining and warming your skin. Now imagine yourself wearing your favorite, most comfortable clothing. Just you, and you alone, enjoying the freedom of being. Noticing how beautiful the sky is. Clear and blue. A familiar light breeze and the beauty of your favorite natural setting is all around you.

And now notice a path leading away off to one side of you. And you decide to take a walk down this path, because it looks so inviting. You feel so free to be adventurous, to do whatever you like. So begin to walk down this beautiful path and just enjoy these good feelings. As you continue down the path, you notice that ahead of you there seems to be a clearing beyond the trees.

As you come closer to the end of the path, you can see that before you are three terraces, leading down to a wide clearing. As you step out on to the first terrace you notice that at the bottom of the clearing there is a beautiful garden, with all of your favorite plants and flowers. It seems so colorful and inviting. But to get there you have to walk down three sets of steps, with five steps each. In a moment, I'll help you to walk down those steps. With each step you take, just let yourself become twice as deeply relaxed as you are now. Just let go of any muscle tension whatsoever with each step, becoming more and more deeply relaxed and letting the scene become more clear, vivid, and inviting to your mind.

Alright now, I'll just count each of the steps down to the second terrace. With each step you take just tell yourself, "I'm going two times deeper relaxed." Okay, one . . . and you take that first relaxing step . . . and two . . . deeper now . . . three . . . more relaxed . . . four . . . and on the next step you arrive at the terrace feeling twice as relaxed and . . . five . . . take a moment to have a deep breath, breathing deeply in . . . and now exhaling and letting that relaxation flow through every part of your body, just enjoying the sun on your skin and the beauty of this place you are creating.

In a moment, I'll help you to go down the next set of steps, helping you to become even deeper relaxed.

Alright, one . . . and you take that first step, relaxing even more . . . and two . . . telling yourself that *"I am* going two times deeper relaxed again" . . . and three . . . feeling relaxed and comfortable . . . four . . . much deeper . . . and five . . . standing now on the third terrace, with only one more set of steps before you enter your garden. Let's go there now, and with each step you take, please tell yourself, *"I am* now entering a wonderful state of deep, healing trance."

Alright, now. one . . . telling yourself "I am entering a state of deep, healing trance" . . . and two . . . more and more at ease and comfortable . . .three . . . almost there now . . . four . . . and on the next step please tell yourself, "I am in a state of deep, healing trance" . . . and five. As you breathe deeply and enjoy the pleasant sensations you are creating, you may tell yourself that you are feeling well in mind, body, and spirit.

Enjoying these sensations, just take a look at your garden and notice that in the middle of all of this beauty there is a small fountain with a very comfortable looking chair next to it, just waiting for you to take a seat and relax all of your troubles and discomforts away. You may choose to just take your shoes off and enjoy the feelings of the lush grass beneath your feet and between your toes as you walk through the garden to that comfortable chair. Enjoy those feelings now as you walk slowly and easily towards that chair.

As you come toward the fountain and listen to the soothingsounds of the gurgling water, you can just take a seat in this chair. As you settle in, just notice how calm, peaceful, serene, and tranquil your mind feels, as your body becomes even more relaxed. You close your eyes and enjoy the feelings of warmth on your body. You begin to notice the light of the sun gently coloring the inside of your eyelids with soft oranges and yellows, making them feel so comfortable that you just let your mind relax as your thoughts drift far, far away. You would not open your eyes now if you could, you feel so comfortable.

And then the most interesting thing happens. The warm relaxing light that you saw on the inside of your eyes seems to grow, to expand. You feel it, now, surrounding your entire head, bathing it in a soft, comfortable, peaceful, and healing light. It feels purifying. As you enjoy this light, you notice that you can actually cause it to grow and to move. Little by little you can feel it flowing over your face and expanding into your neck. Feel it as it moves now across your shoulders in the front . . . and now across the back, suffusing your upper body with comfort and washing away any tension or discomfort. This light does indeed feel healing.

And you notice that the deeper you relax, the stronger it grows. It takes so little effort to help it expand. So you take a nice deep breath and hold . . . and hold . . . and as you exhale, just let that light grow and flow down through your arms and across your chest, soothing away any discomfort that may have been there before like a warm bath of light. You are beginning to feel more comfortable in your body.

Notice how it gently washes over your abdomen and lower back, bathing them in this soft, healing light, relaxing them deeply and washing away any discomfort. Like a liquid light it now flows down over your thighs, relaxing them deeper than ever as you sleep. As it continues flowing down, you can feel it moving through your knees and down into your calves, relaxing them even deeper. Just take a moment to let those sensations of deep, healing relaxation go even deeper and stronger, washing away any discomfort that remains before it continues on down to your feet. Just take a long, deep breath . . . and hold it . . . and hold . . . and as you exhale let that light grow stronger and stronger as it begins to flow down into your feet, relaxing your whole body even deeper, washing away your troubles, and any discomfort.

As you feel the light throughout your body, you notice that it seems to keep flowing, from your feet up to your head slowly . . . and then back down. Each time it circulates, it helps you to feel more and more comfortable and free. Let that light circulate over and through your body again now, and practice moving it throughout your body, stopping any place you would like to grow stronger. When you stop it there, just take another deep breath, and when you exhale and relax your body even more, you may notice how much stronger you can make that light grow, with just a thought as you exhale. How you can easily enjoy just a little more relaxation and comfort, and how it can help you to forget about any sensations that bothered you before for a few moments more.

Those moments of forgetting about the other sensations can begin to happen for longer and longer periods of time each day, until noticing any sensations of discomfort becomes just a reminder for you to take that deep breath, imagine that light growing strong once again, and exhaling, breathing light and comfort into your body. Please take a few moments now to relax and enjoy the comfort in your body, mind, and spirit, breathing deeply as you pay attention to the rhythm of your breath. And now notice the different sensations you are enjoying from this healing white light. I'll just let you enjoy this in peace for a few moments, and you can practice letting that light grow stronger and more purifying. That moment of silence begins . . . now . . .

(wait quietly for approximately 90 seconds)

Okay, I'm back now. In a moment, I'll just count slowly from five up to one, and with each number I say, just let yourself come back up to your everyday state of awareness, holding on to these pleasant sensations in your body, keeping them with you.

Five . . . slowly, easily, and gently feel yourself becoming more aware of the sounds around you . . . four . . . your eyes are clearing under your eyelids . . . three . . . holding on to those good feelings as they continue to grow stronger, your body filled with a wonderful, new energy . . . two . . . and on the next count you may open your eyes, feeling refreshed and relaxed, with pleasant thoughts and feelings spreading through your mind and body . . . and one . . . gently open your eyes, feeling wide aware, relaxed and comfortable.

CHAPTER TWELVE

Birthing Your Child Using Hypnosis

Author's note: For as long as time can remember, women have been giving birth to children while suffering incredible pain. I asked our good friend Melissa Barnes, Certified Master Hypnotherapist, to share with you her experiences and research into reducing the pain of childbirth using hypnosis. Melissa is a wonderful hypnotherapist and a tremendous teacher. I first met her at the National Guild of Hypnotists convention in New Hampshire, but never got the opportunity to sit down with her until we met again in Chicago. There, we sat down and talked about childbirth and the amazing true stories of women whose birthing experiences have changed them forever. Without further ado, I give you our friend Melissa Barnes.

The self-hypnosis techniques described in this chapter are meant to function as an aid and companion to contemporary medical practices regarding childbirth, not an alternative.

Hypnosis in Childbirth

Most people have an idea in their minds of what a "normal" birth is. The images we see on television and in the movies, what we read in books, the stories we hear from those who have experienced it, all paint the same picture: the woman suffering through many long hours of labor, clutching her husband's hand, cursing him with each contraction, asking for drugs when she can't take it anymore.

What if it could be different? What if it could be a calm, peaceful, joyous experience? What if couples could learn not just to cope with the pain, but ways to reduce or even eliminate it in the first place?

Hypnosis can provide a range of tools that can help you work with your body's natural labor process, using the power of your mind and imagination to make the experience safer, easier, and more comfortable.

In order to understand how best to apply the tools of hypnosis, you must first understand how the body is designed to work during childbirth. Strong longitudinal muscles make up the outer layer of the uterus, lying lengthwise from the top to the bottom—these are the muscles that contract during labor. Circular muscles form another inner layer, wrapping around the uterus and becoming thicker towards the bottom, or neck, of the uterus. In the absence of fear and tension during labor, the circular muscles remain relaxed and yield to the contraction of the long muscles, opening and drawing back to allow the baby to pass through the neck of the uterus. But, when tension is present, these circular muscles are also tight, and the long muscles must work that much harder to overcome the resistance offered by these circular muscles. Now, instead of working in harmony as they were designed, the two muscles are contracting in opposition to each other, creating pain and forcing those longitudinal muscles to expend more energy to get the same result.

Which brings us to one of the first and most important ways you can use hypnosis to improve your birth experience-relaxation.

Practice Hypnosis for Relaxation

As you begin preparing for your birth with hypnosis, keep in mind your final goal. That goal is not control. Birth is an instinctual and physical process. To try and control this process will only set up resistance and tension in the body. Instead, think of your goal as release, turning the birth over to your body so your body can do what it was designed to do naturally. By learning to relax your body and mind through hypnosis, you will allow your body to do the work it needs to do without resistance, maximizing the efficiency of those longitudinal muscle contractions and minimizing the resistance of the circular muscles. This will also conserve your energy for later in the birth, when it will be needed during the second stage.

There are two basic kinds of self-hypnosis relaxation exercises you can practice, and many different techniques you can use for each one. By practicing self-hypnosis, you gain the skill to reach a deep level of relaxation in a short amount of time. You will want to practice these exercises until they become so automatic you won't have to think about them in labor.

Progressive Relaxation

The goal of the first exercise is to reach a nice, complete physical and mental relaxation. Set aside about a 30-minute session each day to work on this. This is a good time to involve your birth companion. They can help you deepen your relaxation, and you can get used to responding to their voice. In essence, you are learning to hypnotize yourself, and your partner is learning to be the hypnotist, to help you deepen and maintain your state.

Find a place you where won't be disturbed for 30 minutes or so. You may find it helpful to dim the lights and play some soft, relaxing music. Choose something where the tempo stays at a nice slow, calming speed. Nature music is often great for this—a babbling brook, rainstorm, or ocean sounds. Find something that really works for you and then use it every time you practice. Soon it will act as an anchor, and you will only need to hear a few measures before you naturally slip back into that state. The music is not a necessary part of the hypnosis, though, so just skip it if you find it too distracting or you forget to bring it for the big event. These techniques will work just as well without it. One client found her skills as a musician led her to mentally transcribe the notes she heard into sheet music, taking up too much mental concentration to relax! She did much better with silence.

Now get into a comfortable position. There are a couple different ones you can use for this exercise. You may want to practice them all, since you'll want to change positions during labor.

You can lie comfortably on your back, especially during the early part of your pregnancy. Later in pregnancy, avoid lying flat on your back, as the weight of the baby will press against a large artery in your back, decreasing blood flow to the uterus and your baby. Instead, prop yourself up with pillows, so that your back is elevated. A recliner is good for this position. Pillows under the knees and arms may also feel comfortable.

Many mothers favor the lateral position, especially during the later stages of labor and even the actual birth itself. Lie on your left side, with your left shoulder and head supported by pillows. Let your left arm lie comfortably behind your back. Bend your right leg slightly and support it with pillows so that it is even with your hips. Those of you with body pillows may have already discovered the comforts of this position for sleeping at night.

You can also practice these relaxation techniques while sitting. Just make sure that your whole body is supported and that your head and neck won't fall forward or to the side as you become relaxed. You may have experienced that before when dozing off in the car, and it's not comfortable. Another variation of the sitting position is to straddle a chair and rest your arms and head on a pillow across the back. This position has the added benefit of giving your birth companion access to your back for soft massage.

So now you're in a comfortable position, the lights dim, music playing. One method of hypnotizing yourself is the progressive relaxation induction. Close your eyes and imagine each part of the body relaxing, starting from the head and moving down the body to the toes or starting at the toes up to the head, whichever you find easiest. Your partner can help you relax by speaking softly and naming each part of your body to relax, concentrating on any areas where they observe any tension. You may enjoy having your partner lightly stroke you along the arms, legs, or back. Experiment and give your partner feedback on what particular things really helped you relax.

Focus on your breathing. Take nice, slow, even breaths, filling your lungs completely so that you can see your stomach rise and fall with each breath. Exhale just as slowly and smoothly.

Think of a place in your mind where you can relax completely. Maybe resting on a warm summer beach, maybe sitting in the shade of a tall willow. Perhaps this is a place you've been, maybe a place you only imagine.

(Note: after your first practice, share as many details about that place as possible with your partner. The next time you practice together, they can help you deepen your relaxation by taking you on a trip through your special place.)

When you near the end of your practice session, your partner can observe your level of relaxation. Your breathing should have slowed and deepened, your muscle tone smoothed. Picking up an arm, it should feel completely loose and limp. The eyelids fluttering, or rapid eye movement is also a wonderful sign.

Before ending the session, imagine an anchor of some kind that you can use as a trigger to bring yourself immediately back to this same state of relaxation.

(Note: If you've ever seen a stage hypnosis show, you may have noticed how the hypnotist is able suggest some kind of trigger, like snapping their fingers or saying the word "sleep," so the volunteers on stage can reenter hypnosis immediately without the long induction. You can easily learn to do this yourself. Imagine your trigger for self-hypnosis. For example, some clients imagine themselves taking a deep breath and counting backwards from 3 to 1. Other clients imagine taking a deep breath and touching their first finger and thumb together. Just make it simple. Your intention to enter self-hypnosis, coupled with your trigger, will allow you to reenter the state much more quickly.)

> Now just easily bring yourself out of hypnosis by counting from 1 to
> 3 and opening your eyes.

Your partner may also count you out of hypnosis, or you can mentally count the numbers yourself.

If you have access to hypnosis audio tapes, you can practice with them as well. You will still want to spend some time practicing hypnosis with your birth companion, though, since theirs is the voice you will be responding to during the birth.

You may be pleasantly surprised by your baby's reaction to your hypnosis practice. Mothers often comment to me that their babies can be quite active, but then the hypnosis will put them right to sleep. In fact, more than one has admitted to using the hypnosis tapes to get a rambunctious kicker to settle down so its mother could sleep.

Using your Self-Hypnosis Trigger

In order for the self-hypnosis to have any practical value to you during labor, it has to be immediately available. Considering that each surge is only a minute to a minute and a half, long, it is pretty obvious that you need to be able to enter the state immediately.

Hypnosis is a skill. Like any skill, it becomes easier the more you practice. You may notice after only a few sessions of the progressive relaxation induction above that each time you practice, you reach the same, or an even deeper, level of relaxation much quicker than the time before.

In the same way, your self-hypnosis trigger will become more effective the more you use it. You have already spent time imagining yourself using the self-hypnosis trigger to bring yourself immediately into the state of self-hypnosis. Those mental rehearsals have trained your mind to respond to your trigger in just that way. Now, all you need to do is use the trigger just as you imagined it.

You can practice self-hypnosis anywhere: while riding (not driving) in the car, sitting in your doctor's waiting room, before you go to bed at night, or when you wake up in the morning. Anytime you have a couple minutes to spare. Television commercials can be a perfect practice break. Two to three commercials are about a minute to a minute and a half long, about the length of a contraction. (You weren't going to do anything with that time anyway.)

Get comfortable, close your eyes, and use your trigger just as you imagined it during the progressive relaxation induction. You can increase the effectiveness of your trigger by using it at the moment you exhale. You should feel yourself sink immediately down to that state you experienced before. Again, focus on keeping your breathing relaxed and deep, inhaling all the way down to the stomach, so you can see the stomach rise and fall. You can also use any of the deepening techniques found later in the chapter during these self-hypnosis practices. Then, after a minute or two, count from 1 to 3 and open your eyes. Soon, you should be adept at entering and exiting the state of hypnosis on your own, using your trigger. This is the technique you will use during actual labor contractions.

Preventing Fear During Labor

One of the biggest causes of tension in the body during labor is fear. Many childbirth preparation classes speak of the Fear-Tension-Pain syndrome theorized by Dr. Grantly Dick-Read, the father of Natural Childbirth. He believed that fear-created tension is the primary cause of pain in birth, and he maintained that eliminating fear would also eliminate much or all of the discomfort of labor.

Think of a time you, or someone around you, was afraid, perhaps at a scary movie. The body tenses, tries to curl up into itself, make itself smaller. Breathing becomes more rapid and shallow, sometimes even holding the breath at some moments. The heart races. All of these primal reactions are preparing the body to fight or flee. In the case of labor, however, neither reaction is useful. In fact, in a birthing mother, nature has designed the fear response to slow or stop labor, allowing a threatened animal to find another, safer birth location.

Fear releases catecholamines, stress hormones, into the body. These hormones constrict the lower circular muscles of the uterus, again forcing the longitudinal muscles to contract against resistance. During labor, the body naturally releases endorphins into the blood stream, hormones that have a tranquil, analgesic effect. In essence, these are the body's own nat-ural epidural. These endorphins are released steadily throughout labor, increasing during contractions and as the intensity of the labor increases. Fear-released catecholamines block the effect of these endorphins, inter-fering with the body's own pain control system.

This becomes a vicious circle. As the mother approaches her labor in fear, the circular muscles constrict, catecholomines block the body's natural anal-gesic, and she experiences pain during contractions. This creates more fear, so she tenses up even more in anticipation of the next contraction, experi-encing even more pain. When pain is expected, pain is experienced.

Understand the Physical Process

One of the first things you can do to reduce your fear is to understand the physical process of labor. People generally fear the unknown. The more you learn about how the body is designed to work during birth, the more relaxed and confident you will feel as you approach your birth. By understanding how the body operates during labor, you will find it easier to release and trust your body. You will be better able to respond to the cues your body gives you, allowing you to work with, rather than against, your body.

Take classes and read books that focus on birth as a natural process rather than as a medical event. Many of the facts you learn will provide you with comforting imagery of how all aspects of your body work in har-mony to accomplish the act of birth. For example, throughout the later months of pregnancy, hormones have softened the cervix until it is as soft as your earlobe. The onset of labor releases hormones that stretch and lubricate the vaginal walls to accommodate the baby's passage. The soft spots of the baby's head, the fontenals, allow the skull to compress and mold to fit the birth canal. The pressure of the baby's head numbs the area around the perineum.

Prepare your body physically for birth by doing the exercises they teach you in your childbirth classes. Kegel and squatting exercises will help prepare the muscles you will use in birth. Perineal massage will help stretch the tissue of the vagina to reduce the likelihood of tears.

Release Your Own Fears

Next, make an honest inventory of any fears you may have surround-ing the birth. What kind of birth stories did you grow up with and how did they affect your expectations for this birth? What were your past birth experiences like? Your family members' experiences? Take into consideration any fear surrounding other aspects of the baby's arrival, not just the birth. Any fears about becoming a parent. Concerns about how your relationship with your spouse or other children will change. How the new baby will affect your career, your finances.

Releasing any fears you may be holding on to, whether on a conscious or unconscious level, is a vital part of preparing yourself for birth. Ideally, it would be worth the investment to visit a local, qualified hypnotherapist for a fear release session. If that is not possible for you, your partner can walk you through some fear release imagery during your progressive relaxation practice.

> ***Release all fears of childbirth before labor to experience minimal discomfort.***

Imagine yourself somewhere safe, and you have a book filled with any fears or anxieties surrounding this birth. As you turn the pages of the book, imagine the color from each image on each page fading to black and white. Put those images and fears into a new perspective—they are someone else's experiences, or your own experiences, before you learned these new tools. Turn to the last page and see that the page is blank. Realize that this birth has not been written yet. Tear out the pages before it, the fears that are now part of your past. Release them and send them far out of your mind, whether by burning them, or shredding them, or letting the wind carry them far from your sight. One client used the image of the sheets of paper transforming into a flock of doves and flying off beyond the horizon.

Now return to the blank page in front of you and allow it to fill with the full color picture of this birth. Imagine yourself calm and relaxed, releasing and letting go to the body that performs just as it was meant to. Enjoy the moment you greet your child for the first time. Close the book and savor the excitement you feel when looking forward to the birth of your child.

Deepening Techniques and Imagery

You can use any of the following techniques to deepen your state of hypnosis either during your practice sessions or during your actual birth.

Down the Stairs/Elevator

Imagine being at the top of a staircase, or getting on the elevator at the top floor. Count backwards from 25 to 1 and imagine that each number is another step or another floor, each step or each floor taking you deeper into hypnosis. You may even feel as though you are sinking into the chair or bed.

Open Blossom

During contractions you may find it useful to imagine a flower opening, a rose, or whatever kind of flower you like. Imagine the petals slowly uncurling and spreading wide. Imagine it in as much detail as possible: the warmth of the sun on each velvet petal, the dew sparkling on the tips. Imagine yourself opening as the flower opens. Imagine the cervix opening, widening, and the tissues of the vaginal wall stretching and opening to receive the baby.

Waterfall or Ocean

Water often has a calming tranquil effect for laboring mothers. Besides the relief of taking an actual bath or shower, you can use the image of water to help you relax.

You may imagine a waterfall or running stream. Or you may prefer to imagine the ocean. Contractions themselves are often compared to ocean waves: surging, reaching a crest, then ebbing away. You can imagine yourself floating on the ocean, relaxed, rising and falling with each wave, but still floating and relaxed.

Deep Breathing/Satin Ribbons

With each contraction, really focus on making the inhale slow, smooth, and deep. Imagine that, as your stomach rises with each breath in, you are working with those longitudinal uterine muscles as they contract up and draw back the relaxed circular muscles. Think of those circular muscles as soft ribbons lying across your uterus and imagine with each contraction that those long muscles are drawing them up and back.

Hypnosis to Control Pain

Everything you experience, pain included, is experienced by the mind interpreting the signals your body sends to it. Physical experience has an emotional component, which means that your mind can influence what your body feels. Think of the athlete who gets injured during the game, but doesn't feel pain until the game is over. Or the power of a parent's kiss to make a child's scratch feel better. Drug studies must account for this mind-body effect through control groups, since some people will get better through belief, through the power of their imagination to affect their body. What if you could harness the power of the placebo effect at will?

Glove Anesthesia

While in hypnosis, imagine that you are dunking your hand in really cool water, or rubbing ice across it. Imagine that hand becomes very numb, almost like the sensation of when your hand falls asleep. Now imagine you can transfer that feeling of numbness anyplace you want by either mentally or physically touching your hand to that area.

Your partner can also gently stroke your arm upward from the hand as you imagine pulling that numbness into the rest of your body.

Mind-Body Control Room

Imagine that in your mind there is a control room. You can walk through the door and into the operations center of your mind. The room is filled with machines and dials controlling every physical sensation in every area of your body. You can practice by finding a control for tingling in your hands and then turn it up a bit. Notice the sensations in your hands as you do this. The more you imagine them tingling, the more they begin to feel that way. Then turn the dial back to normal. If you can use your imagination to create sensation that wasn't there, you can also use hypnosis to reduce sensation that is there. During labor, you can imagine walking into the control room and adjusting the dials to your comfort level.

Other Uses for Hypnosis before Your Birth

Hypnosis can help relieve other ailments of pregnancy as well. Some mothers find it extremely helpful for morning sickness, either by directly suggesting relief of the nausea or by dealing with any emotional reasons that may be causing it. Some morning sickness can be attributed to expectation and imagination, as this culture considers it a necessary accompaniment to pregnancy.

For some mothers who experience backaches or high blood pressure, tension or stress can be a contributing factor. They can experience some relief simply from the relaxation offered by self-hypnosis.

Insomnia, too, can be relieved. Often practicing self-hypnosis or progressive relaxation just before it is time to sleep can relax the mind and body enough to overcome insomnia.

A 1992 study by the University of Vermont found hypnosis effective in turning breech babies. Using hypnosis, mothers visualized the uterus relaxing and the baby turning downward in preparation for birth. In this manner, 81 out of 100 of the breech babies turned spontaneously. In a comparison group of 100 women, only 26 spontaneously turned and another 20 turned with the aid of ECV (external cephalic version).

Lisa's Birth Story

Lisa's first two labors were short and intense, with none of the usual build-up typical of most labors. "I started in transition and stayed there." She had a six-hour labor for the first child, three hours for the second. She hoped hypnosis would give her some added tools for this third labor.

This one started quite differently from her previous two. She lost the mucus plug and began having regular contractions, approximately every 15 minutes. Like their previous two births, they had planned for a home birth. Knowing her previous track record for fast births, they called the midwives right away, at 5:00 A.M. The contractions continued closer together, strong enough to get her attention, too strong to want to walk through them. Lisa and Michael used the relaxation and breathing just as they had practiced, the music playing in the background. She found the long slow inhales really felt good with the contractions and described this part of her labor as painless. Sometimes, after a contraction, she would ask her husband if she looked like the women in the videos, because that's how she felt.

Shortly before noon, her labor stopped, and she had the chance for a nice long nap. Most of the birth attendants went home for the time being to wait for labor to start again.

About 4:00 P.M., she had one really strong contraction, but no more until almost 7:30 P.M. The rest of her labor, from 7:30 P.M. until the birth at 8:55 P.M., remained intense, with the contractions very strong and very close together. At this stage, she found that what worked best for her were low guttural moans that vibrated deep in her chest. She adopted a hands and knees position, focusing on the exhale with each contraction and making the moans resonate low and deep throughout her body. Allowing the muscles of the uterus to do all the work, she breathed her daughter, Amay, into the world without any active pushing. The head slipped gently through the rim of the perineum. The cord was wrapped twice around the neck, so the midwife tilted the head carefully to one side in order to let the body fold out behind it, then once completely delivered, easily unlooped the cord from the neck. Helping Lisa to turn onto her back, they laid Amay on her stomach. From the first, the baby was calm and quiet, her eyes wide open and taking in the world around her.

Afterwards, Lisa thought back on her experience. She believed that hypnosis might have helped her slow her labor down, allowing her to use the tools she had practiced. She described the last hour and a half as painful, but no more than she had skills to cope with. She thought that if they could have slowed the labor a little at the end, with warm water, that perhaps she could have continued using the breathing and relaxation as they had practiced. But with the intensity she experienced at the end, she was able to release and trust her body, finding the low instinctual moaning to be the better coping tool for her in that situation. She chose not to use the imagery during her labor, saying that she knew she could use her imagination to take her somewhere else, but that there was no where else she wanted to be in that moment.

Giavonne's Birthing Experience

Giavonne Mitchell recently gave birth to her beautiful baby, Kayla Franchesca, with the help of a hypnotherapist and some simple self-hypnosis techniques. Here is her story.

"The decision to forgo pain killers, or other pain blocking procedures provided by modern medicine, was not easy. Years of conditioning had me convinced childbirth was going to be one of the most agonizingly painful experiences of my life. My mom verified this by recounting her agony. My friends also enthusiastically encouraged the pain free route and television shows epitomized the entire nightmare with their garish scenes of grossly violent and hateful women spewing invectives at their speechless husbands, doctors, and nurses.

The chaotic picture captured on the silver screen was not what I wanted for myself, or my husband, Callum, and our unborn child. After consulting with a midwife, I was referred to a woman who worked with pregnant mothers using a technique she called "Birthing with Hypnosis."

My husband and I paid our first visit to our new birthing coach, Debbie, nearly two months before my projected due date. We settled into two very comfortable reclining chairs while Debbie showed us a few videos sent in to her by some of her grateful past clients. These women gave birth without medical intervention. Equally encouraging, these women weren't biting or scratching or moaning for pain killers.

Instead, we witnessed women (one of whom had experience a prior birth the standard clinical way—c-section, due to impatient doctors) easily talking with their friends, family, children, and midwives throughout their labor and delivery. We saw women completely in unison with their husbands, women entirely in control and without calling for painkillers!

The technique Debbie taught was simple and easy to follow. Since she would not be present for delivery, it was her intention to give us the tools we needed to stay calm, in control, and unified. After three two-hour sessions, Debbie concluded her teachings and gave me a tape to listen to. Instructing me to listen to the tape daily until the time of delivery, Debbie waved good-bye and urged us to share our experience with her upon the birth of our child.

On delivery night, I was calm and prepared. I had listened to the tapes and practiced her techniques often. Debbie had cautioned that pain might still be inevitable, but if I practiced the self-hypnosis technique, I would ease through delivery without trauma to myself or my body.

Contractions and labor pains are, by far, the most painful things I have ever experienced. I was amazed that the human body could elicit such pain and endure it! I calmly told my husband this much while right in the middle of one. That was the amazing thing about the effect the birthing technique had on me. I was capable of listening to my body, knowing when I was dilating, sensing the impending descent of my baby, and withstanding the tremendous pain, while maintaining a distant, almost third person view of my child's birth. I chatted with the nurses, a friend, and my husband. We worked through it together. No yelling, no crying, no episiotomy, no hemorrhoids. Nothing but a beautiful baby girl and one heck of a proud father and mother.

I highly recommend this birthing method to anyone who is expecting a child!"

Finally, in the list of testimonials for using hypnosis to ease the pain of childbirth, Kevin's wife, Katie, has a story of how hypnosis helped her give birth to Mark James.

Katie's Birthing Experience

"My first labor and delivery lasted twenty and one-half hours. It was both emotionally and physically devastating. When I became pregnant with my second child, I found myself longing for a less stressful, less painful birthing process.

I was aware, through Lamaze classes, that self-relaxation offers benefits throughout the pregnancy for alleviating stress and reducing general aches and pains. I used self-relaxation techniques every evening before falling asleep. At about twenty weeks, I had a labor/birthing audio tape made by Kevin that was tailored just for me. The tape was a wonderful way to relax and take the time to think about the labor experience I really wanted. The tape referred continually to my courage, my calm, and my ability to relax and gently push the baby out of the birth canal.

My due date was November 10, 1997. Around 5:00 or 6:00 in the morning on November 10, I began experiencing the strong contractions that I knew were the beginnings of true labor. I rose out of bed and took a shower. With my first birth, I had called the hospital right away to report contractions and the nurses had told me to come right in. I had only been dilated to 3cm and had had a long, tortuous experience ahead of me. I knew I did not want to make the mistake of going in too early again. I wanted to be comfortable at home, able to eat lightly, watch movies, walk around the house, and relax.

I did not listen to my birthing audio tape at any time during my labor experience but I felt as if I were in trance throughout. I felt calm, prepared, and ready to push my baby out when the time came. It was as if the contractions were a trigger for me to relax.

From 7:00 A.M. until noon, the contractions came and went, getting stronger and then subsiding. I massaged my nipples to help bring on stronger contractions when they seemed to subside. At about 1:00 P.M. I noticed that it was getting more difficult to walk through the contractions. It was not 'painful,' but the uterus became really tight. I would have to go down on my knees and wait for the easing of the contraction.

At 2:45 P.M., when the contractions were coming two minutes apart, I finally told Kevin that it was time to call the hospital. He called and, wouldn't you know it, there were no birthing rooms available! They were sending us to a different hospital almost a half-hour away. And what about traffic? And our daughter was scheduled to come home on the school bus in twenty minutes. Who would meet her? Through all this stress, I repeated the mantra in my head, 'calm, courage, relax, calm, courage, relax.' Kevin frantically made phone calls and got a friend to rush over to meet our daughter.

We literally raced for the car thinking I had let the labor progress go further than I should have. The contractions continued very strongly in the car and I remember some discomfort and pain, but more a dull pain as the uterus stretched. I pictured in my head the uterus stretching to release my baby. Kevin dropped me off at the main door at 3:45 P.M. and I found my way up to labor and delivery, calmly breathing through contractions on the crowded elevator on the way up to the fourth floor.

The intake nurse took a look at my calm face and sent me to triage to be assessed. Was I really in labor? After a twenty-minute wait, a nurse came in to check me. She looked at my calm face and said, 'Do I need to check you now? You don't look like you're in labor.' I said, 'Well, yeah, why don't you go ahead?'

Seconds later she was saying, 'The amniotic sac is bulging and you're dilated to six! You're going to have a baby within the hour! Let's get you moved to a birthing room!'

The contractions continued as I was prepped for delivery. They got consistently stronger and harder. Finally, the nurse asked if I would like her to break the bag of waters. I said, 'Yes, if that will make it go faster.' Contractions continued but I was able to stay focused with my eyes open (with my first baby I had my eyes clamped shut so tight from the pain the nurses had to urge me to open them and look at my baby!).

There was no time for anything except getting ready for the next contraction and bearing down. The nurses helped hold my legs and arms, and counted 1 to 10 as I pushed. When I didn't think I could get through the pain of a contraction, I would think, *calm, courage, relax . . . calm, courage, relax.* I pushed through about ten contractions. Our baby Mark James was born at 4:43 P.M.

I used self-relaxation after the delivery to distract myself from the pain of episiotomy repair and the uterine massage, which is done to help make the uterus shrink to its normal size.

This birth was a truly rewarding experience because, instead of dreading another long and painful labor, I was able to picture a calm, stress-free delivery. Self-hypnosis helped me achieve that."

CHAPTER THIRTEEN

Prosperity Consciousness

It used to be said that, "love makes the world go 'round." Today that might still be true, but if anything else does, it's money. Money is so important to the security, stability, freedom, and peace of mind of any individual that we have decided to really put some time into understanding prosperity. We want you to do more than understand financial freedom, we want you to experience it!

Prosperity means different things to different people. A good friend of mine (K.H.), likes to define prosperity as having the means to live the way you want to live. She chooses to live a life that would best be called "Voluntary Simplicity." She also considers herself very prosperous . . . and she is. With no children, she and her husband live comfortably in a rustic setting in central Minnesota. They probably earn less money than the average American working couple and live a far better life in terms of health and happiness than that same American couple. They also feel comfortable with their lower income because they keep their expenses under control and do not use credit cards and do not have debt of any kind. This lifestyle is typical of those who live within the "Voluntary Simplicity" movement.

A lifestyle of simplicity and one that is marked by a self-sustaining experience is attractive to many people and not so attractive to others. My lifestyle is different in some ways to my friends' style of living and similar in others. Like my friend, I no longer utilize long-term debt to make my purchases (with the exception of my family home). I make a living that provides income that is significantly higher than that of the average American. I also drive a new car and have many of the unnecessary luxuries of life like cable television, multiple televisions, several computers, as many bathrooms in the house as people who live there, and well, you get the idea . . . I'm easily living within my means and could eliminate many monthly expenditures if I wanted to, but I don't. What about you?

Is It Okay for You to Have Money?

When someone makes more money than you do, do you judge that person negatively or positively?

How much money is the right amount of money for you to have?

How much money is the right amount for other people in your life to have?

When does working become an endless pursuit of money?

What does it mean when someone has what you consider to be "a lot" of money?

Money is a representation of the value that is being offered by one person or group to another person or group in exchange for a service or product that is being performed or received. A cashier at a department store will receive less money for his services than a medical doctor will for hers because the economy of the nation perceives that service as less in value when contrasted to the medical doctor's. There are three basic ways to make more money within the context of your work. You can perform more service, higher-quality service, or faster service. There are also numerous strategies, both mental and physical, that you must be able to understand and perform in order for you to become financially prosperous.

It is a rare person who is able to be successful in making money without understanding money, and very few people understand how money works and what it really is. In this chapter, we will show you what money is, how it works, and how you can build a prosperous future. Once you understand consciously how money works we can then work with the unconscious mind to create a prosperity consciousness to live a full and pleasure filled life.

> *Self-hypnosis will help you create a prosperous life once you understand money and the creation of money.*

You were told long ago that you should save ten percent of your weekly income. You were assured this would make you rich, but it didn't. What happened? Did you get discouraged because the money you thought was going to come your way didn't? Your advisor's lack of knowledge about what to do with that ten percent was probably part of the learning experience. Your advisor didn't know, because your advisor had not succeeded in saving his way to wealth.

What is Money?

Do you know what money is? Do you know how money "works"? Do you know how you can get more of it without significant risk? Do you know how to make your money multiply?

The ability to create, manage, and spend money wisely is inherent to living a life by design. We will begin by looking at what money is. By considering a thumbnail sketch of the history of money, you will discover some of the challenges inherent in designing a lifestyle that will help you create wealth.

Long ago there was no money. If you wanted pheasant for dinner, you would trade something for that pheasant. You traded a string of beads you had made that day for the pheasant. What you did not grow or make yourself, you traded to someone who did make or grow what you wanted. Two thousand years before the birth of Christ, the concept of money began. Some 1,300 years later, money became standardized, at least in the country of Greece. Aristotle noted,

> "The various necessities of life are not easily carried about, and hence man agreed to employ in their dealings with each other something that was intrinsically useful and easily applicable to the purposes of life, for example, iron, silver, and the like. Of this the value was at first measured by size and weight, but in process of time they put a stamp upon it, to save the trouble of weighing and to mark the value."

Those looking for an extra advantage over those they did business with would shave off portions of gold and silver from the "nuggets" that were used as a means of exchange. This was the first "inflation." The Roman Empire fell, in part, because of this "shaving." Copper coins that originally weighed a pound eventually were shaved to less than one ounce. Similar dishonesty occurred worldwide in developing countries. This brought in the notion of weights and measures. Metals (iron, silver, gold, and copper) were in demand for several reasons. Metals were essential ingredients in fine jewelry, objects of worship, tools, weapons, and so on.

In the 18th and 19th centuries, gold became the standard unit of exchange in the United States and many other developed countries. The problem with metals as a standard was that metal was very heavy to carry around. Carrying gold and silver was clumsy and not effective for trading goods.

Money is a Belief

Enter paper. Various governments began to store precious metals and issued paper imprinted with various amounts in terms of dollars, pounds, francs, etc., on the paper. It was "monopoly money" with one exception. There was an equal amount of "monopoly money" in print as there was value in the metals in government storehouses. The paper itself was worthless, but the governments issuing the paper "vouched" for the value of the paper. They created a belief. It wasn't long before the metals backed very little of the money.

Once beliefs are created, then those who wish to take advantage of believers enter. Instead of people shaving gold and silver in financial exchange, as was done centuries ago, banks formed to create an area of exchange. It was here that shaving would begin again. Banks created another belief. If you brought your paper to let them keep it safe for you, they would return it to you on demand with interest. Of course, your money was not safe. It was being loaned to other people to build and speculate in other pursuits. This process is certainly beneficial to growth, but it also opens the way for corruption and erosion of the value of money.

As time passed, governments would issue more currency (creating inflation) and spend money without having anything to back up the paper they were distributing. This created federal deficits (spending more money than was being taken in from taxes). Money was no longer real. The belief had become invested in an illusion.

For some reason unbeknownst to this author, most countries allowed the creation of central banks. Central banks in the United States are part of what is called the Federal Reserve. When the United States needs money, say one billion dollars, they ask the Federal Reserve for a loan. The United States then owes the Federal Reserve one billion dollars plus interest. However, the government does not produce income, so it cannot pay back the Federal Reserve. Therefore, the United States taxes its people for part of the money and then borrows money from its citizens by issuing bonds. The bonds promise to pay the citizen interest on the loan to the government. This money in turn is paid to the Federal Reserve to pay the interest the government owes to the Federal Reserve.

Who Benefits in this Transaction?

The cost of printing one billion dollars by the Federal Reserve is approximately $1,000.00 in paper. Most of the difference is profit to the owners of the banks. The government benefited because it can spend money without responsibility for the repayment. Because the government is essentially a non-producing entity, it can only collect taxes and place the burden on the person paying taxes.

The loser, unfortunately, is the citizen. However, it does not end here. This may seem very distant and unreal to you. Consider the following and realize why learning to create money in a purposeful fashion is critical to living a life by design: The Federal Reserve, in large part, determines how much you will be paying in interest for the next home you purchase. They have the right to set interest rates to smaller banks at any level they wish. Smaller banks then loan you money. When interest rates go up, smaller banks do not benefit significantly, but the Federal Reserve certainly does. Additionally, the Federal Reserve is loaning your money to the bank you do business with. You then pay an unreasonable interest rate for your new home. Here's what happens.

True Cost of a Home

You decide to purchase a new home for $135,000.00. Unless you have cash on hand, you will borrow the money from your banker. In the year 2000 the interest paid on new homes was a relatively reasonable eight percent. Most homebuyers take advantage of the traditional 30-year mortgage as their timeframe to repay the $120,000.00 (assuming $15,000.00 for a down payment). The homebuyer will pay $881.00 per month in principal and interest only, for 30 years. The total of principal and interest payments on the home over the period total $317,000.00. A $135,000.00 home, financed at eight percent for 30 years, really costs you $317,000.00!

Approximately 7 years into a mortgage, many people decide to move into a new home. When they begin looking, they will most likely believe they have built a significant equity position in their home. Having lived in a home 7 years, one would expect to have nearly 25 percent equity after seven years (7/30). However, you have not paid 7/30 of your loan. Loans are not paid off in equal monthly proportions as your stable monthly payments lead one to expect. By the 7th year of a 30-year mortgage, you still owe about 90 percent of the original principal. You have built very little equity in your home.

Playing and Winning the Money Game

What all this means is that you have been entered into a game in which the odds are definitely tilted in favor of the house (the government and those loaning the money). Living a life by design means that you can play the money game and win for you and your family while not creating losses for others. Playing to win, however, does take some strategic planning.

Winning means building a surplus of those illusory dollars so that when you decide to "retire" or lead a more independent and less structured life, you can. It is still a rarity to find someone who is planning their retirement 20 or more years in advance. In the 21st century it is more important than ever to do so. The taxes that were taken from your payroll checks for social security simply will not be available for you when you retire, barring a miracle equivalent to the parting of the Red Sea.

It is enticing to note here that the earlier you begin taking control of your money, the earlier you are likely to begin truly enjoying the rewards money can buy. As it turns out, time and interest (return on investment) are more important than the amount of money you invest for your ultimate "freedom" years.

As with every aspect in life by design, you want to know where you are before attempting to set goals, directions, and plans to move ahead.

Do You Have a Budgetary Crisis?

Is your personal budget a microcosm of the United States? As of this writing in the year 2000, the United States is 6 trillion dollars in debt. That's approximately $22,000.00 per human being in the United States.

Compare this to a family budget. If you bring in $50,000.00 per year before taxes, owe $250,000.00 in debts, and spend about $50,000.00 after taxes, you are in the same shape as the government. (This completely excludes what you personally owe the national deficit and debt. No one knows when this rapidly growing credit card payment will come due.)

Fortunately, most people budget far better than our government.

Unfortunately, most people are in debt and are operating at a net loss each year. It is impossible to live a life of your choosing in this situation. Life by design means that you are in charge of your life. When you are in debt, you are not in charge of your life. How do you know if you are in debt?

Make a balance sheet with assets and liabilities listed and discover whether your financial worth is positive or negative. If it is negative, you are in debt. Fill in all of your assets and all of your debts. Think of everything. An asset's value is what you could sell it for today.

A book may have cost $30.00, but you cannot sell a book for $30.00. A used bookstore will give you $2 for such an item. A $4,000.00 ring is really worth about $400.00. Jewelry is worth roughly 10 percent of retail. The same is true for many seemingly good "investments."

One of the things you need to know about your money is how much discretionary money you have available to you, after your expenses. It is your "flex" money. All flex money should generally be used to pay off debts (including credit cards) that have no asset backing up the debt.

In other words, if you have a $2,000.00 credit card bill and it is simply accumulation of small debts and purchases it needs to be paid off as soon as possible. Credit cards charge 15 percent or more for interest and every dollar you pay off has a 15 percent guaranteed return on investment. That makes this a priority. High interest credit cards should be paid in full, first. Then, those cards that carry lower rates should be paid off.

How much of your monthly income should you be keeping to enjoy your life tomorrow? If you are more than 10 years from retirement, you probably want to save 10 percent of your income as a minimum. If you are less than 10 years from retirement you want to save (invest) more than 10 percent per month. If your retirement will begin after 2015 you cannot be certain that there will be "social security." There is no reason to believe that the fund will be solvent at that time. Therefore, your investments and savings will need to augment any pension plans that you are offered. If you have no pension plans sponsored by an employer, you are going to need to design your entire financial security yourself.

How to Become a Millionaire

Materialism is not what life by design is all about. Living a life of joy and happiness is what design is about. In order to truly live a life of your choosing you want to plan your finances so the lack of money does not become burdensome.

When you decide to live your life with fewer obligations (some people call this retiring) you will want to have money waiting for you to live comfortably. One million dollars is a reasonable dollar figure to be able to retire on, as long as you continue to care for your financial situation in retirement.

You do not have to earn one million dollars each year to be a millionaire. You can attain the millionaire status with a very small amount of money each month over time. Each month, take at least 10 percent of your gross income and immediately invest it in stock mutual funds. Over the last six decades, stocks, in general, return over 10 percent per year. There are certainly ups and downs, but nothing matches the performance of investing in corporate America. You can begin to invest in stocks through mutual funds. A mutual fund is a pool of investors that purchases stocks or bonds or both. You can invest in mutual funds with no commission charge. These are called no-load mutual funds. If someone tells you that you need to pay a commission for a mutual fund, simply find a fund that is doing better or as well that you can invest in for free. There are thousands of them. Some well-known companies that offer no-load mutual funds include Fidelity, Vanguard, Scudder, and American Century. There are many others. To find out the phone numbers of various mutual funds, buy a copy of *Investor's Business Daily* at your newsstand and look at the listings of mutual funds. The phone numbers are listed by the company names. Call the funds that look interesting and ask for a prospectus. Most of the daily business papers tell you the returns that mutual funds have accomplished up to date.

By investing monthly in mutual funds that are well managed, you will eventually build your wealth to the level of a millionaire. It sounds far fetched, but see how easy it is.

Formula for Becoming a Millionaire

$$TDR=W$$

That formula is the key to wealth (W). Time (T) multiplied by dollars (D) multiplied by your return on your investment (R) equals wealth. To be more specific, let us set a goal to have a million dollars invested in mutual funds. Here is how you can become a millionaire. The first chart will reveal how old you will be when you will have $1,000,000.00 in mutual funds that have historically returned about 10 percent per year. These are large cap stock funds that invest in larger companies. The second chart will show you when a 12 percent average yield will turn you into a millionaire. Over the past several decades, small stocks have returned approximately 12 percent. As you look at the charts, remember that $2,000.00 per year is only about $167.00 per month. It doesn't take much to build a small fortune.

Ten Percent Average Return

Your Age	Dollars Per Year Invested	$1,000,000.00 Age
25	2,000.00	65
30	2,000.00	70
35	2,000.00	75
40	2,000.00	80
25	2,500.00	64
30	2,500.00	69
35	2,500.00	74
40	2,500.00	79
25	3,000.00	62
30	3,000.00	67
35	3,000.00	72
40	3,000.00	77
25	3,500.00	60
30	3,500.00	65
35	3,500.00	70
40	3,500.00	75
25	4,000.00	59
30	4,000.00	64
35	4,000.00	69
40	4,000.00	74

Twelve Percent Average Return

Your Age	$ Per Year Invested	$1,000,000.00 Age
20	2,000.00	56
25	2,000.00	61

Your Age	$ Per Year Invested	$1,000,000.00 Age
30	2,000.00	66
35	2,000.00	71
40	2,000.00	76
20	2,500.00	54
25	2,500.00	59
30	2,500.00	64
35	2,500.00	69
40	2,500.00	74
45	2,500.00	79
20	3,000.00	52
25	3,000.00	57
30	3,000.00	62
35	3,000.00	67
40	3,000.00	73
45	3,000.00	77
20	3,500.00	51
25	3,500.00	56
30	3,500.00	61
35	3,500.00	66
40	3,500.00	71
45	3,500.00	76
20	4,000.00	50
25	4,000.00	55
30	4,000.00	60
35	4,000.00	65
40	4,000.00	70
45	4,000.00	75

Your specific goals may vary quite a bit. Your specific investment vehicles may return more than 10 or 12 percent. As you can see, it takes very little to develop an investment fund that is going to meet your financial needs in retirement. Remember, this is only one investment vehicle. There is another excellent vehicle that you can begin now if you are buying your home.

How to Save $5,000.00 Per Year

What is not included in the charts above is the equity you build in your home. Equity is an asset that is as real as money you invest in stocks or the furniture in your home. Equity is the value of a house minus what you owe on the house.

Imagine that instead of taking out a 30-year loan on the $135,000.00 home we discussed earlier, that you would take out a 15-year loan. How would that change the numbers? Your monthly payment of principal and interest on a 15-year loan of $120,000.00 would be $1,147.00 per month. That compares with $881.00 per month using the 30-year mortgage. Your total payments would be $206,460.00 instead of $317,000.00. A savings of over $110,000.00! Better yet, you probably will pay about one-half percent less in interest on your loan with a 15-year loan. That means that your actual principal and interest would be $1,113 per month. That is only $231 per month more for your home and your total payments will be $200,340.00. You save $115,000.00 by paying your mortgage off in 15 years instead of 30 years.

What would you do with $115,000.00?

Even though you are paying $231.00 per month more for your home, *all* of that money is going to equity in your home. This is how to play the banker's game. You get the best possible interest rate and the most favorable terms and end up saving $7,000.00 per year over 15 years by paying off your mortgage in more financially logical terms. If you are not buying a home, you can refinance your current loan using a 15-year mortgage. If you are going to live in your home for more than two more years, you will rapidly recoup your closing costs and then quickly build equity in your home.

If refinancing is unwise because interest rates are higher than when you bought your home, you can most likely make principal payments in addition to your regular payment each month. Your lender will take these principal payments right off the balance of the loan. Even investing $100.00 per month extra can cut years off a mortgage. Ask your lender for an amortization sheet showing how much of your money goes to principal and how much goes to interest.

Creating Money Out of Thin Air

You can create money out of nothing by making a few phone calls or doing just a few simple tasks. Here are a few examples.

1) Are you paying 18 percent on a credit card with $5,000.00 charged to it? Call your bank and ask for a consolidation loan for your debts. The rate will probably be about 10 or 12 percent. If it's 12 percent, you'll save 6 percent per year, or about $300.00, all for making a phone call.

2) Take the $3,000.00 sitting in a savings account and move it to the highest paying money market account in the country. If the savings account is paying 2 percent, the best money market account is paying closer to 6 percent. That 4 percent difference will net you over $100.00 this year.

3) Call your insurance agent. Add "Towing and Road" coverage and drop your auto club. Save about $30.00 per year. (While you're on the phone with your insurance agent, make sure your automobile liability coverages are higher than the value of your home.)

4) If you take a lot of photographs, you can save 50 percent or more by using mail order developers. The quality of the pictures is normally acceptable and if you shoot one roll of film per month you will save about $50 per year.

5) When you go to the store, know what you want to buy before you get there. By stopping impulse buying, you can save $1,000.00-$3,000.00 per year.

6) Buy birthday and anniversary cards by the box and not individually. A box of 20 cards retails for about $7.00. Twenty cards individually bought sell for about $40.00. You save $33.00.

7) Switch from annual fee to no-annual fee credit cards. Make it your policy to never pay for an annual fee card again. Switch three cards and save $70.00.

8) Learn how to do simple repairs at home yourself by buying a "fix-it" book. This can save $60.00 on one unnecessary visit from a serviceman.

9) Change the oil in your car. You will spend about $6.00 and save about $18.00 per visit off the quickie oil shops. Annual savings: $72.00.

10) Ask for a discount on everything you buy, every hotel you stay at, every loan you get. Over half of all purchases could be had at a discount if the right person is asked. Savings? Varies.

11) What are you currently spending money on now, that is a complete waste of your hard earned money? (Cigarettes, alcohol, impulse items, etc.)

_____

_____

Completing this exercise made you aware that you can literally create money out of nowhere by simply saving, instead of spending. Once you begin saving, you can then begin investing!

Always Pay Yourself First

When you are working 40-50 hours per week, you deserve to keep some of the money that you are earning. When investing, remember you are taking the money you have earned and making it grow for your future use. Advertisers have convinced many people to "spoil yourself" by spending money on fleeting moments of pleasure. Reconsider the advertisers message and spoil yourself with a lavish lifestyle when you truly want it and deserve it.

When you get paid, send 10 percent directly to your money market fund or your bank account. It's your money, you earned it. The government is taking far more than 10 percent, aren't they? Did they earn it? Do you deserve at least half as much as Uncle Sam is getting? That's right, you're seeing it more clearly now. You earned your money and you deserve to keep it for your use in the future. You are investing in yourself and your future.

Understanding Mutual Funds

Mutual Funds can be mysterious at first glance. Here is a simple thumbnail sketch of what mutual funds are. For more detailed information about mutual funds ask your librarian to direct you to some good books on investing.

A family of Mutual Funds is like a family. You have parents and children. In a family of Mutual Funds you have fund managers and their funds. Thousands of investors send these funds money to invest. Your money is pooled with these investors and, through this process, you are able to own a diversified portfolio from the very beginning of your investing days. Earlier in this chapter you learned that Fidelity, Vanguard, Scudder, and American Century are all families of funds. Each of these companies have dozens of funds.

There are many types of funds. Some fund managers run funds that invest in large capitalization stocks like Caterpillar, Disney, and IBM. Other funds invest in small stocks. These are typically called "growth funds." Funds investing in bonds are, not surprisingly, called bond funds. However, much like children, the names of funds do not tell you what is inside the fund. Fidelity Magellan Fund is well known as one of the world's largest mutual funds. However, you have no idea what this fund invests in until you request a prospectus.

What to Invest In

By taking a trip to the library you can look up various mutual funds in the *Morningstar Mutual Fund Guides.* They rate various funds and explain the risk and reward potentials for thousands of funds. Look for Morningstar's four star rating or better picks, and you will improve your odds of making an excellent decision. What is a good fund today may not be good tomorrow. Becoming even a little familiar with a few of the major families of funds and their track record will greatly help you choose where to send your money.

Ultimate Risk?

There is an element of risk in investing in mutual funds. A major stock market crash could drain your portfolio. Historically these crashes have been relatively short lived and the markets recover in general, as do most specific stocks. History has taught us that stocks are the best place to invest (along with real estate), and with mutual funds, there is little need to worry about diversification as you are buying into a "pre-diversified pie." Each dollar you invest is literally diversified instantly.

Other Investments

Real Estate is the most lucrative investment for most investors once a portfolio of stocks or mutual funds have been developed. There is not space in this book to cover the various aspects of real estate. Your home is certainly a solid investment if you paid a fair price and get average or better appreciation. There are numerous books that detail investment real estate. However, before jumping in, it may be wise to develop a solid portfolio of mutual funds. The instant diversification takes most of the major risk out of the process and the objective here is not to speculate but to create and design a wealthy future to live in.

Land, like real estate, is best left to the experts that know what they are doing. Buying undeveloped land can be boom-or-bust. Early in your investing career is not the time to take such a risk.

Collectibles and miscellaneous investments are usually not a good investment. One example would be that of baseball cards. Baseball cards were big money collectibles in the 1980s. However, in the 1990s the value tapered. Old cards in mint shape are still valuable, but the new products are unlikely to produce much of value because of the popularity of card collecting.

Jewelry and diamonds are poor investments. The day you buy a diamond ring its value immediately drops about 80-90 percent regardless of what the "appraisal" says.

Gold and platinum have some potential in scenarios that put the United States in a financial crisis. Because the United States will someday have to pay the national debt and erase deficits, inflation will once again rear its ugly head. This makes gold, silver and platinum worth holding as a tiny percentage of your portfolio.

Stamps and coins are cyclical in their collecting value. Like baseball cards, when the hobby is popular, it is far less profitable. When it is out of vogue it is far more profitable.

Lotteries and games of chance are not investments. They are entertainment and they are designed for you to lose most or all of your money.

What is Money?

Money is something that two parties agree has value in expediting a transaction of goods or service. Because it takes agreement, it is a belief. Money is not the root of all evil. The love of money is. To become addicted to a belief is to severely limit your ability to function in life. Ignoring money is as foolish as chasing after money. Most of the people who are in prison today are in prison for something that in some way had to do with money. Most of the people who live lives by design have a great deal of money. The difference is the sequence of events and the goals involved. Money itself only solves a few problems.

Living a life by design can mean doing what you love and getting paid for it. It can also mean doing what you don't like a little longer while you become a master of what you wish to do.

People who misuse money idolize it. It is not viewed as a product of happiness but the reverse. People who end up in jail often believe that money would have made them happy. It would not have. Doing what you love and designing your life is what will give you long-term pleasure. Prosperity is a by-product of intentional thinking, sound investment and giving great service and/or products to others.

Visualize into Prosperity

Close your eyes and go out into the future until you come to a time when you experience life in such a way that you have the right amount of money . . . the right amount of financial resources and security . . . to help you live the life you want to live . . .

Notice what you observe around you . . . who is with you . . . what they are doing . . . what kind of environment you are in . . . what people are saying and what you are doing . . .

How does it feel inside to be comfortable . . . and secure . . . knowing that you have no financial worries . . . what do you feel inside?

Now go inside and float up out of this experience and go backward in time, back toward the present until you come to the moment where you changed your thinking . . . your work . . . your investing patterns . . . your use of credit . . . see, hear, and feel what it was that you began to do differently . . .

Go forward into the near future and see what kinds of service you offered to people . . . what job changes or additions to your work load that you made . . . what changes in life you made to end up with such a wonderful future . . . that made you feel so good inside . . .

Go a little further into the future and see what other services or products you work with . . . and see what it is that really changes your financial life . . . and do that now . . . good . . . take your time and experience everything you see, feel, and hear . . .

There are some events in the future that you want to experience more closely . . . there is a time when you really started paying off old debts . . . go to that time now and see how it feels to actually get out of debt . . . notice how that feels inside . . . now . . .

There is another time in the future . . . that you begin to invest money into your future . . . money that is for you and not for the rest of the world . . . when do you start taking care of yourself . . . paying yourself . . . the money you so richly have earned? Notice that time and see how that feels inside . . . now . . .

There is yet another time in your future . . . when you use your time more profitably . . . when you get paid much more for every hour you work . . . go into that time period now and see what it is that you are doing to produce more value per hour of work . . . good . . . what are you doing . . . that you will need to prepare for . . . either with education . . . self-study . . . or prepare for in some other way? Go there now and see what you will be doing that will change your life and determine what it is that got you to that point . . . now . . .

You persist until you succeed . . . and you continue . . . even when others get lazy or unmotivated. Go to a time . . . now . . . in your future . . . where you no longer feel the need to be lazy because the reward is now worth the price of being active and doing . . . and working . . .

And go to a time in your future when work is rewarding . . . in some important way to you . . . and go there now . . . to a time when you feel not only financially rewarded by what you do . . . but emotionally or spiritually rewarded by what you do. And how do you feel inside . . . now . . . ?

And . . . as you gather all of these lessons and experiences . . . bring the realizations back with you to the present as you re-orient yourself into the present . . . hearing all the sounds around you . . . becoming more aware of what you feel . . . now in the present . . . and when I say "one" you can open your eyes, wide aware and refreshed . . .

Three, hearing all the sounds around you . . . two, feeling so much better and more certain about your future . . . and one, wide aware and refreshed . . . feeling so good inside . . . eyes open and completely aware . . .

CHAPTER FOURTEEN

Accelerated Learning and Memory Enhancement

Learning is something that most people do fairly well . . . but only fairly. Our opportunity to learn more, faster, and easier is something we can start to take advantage of immediately. Almost everyone fails to utilize the hypnotic tools that are available to them in the learning process.

Most people are shocked when we tell them that their IQ can be raised. It was once thought that IQ was set like the Ten Commandments . . . in stone. Such is not the case. In Minnesota, we have taught thousands of people, young and old, how to learn faster and more efficiently. We have discovered that by using simple hypnotic techniques, we can increase IQ by up to 10 percent and retention of facts by as much as 300 percent in some tests.

What Are the Secrets?

For years, hypnotherapists have known that certain types of music have trance-like effects with their clients. Some kinds of music enhance dissociation, some kinds enhance association. Some music excites. Other kinds of music measurably relaxes clients. Could it be that there are kinds of music for enhancing learning states of mind? What other strategies and mental manipulations outside of music could be used? There are a number of strategies you will want to learn in order to be able to optimize your learning ability. Each strategy, independently, will assist you measurably. Synthesize them and you will amaze yourself and others.

Utilization of Mind-Expanding Music

It may or may not surprise you that music directly affects how you learn and remember. There are certain types of music that have been scientifically researched to increase IQ and enhance learning (at least while the music is being listened to). Various pieces from the works of Mozart, Bach, Vivaldi, Beethoven, and Pachibel have been cited as increasing learning speed and IQ.

The most famous study of the effect of certain types of classical music on learning and memory was done at the University of California at Irvine. Mozart's "Sonata for Two Pianos in D Major K 448" was the piece of music studied. It was contrasted to students listening to no music, and also to a group of students listening to a relaxation tape for ten minutes, both before taking the spatial component of an IQ test. Those students listening to Mozart tested out at 119. Those listening to the relaxation tape tested at 111. Those listening to nothing tested at 110! The bad news, as mentioned above, is that the gains are not maintained for long after the music is turned off! The good news is that we know music (at least certain types of classical music) raises IQ.

Does music do more than raise IQ? Absolutely. Some remarkable results were found in an eight-month study examining the effects of music lessons on students. One group of students took music lessons and other students in the research project did not. Tests showed that music helped accomplish various tasks, including putting puzzles together. In order to put a puzzle together the student needed to have a clear mental image of the puzzle to do the task quickly. In fact, those students who had music lessons performed 80 percent better on object assembly tasks when compared to the norm. However, music is not the only magical element in achievement. In other tasks, there was no difference between students who had been given music lessons and those who had not, including tasks that did not require mental imagery.

There is much more, though. Dr. Georgi Lozanov pioneered the accelerated learning movement and recorded his research in the groundbreaking book,*Suggestology and the Outlines of Suggestopedia.* Lozanov, a Bulgarian psychiatrist, was the first to fuse hypnosis and music in creating accelerated achievement in learning.

Lozanov created the concept of learning concerts by blending verbalization of reading assignments with relaxation and music. There are two kinds of concerts that Lozanov developed. One was the Active Concert, wherein material that is to be learned is read with emotional flair, in correspondence to the highs and lows of the music it is "scored" to.

The other kind of concert Lozanov developed was the Passive Concert. This reading was simply articulated softly and quietly with a baroque score in the background.

Both types of hypnotic concerts have proven to be very effective in learning something as complex as foreign languages! In both cases, the recall of terms and phrases is impressive and effective in the long term.

Lozanov (the creator of the mind model discussed earlier in this book) and his fellow researcher, E. Gateva, spent thousands of hours researching both trance and music in creating a learning technology that is now modeled all across the world. Here are a few samples of the pieces of music that accelerate achievement.

Active Concerts

Beethoven	Concerto No. 5 in E-flat Major for Piano and Orchestra, op. 73 ("Emperor")
Brahms	Concerto for Violin and Orchestra in D Major, op. 77
Haydn	Concerto No. 1 in C Major for Violin and Orchestra
	Concerto for Violin and String Orchestra, No. 1 in C Major and No. 2 in G Major
	Symphony No. 67 in F Major and No. 69 in B Major
Mozart	Concerto for Violin and Orchestra; Concerto No. 7 in D Major
	Concerto for Piano and Orchestra, No. 18 in B flat Major
Tchaikovsky	Concerto No. 1 in B-flat Minor for Piano and Orchestra

Passive Concerts

Bach	Choral Prelude in A Major and Prelude and Fugue in G Minor
	Fantasy in G Major, Fantasy in C Minor, and Trio in D Minor
	Canonic Variations and Toccata
	Symphony No. 2 for String Orchestra
	Symphony in C Major
	Symphony in D Major

Corelli	Concerti Grossi, op. 6, No. 2, 8, 5, 9
	Concerti Grossi, op. 4, 10, 11, 12
Handel	Concerto for Organ and Orchestra

Water Music

| Vivaldi | The Four Seasons |
| | Five Concertos for Flute and Chamber Orchestra |

Making Your Own Hypnotic Concerts

You will be amazed at how easy it is make your own Hypnotic Concerts. Here is the step-by-step plan.

1. Acquire the pieces of music that are proven to enhance learning and memory.
2. Verbalize what you want to learn into a tape recorder in either a passive or active voice as discussed above.
3. Close your eyes and relax before you play your concert.
4. Allow yourself to be alert. Focusing your mind on the concert, allowing it to fill your mind.
5. When the concert is over test your recall to ensure that learning has taken place!

Music's power, beat, and rhythm have induced trance for millennia. Now we can change the way we learn forever with the right music.

Learning In Multiple Modalities

We learn from hypnosis that the more sensory modalities we can access, the more likely the hypnotic experience is to be useful in changing the person's future. The same is true for learning and memory. Many people simply read a textbook or learn something from a lecture. Long-term retention in these situations is slight. Did you go to college? About one in four Americans graduate college with a degree. Most of them can not remember anything they learned in college. Even fewer can remember the names of the majority of their professors and instructors. The college learning environment is not conducive to long term learning.

What Is?

You and I learn better when we see, feel, hear, touch, and do something. It has been said that we remember about:

20 percent of what we read
30 percent of what we hear
40 percent of what we see
50 percent of what we say
60 percent of what we do
and
90 percent of what we see, hear, say, *and* do.

Therefore, when we are learning any new material, we want to fully utilize all of our sensory systems. When you read a book for the purpose of learning, you should pause once in a while. Close your eyes and internally dialogue with yourself, commenting to yourself about what you are learning and how you will remember it. You also want to see yourself, in your mind's eye, utilizing the information you are learning. Make sure you fully experience the use of everything you are learning in your mind. Thus, your learning experience will become more vivid and real to you. If you can imagine yourself teaching others the material you are learning, you will benefit even more from the experience. Preparing to teach is one of the finest ways known to learn.

Use Mental Imagery to Enhance Recall and Learning

Imagery is a pillar of good hypnotic trance work. Throughout this book, you have experienced how to make many different kinds of pictures in your mind. You have learned how to manipulate those pictures to make the images work in your favor. Now you will learn two fascinating hypnotic memory tools. The first is exaggeration, and the second is association. Blended together, you can remember almost anything.

Imagine that you have a list of items to remember. Here is your list:

Hitler	Tomatoes
Love	Diamonds
Mom	Spain
Boxer	Bull
Airplane	Chair

Repeating the list over and over would help you remember some of the words for the short term but you wouldn't retain the list for long. However, creating a metaphor, or an exaggerated story using associative techniques would permanently embed the list into your mind. Read this story and see if you do not remember the list easily and clearly by the end of the chapter.

Hitler raises his right hand high into the air. As you look at Hitler's hand you are shocked to find the word *love* written in big red letters on his hand. As Hitler turns and looks at his hand he does not see the letters but sees a picture of your *mom* in his hand. Your mom has never looked better and she pops out of Hitler's hand onto the ground growing to her full height like magic and immediately knocks Hitler to the ground with a blow to the chin. Mom is ready to take on the next heavyweight contender and a *boxer* mystically appears as Mom turns around. She immediately strikes the boxer so hard that he flies onto the top of the biggest *airplane* you ever have seen. Mom blows like the wind and the airplane takes off into the sky. As the plane ascends the boxer falls off the plane into a huge crate of *tomatoes* rendering the boxer unconscious. You go to look at the tomatoes and, as you come closer, they turn into huge *diamonds*. You grab a handful and jump so high into the sky that you land on top of the airplane, which is flying to *Spain*. The airplane lands in an arena where a *bull* is charging you. You sit on a *chair* and look at the bull with ferocious eyes and the bull stops dead in his tracks . . . and you remember all ten words!

That which is difficult to remember comes easy when you create an exaggerated story or a metaphor. Not only can you remember lists, you can remember steps, functions, processes, and just about anything you need to remember, using this hypnotic technique.

If you put your story to the music we discussed earlier in the chapter the memory becomes even more firmly embedded into your mind. Try it with this list of ten words, then test yourself.

Jack of Spades	Fireplace
Desk	Tree
Run	Jump
Dog	Nuclear Power Plant
Table	Nurse

Now, make up your own story, exaggerating its contents as much as you possibly can. Then read your story just one time. If you do not use gross exaggeration the story will not help you remember the word list. You must exaggerate, and in great proportion. This is what makes the memory so . . . .well, memorable! When you are done reading your story, close your eyes and remember it. Amaze yourself now!

How did you do? Most people remember 9 or 10 words out of every 10 words that are on the list. You can try this on your own with 20 or 30 words and you will find that you can remember them easily.

Have the Right Attitude about Learning!

What is the right attitude about learning? The attitude, in part, is that you are going to benefit from what you are learning! So, what is it that you get out of learning? How does it help you? Always answer those questions before you begin learning. What's in it for you? If you find a reason to learn, a real reason that really benefits you, then you will learn more readily than you thought you could.

Meditate into Learning

Before you begin a serious learning project, you may want to induce yourself into a light trance by reading, or listening to an audio tape of, this meditation.

Take a deep breath in and slowly release it . . . take another deep breath in and let it go even further. Allow yourself to enter what is called a learning state. Remember a time when you learned something that was fun . . . easy to learn . . . so easy that you could not believe other people wouldn't "get it." Remember that time when learning something was easy . . . now . . .

Was it riding a bicycle? Playing a card game? What was it that was so easy to learn? Was it easy to play a board game . . . or a sport . . . or a subject in school? Think of a specific time and go there . . . now . . .

Allow yourself to be there now . . . and remember everything you saw, felt, and heard . . . as you begin to re-experience a specific time in your life . . . when you understood something easily and quickly. Take your time and be there now . . . walking through the event . . . moment by moment in great detail . . .

Good . . . now . . . how did you feel inside as you were learning what it was you were learning? When you have that feeling . . . and it is clear and strong . . . take your thumb and your index finger and touch them together . . .

Good . . . now . . . as the feeling subsides, release the thumb and the index finger . . .

Return to another time . . . a different time . . . when you found that learning something was particularly easy. Allow yourself to be there now . . . and remember everything you saw, felt and heard . . . as you begin to re-experience a specific time in your life when you picked up on something easily and quickly. Take your time and be there now . . . walking through the event, moment by moment in great detail . . .

Good . . . now . . . how did you feel inside as you were learning what it was you were learning? When you have that feeling . . . and it is clear and strong . . . take your thumb and your middle finger and touch them together . . .

Good . . . now . . . as the feeling subsides, release the thumb and the middle finger . . .

Return to yet another time . . . a very different time when you found that learning something was particularly easy. Allow yourself to be there now . . . and remember everything you saw, felt, and heard . . . as you begin to re-experience a specific time in your life when you picked up on something easily and quickly. Take your time and be there now . . . .walking through the event, moment by moment in great detail . . .

Good . . . now . . . how did you feel inside as you were learning what it was you were learning? When you have that feeling . . . and it is clear and strong . . . take your thumb and your ring finger and touch them together . . .

Good . . . now . . . as the feeling subsides, release the thumb and the ring finger . . .

Now . . . touch all three fingers to your thumb at the same time and take a deep breath in . . . good. How do you feel inside? That's right . . . good . . . and release the fingers and . . . now . . . one more time. Touch the fingers to the thumb and experience how you feel inside . . . and this time realize that each time you need to learn something that is important, you can touch your fingers to your thumb and you will feel just like you do . . . now . . . inside. And it makes learning easy and remembering what you learned fun . . . good . . . now . . .

Allow yourself to become more aware of the environment around you and return to your reading or whatever it is you want to do . . . now. Wide awake and refreshed . . .

CHAPTER FIFTEEN

Interpreting Your Dreams

Throughout history, dreams have been the subject of much intrigue and mystery. Dreams have been used as the center of psychological analysis, as the basis for prophecy, and as the topic of fascinating conversations among friends.

There have been extensive research and speculation around the subject of dreams and their interpretations, and yet none of it is fully conclusive. However, we are quite certain that dreams occur most often, and most vividly, during REM sleep. REM sleep is evidenced by the rapid eye movement that gives it its name The first dream cycle occurs approximately ninety minutes after we fall asleep, and repeats about every ninety minutes thereafter. Dreams may last from five to twenty-five minutes in each of the given periods.

Dreams appear to be a most elegant avenue for the unconscious mind to communicate with the conscious mind. As has been discussed throughout this book, the unconscious mind stores every experience that a person has throughout their life. These experiences include all the input from the physical senses—sight, hearing, taste, touch, and smell. It also includes all the thoughts and emotions that a person has, both real and fantasized. Also stored in the unconscious mind are extensive data that the conscious mind is completely unaware of. These might include the autonomic functioning of the body, health conditions, telepathic communications, energy sensing, and other subliminal information that has been received unwittingly.

While the conscious mind is busy paying attention to all that it does during a given day, the unconscious mind is busy gathering in all the information that is bombarding it. It is apparently stored somewhat randomly, yet it alone knows its own filing system. The information is interconnected in a way that is illogical to the rational mind, but makes perfect sense within its own system. Dreams, stream of consciousness thinking, and reverse metaphors are all methods for the unconscious mind to put those various bits of information into context. In this way, the apparently random bits of information are organized without the barriers and limitations of the rational mind.

Dreams are particularly instructional. Because they allow the unconscious mind to communicate directly with the conscious mind, you are given the opportunity to gain tremendous amounts of information and insight concerning your life. These insights may help you to remember forgotten information, give you ideas for solutions to your problems, help you to understand your emotions and motivations more fully, and to sort out and organize your thoughts.

Dream a Little Dream . . .

The following dream was recorded by one of our recent hypnotherapy certification graduates, Rebecca Phifer. You will see that it is rich in symbolism and meaning. Enjoy reading the dream for now. We will decipher the symbolism later in the chapter when we discuss interpreting dreams.

> I am outside, during the day, and I am surrounded by a field of beautiful fragrant flowers. The ground that I am standing on is a piece of earth that is floating in the sky. It is flat, a jagged round shape, and the earth beneath falls away to a point. It is gently floating through the sky. There are wispy clouds around, but no other objects. I am standing on this piece of land, looking at all the beautiful flowers that have bloomed. It is spring, and the flowers surround me completely.
>
> I walk to the edge. I think there is more land underneath my feet, but I am wrong and I fall off. I'm falling. Suddenly I have wings and I can fly back up through the sky. I am doing aerodynamic acrobatics, tumbling, turning. It's so fun.
>
> Slowly I float down to some land. It's really dark land. Dark, rich, fertile soil. It feels almost scary in a way. I walk along. There are no plants, just dark rich soil. It begins to slope downward, becoming really steep. I can't walk, I just start to slide down. I slide into a cavern that is lit up brightly. It's so bright that I can't see. All I notice is bright light inside a

cave. Really bright. It feels good, but also I wish I could see something else. I see nothing but warm light. I am bewildered. I can't climb out because it is so steep.

Since I can only see light, I don't know where to go. It's just like being in the dark because I am walking with my hands in front of me, feeling the way. Being in the light is like being in the dark. I am stumbling around and I don't know if the ground is level. Will I fall? Gingerly, I am putting my feet in front of me. It feels like I am going deeper and it is still bright.

As I am going, the space gets smaller and smaller. And I get smaller and smaller. I am becoming a ball of light, rolling around like a roller coaster ride. Finally I come out at the end.

I am in something that is a cross between a jungle and a forest. It is really green and lush. I unroll myself and become a person again. I like it. There is color here. It feels good. I like to be able to move my arms and legs and look around. I can smell the air, clean and fresh like it just rained. It's alive. It feels so good to be alive.

I am in a river now, swimming and flowing along. It is cleansing and refreshing.

Remembering Dreams

Emotions appear to be the catalysts for dreams. The feelings that a person is experiencing, whether they are fully aware of them or not, will drive the dream in a corresponding direction and subject matter. Therefore, dreams may elicit any number of feelings, including but not limited to those of sadness, guilt, rejection, abandonment, joy, surprise, fear, comforting, and acceptance. In like manner, we can use emotions to direct our dreams to give us particular needed information, and to help us remember what those dreams are. We will discuss directing dreams in just a moment. Let's look now at how we can remember them.

Some people seem to just be more adept than others at remembering their dreams. Do not worry. If you are one of those people who think they never dream, or who only remember dreams once in a while, there are methods that you can practice that will make it easier and easier to remember your dreams.

Everyone dreams. Remembering your dreams will become easier.

And why should you remember your dreams? There is a philosophy that if you were supposed to remember your dreams you would. However, it may go beyond that. Perhaps you are supposed to remember your dreams and you do not want to.

Why would a person not want to remember their dreams? Perhaps for the same reason we would prefer to forget many things. Maybe there is something that we do not want to face in ourselves—fear, guilt, health conditions, or the need for change. For those of you who might fall into this category, as you read and work on the topics of the other chapters of this book, you will be more prepared and willing to look at your dreams.

Another reason we forget our dreams in the morning is because we are too busy, either mentally or physically, or both. When we awaken in the morning, if we immediately start thinking and worrying about the day's activities or some other subject that is bothering us, our dreams are pushed right back down into the unconscious, along with all the other repressed and forgotten memories.

Therefore, it is vital to the remembrance of dreams to awaken slowly and calmly, focusing your attention immediately on your thoughts and feelings in the present moment.

Keeping a Dream Journal

Generally, the dreams that occur closer to the morning are the ones most frequently remembered. For this reason, it is a good idea to keep a dream journal near your bed. A dream journal can be any type of notebook, plain or fancy. You will also need a pen, preferably one that writes in any position, and a source of dim light. You do not want to shocked or blinded by the light when all you want to do is to jot down a couple of notes or key words.

Upon awakening, calmly, you can reach for your dream journal and begin to write down thoughts or feelings that may come to you. They may not make sense. They may not appear to be connected to anything. That is perfectly fine and quite natural. But the more you relax and just allow the free flow of words, thoughts, images, and feelings to occur, the more you will begin to remember each morning, the more you will remember of each dream, and the more you will train yourself to remember your dreams. Over time, you will create a habit and your dreams will come to you easily and vividly.

Feelings and moods are particularly helpful in the recollection of dreams. Immediately upon awakening, observe the mood that you are in or the emotions that you are experiencing. As you name them, follow them back to their origins. You most likely had a dream that sparked these feelings inside of you.

Because you are naturally more likely to remember the dreams that occurred just prior to awakening, there are steps that you can take to begin remembering more of those that occurred earlier in the night. You can program yourself to wake up in the middle of the night, either by mental self-suggestion, or by setting an alarm. When you surface from a dream and come to near wakefulness, you can simply turn on your small light, reach for your dream journal, and write a few notes or keywords that will help to jog your memory about the dream in the morning.

Programming Your Mind to Remember Your Dreams

In order to program your mind to automatically awaken you after a dream, you can do the following self-hypnosis exercise just before falling asleep. You may want to record the following script and play it to yourself as you are dozing off to sleep. If you use this tape nightly, you will find that your dreams will become more vivid, and you will easily remember more and more of them.

> As you lay your head on your pillow . . . and begin to relax into sleep . . . focus your energy up in your head. Clearing all thoughts from your mind . . . focusing only on my voice and your purpose of remembering your dreams. Notice how relaxed your body is becoming. As your energy continues to concentrate in your head . . . you become unaware of your body. It relaxes completely . . . All sensation fading away.
>
> Focused completely in the head now. The head clearing of all thoughts except my voice . . . you become curious as to what you might discover . . . by remembering your dreams. It seems like such a fascinating adventure. The discovery of what can be found in the unconscious mind. There is a part of you that already remembers all of your dreams. They are all stored there in the unconscious mind.
>
> If you were really curious . . . you would be able to go into the archives of your mind and retrieve those dreams right now. If you were curious enough. And doesn't it just make you wonder? Perhaps we could take a look right now. Imagine flying over a great labyrinth . . . in which is stored all the memories . . . and information of your unconscious mind. What a wonderful sight.

And as you fly over this labyrinth . . . something catches your eye. It might be a color or a movement. It might be an object or an image. It does not matter what it is . . . whether it makes sense or whether you have ever seen it before. Whatever it is, you become ever more curious about it.

As you move closer to it, you begin to see more detail. You explore and examine. You watch as it changes and evolves. Upon looking at it, a story begins . . . to unfold about this object. It may be a silly story . . . or it may be profound. It does not matter. It is simply a story. And . . . you are most curious about it. You continue through the story until it is concluded. It was a most unusual . . . and curious story. Fascinating. Worth remembering . . . worth writing down.

When the story is finished . . . your thoughts will come back from that labyrinth. Back into your head, back to your conscious thoughts. You will feel the urge to stir . . . and come up to the surface of consciousness. Only so wakeful that you will want to turn on a dim light . . . and write a few words in your dream journal. Keywords that will allow you to immediately recall . . . the nature of the storyline of this dream. When the dream is finished . . . you will want to turn on the light and write down your dream. You will want to remember this dream. You will remember this dream.

You may find yourself restless until you have written down your dream. When it has been written . . . you will easily and gently fall back to sleep to dream another dream. It will be such a pleasure . . . to dream again. To discover another story. To fly and take adventures. The best part of the adventure is remembering it. With each dream adventure it will be easy . . . and natural to come back to the surface . . . and write down the keywords of the dream. So easy. So fascinating. So fun to be curious.

In the morning when you wake up for the day . . . your first thoughts will be about your dreams. They are so fascinating . . . and it is so easy to be curious about them. Images, feelings, thoughts, and memories . . . will be right there in your mind. You will awaken refreshed and energetic . . . and so very curious about the dreams that you have had.

Other Ways to Remember Dreams

Another method of remembering dreams is one that I (M.L.) discovered for myself some years ago. It was a period of time when I was working diligently on remembering my dreams. One morning I did not get much in the way of clues to the previous night's dreams, so I went along with my day and got up. While I was in the shower an old song popped into my head. I found I was singing it to myself over and over. I began to think it was curious, because it was not a song that I had heard recently and I could not think of why it would be in my head. As I started to pay attention to the words of the song, I realized that the words brought back images of the dream that I had experienced that previous night. I had to laugh to myself. My unconscious mind had given me a trigger so that I would remember my dream.

Along that same vein, you may have signals and triggers that you have or can set up for yourself. The bottom line is to pay attention. Pay attention to your random thoughts because somewhere in there you might find clues to the messages that your unconscious mind wants to deliver to you.

Together with self-hypnosis and programming your mind to remember your dreams, sometimes other rituals are helpful. Just like any kind of anchoring, we can program our minds to respond to a certain stimulus to give us a desired response. So if you think that hanging a dream catcher over your bed will help you capture your dreams, by all means include that in your programming for dream recall.

You can program your mind to recall dreams when you touch a certain stone, look at a certain color, smell a particular aroma, drink your morning coffee, or hear a bell chime. You are free to create your own rituals and to designate a certain anchor as the trigger for dream recollection. The more belief and emotion that you pour into that anchor, the more successfully it will work for you.

A natural anchor that you may have already programmed into your mind is right in your body. If you are having trouble remembering your dream, roll over onto different sides, or onto your stomach. If you were lying that way when you were dreaming, it is possible that the emotions or images associated with the dream will be recalled when you resume the same position.

Dream Interpretation

Now that you are starting to collect your dreams, the next step will be to learn how to interpret them. Interpretation is the key to making the dreams meaningful in your life. Since the unconscious is going to all the trouble to communicate its messages to you, you might as well discover what the messages mean to you.

There are psychics, psychologists, organizations, and books that will eagerly decipher your dreams for you. These can be helpful guidelines as archetypes of universe symbols. There are general meanings that are universal across a culture, a gender, or a race. However, for the most part only you will be able to determine the exact meaning, context, and relevance a particular dream has for you. Dreams are one of the most personal and intimate conversations you can have with yourself. It is like the language spoken between two longtime lovers. Only they know the exact meaning and context of their messages.

If you choose to use a dream dictionary or assistance from another person, use them only as a guide or a source of ideas that you can ponder. Ultimately you have to determine the meanings of the symbols found in your dreams. As an example, take the image of a snake. If it appeared in your dream it could have one of many radically different meanings. It could be something scary and deadly, it could mean deceit or threat. It could have sexual connotations, or refer to life, or *kundalini,* energy. If you are a lover of reptiles, it may represent a pet or subject of interest. Snakes have also been linked with magic and mystery. Obviously, only you will be able to judge which, if any of these, meanings is appropriate for you.

One of the most effective ways to decipher a dream is to first write it down. As you write, add in any tangential information that comes to mind. When you have completed the writing of your dream, read back over it. Once again, add in any further information that you come up with. It is fascinating that each time you go over the dream, more details will be made available to you. It is important that you write the dream at the onset, as it tends to solidify your thoughts and recollections. The time it takes to write focuses your mind on the dream and "holds the door open," so to speak. When you are only thinking about the dream, rather than writing it, it is easy for your mind to wander to subjects that you may be worried about in your everyday life.

> *Write down your dreams to optimize*
> *the interpretation of the dream.*

After writing as much as you remember, close your eyes and review the dream once again. This time as you move through the dream, allow yourself to associate with it. In other words, get "into" the dream. Be there. By being fully associated in the dream you will get even further insights as to the meaning and significance of the actions, images, and symbols. Again, you may want to go through it in this fashion a couple more times.

When you have finished viewing the dream, again take paper and pen, and answer the following questions:

What images were in your dream? (Make a list of all the nouns—people, places, and things. This could be extensive.) Next to each of the images, write what you think they represent in your everyday life.

What emotions did you have?

Did your emotions correlate to particular images or was there an overall emotion throughout the whole dream?

What correlation do you notice between the dream and something that is happening in your everyday life?

Was this dream primarily symbolic, a replay of a memory, or informational, as in giving you the answer to a question or problem that you have?

Did this dream appear to be prophetic in nature?

What have you learned from this dream?

How will this dream affect your daily life?

What will you do differently now that you have remembered and understood this dream?

Again, the deciphering of the dream symbols is a very personal activity. With time and practice, you will get very good at understanding them and their meaning for you.

Deciphering Rebecca's Dream

When you read Rebecca's dream, did you think that you understood the underlying meanings of the metaphors? I asked Rebecca to interpret her dream for herself. She gave me the following description, based on the events and circumstances of her life today. How closely you would have "guessed" at the meaning of her dream?

> The flowers and land represented the abundance I am feeling with my new career direction and my hypnotherapy certification. The spring represents things that are growing my life. That piece of earth is my private universe. Where I stand. It is sprouting, growing and smells and looks wonderful. I am standing in the center of it. I feel like I am standing in the center of my rich and abundant life right now.
>
> Stepping off and falling relates to my fear of failure and the unknown. That I might put faith into something that is not there. But, with

my faith, I have everything I need to bring me out. I can soar. All I need is my faith. I can sprout wings and fly. I can do all sorts of amazing feats. It's enjoyable, fun, and invigorating. It gives me the confidence I need.

When I land on the dark earth, it is fertile. It means that I can grow the things that I want in my life. I can create a new life, a new way of being. It's scary to have the power to create and reshape my life.

I was walking and slipped in the cavern. It means that once I get started, things will move along quickly. Almost out of my control. I'll move right into it. Right into the light. I'll know exactly what is what.

But I don't know exactly what that is yet. I'm blinded by the light because I've been in the dark for so long. The light is too much. At first I'm groping, trying to figure things out, and where the path is. I won't know where this path leads me until I get there, learning and feeling it out along the way. But I know I am in the light.

Eventually I turn to a ball of light. I go off with the knowledge, achieving what I need to do. Then I come out of that learning and developing process and onto land again.

The jungle represents being alive and aware. Being in the river means that at that point I will be able to keep up with the flow, and go with the flow. I have it. I know what I am doing and what needs to be done. I won't fight against it. I will be invigorated and relish the beauty and wonder sustained by the flow.

Nightmares

Why is it that we are able to more readily remember our nightmares than our dreams? Frightening dreams will wake us up in the middle of the night, fully remembering every detail. The reason why we are awakened by them, and why we remember them so much more vividly, is because of the emotional charge they carry. The more emotional content an activity has, the more focused upon it we become. The more focus, the more conscious attention. That, along with the adrenaline, makes us very alert and aware.

Nightmares are just as important as dreams and should be remembered and interpreted just as thoroughly. They will give us important, and sometimes life-saving, information to process and perhaps act upon. Nightmares can be based on irrational fears that we have. It is the mind's way of acting out the scenes that your mind is pouring so much "worry energy" into. Nightmares can be negative influences from the spiritual world, and may be reminding you to bolster your defenses. "Bad" dreams may also be your unconscious mind's way of communicating to you a health condition or some other area of your life that needs examining and change.

Nightmares can be reduced by a couple of different methods. The first one is to go over it as outlined above. By writing it, examining it, reviewing it in your mind, over and over, you will become desensitized to the impact of the elicited emotions. A deeper understanding of the nightmare may be all that is needed to banish it from your mind. Once the message is delivered and acted upon, the unconscious mind no longer will feel the need to communicate to you about it.

Another way to rid yourself of most of your nightmares is to program your mind. Remember that, like pain, there is a use for some nightmares. Pain warns us when something is going wrong with our bodies and needs attention. Nightmares, too, may serve the purpose of warning us about impending danger and things that need to be corrected in our lives. However, once the message is received and you want to cease the terror, you can program your mind to ask for assistance.

Calling On a Hero

When my (M.L.) daughter, London, was about six years old, she would frequently wake up in the middle of the night with nightmares. I would get up with her and comfort her. We would discuss the nightmare and I would help her calm down and back to sleep. However, these episodes became a recurring problem. Finally, I asked her to name a person she knew who she felt was a hero. Someone she would trust to save her from any harm. The whole family was practicing martial arts at the time, so she chose our instructor, who was also a close friend of the family. He was a man that she respected, trusted, and felt she could rely on.

I talked to her about calling to him in her dreams whenever she started to become afraid. She agreed to do it. Children are so wonderfully imaginative and open to trying new concepts. For several mornings, she would tell me stories about how she would start to get afraid, and when she called our instructor, he would appear. He would fight the monsters and save her. All was well. Before long the nightmares ceased to occur at all.

Try calling on a hero to assist you through your difficult dreams. Choose a person, real or fictional, that you would trust. They should be capable and strong enough to handle the troubles that you find yourself in during those episodes. Simply determine who that hero is going to be. Then follow these instructions:

> Relaxing and closing your eyes, imagine a picture of you about to get into trouble in a dream. Hold that picture in your right hand. In your left hand hold a picture of your hero coming to rescue you and banish the "monsters." Start by looking at the picture in your right hand. See the picture turning black and white. See it diminishing and fading, shrinking to a dot and disappearing. Immediately look at the picture in your left hand. See it get colorful and bright, growing ever larger until your hero is there beside you, protecting you. Notice how safe that feels. Take a deep breath and hold it for ten seconds. Release it.
>
> Once again, look at the picture in your right hand. See it shrinking to a dot and disappearing. Immediately look to the picture in your left hand. It becomes bright and colorful as it grows larger, to lifesize. Feeling good, feeling safe. Take a deep breath, hold it ten seconds. Release it.
>
> Continue to repeat this process several more times. Do it at least three times and preferably more. The faster you make the shift from the right picture to the left, the more strongly your unconscious mind will learn to remember to bring in your hero during a nightmare.

As it has been pointed out, our dreams play out aspects of our hopes and desires, our fears, and parts of our personalities we may be too inhibited to exhibit during our everyday lives.

Dreams also allow us to learn our lessons in a way that may give us the opportunity to avoid having those experiences in our "real" life. For instance, if we need to learn a major lesson about compassion for others, we may have a very sensory realistic dream about losing a limb, or having some disability that would require us to seek compassion from others. By being able to experience this dream completely, with the full strength of the emotions attached to it, we may not have to actually experience a similar event in our waking life. Our conscious mind receives the message and makes a change in our personality or character. Then the change is registered by the unconscious mind, causing it to believe that the experience has served its purpose. Perhaps in this way, we can avoid having to draw difficult and heartbreaking events into our lives. We can learn through our dreams as opposed to having to face such an experience in our waking life.

Receiving Answers to Our Problems

One of the most fascinating uses for dreams is that of problem solving. It has been recorded throughout history that great minds have used the power of their dreams for inspiration and imagination. Edgar Cayce, Thomas Edison, and Mozart, to name a few, saw the wellspring of ideas that can come from paying attention to their dreams.

This is a concept I was later to read about, but as a child I discovered it for myself quite by accident. When I was in the first years of elementary school I was given tap dancing lessons. Before fourth grade, our family moved from Minnesota to Colorado. Later that year there was a talent show in my school. I entered it, wanting to perform a tap dance that I had learned during my earlier classes. As I was practicing for the show I realized that I could not, for the life of me, remember part of the routine. I tried and tried to figure out what the steps were and just couldn't get it. One night, as I was going to sleep I was replaying the incomplete dance routine in my head, over and over. And then I drifted to sleep. In the morning I woke up thinking about the dance and suddenly realized that I could now remember all the steps. It had been presented to me in my dream.

By going to sleep and relaxing the critical factors of my frantic rational mind, my unconscious mind was able to direct me to my memories of the entire dance routine. After all, the memory was already there. I just had to retrieve it.

What happens when you want answers to puzzles on subjects you have not previously learned, such as the materials to use for an as-yet-not-invented light bulb? The extent of the resources available to our unconscious minds is not, as yet, fully known. Where the information comes from and how we are able to access it is still under continuing research. However, we do know that people have brain storms, get creative inspiration, and invent new things everyday. Wherever that comes from, we do know that it is through the unconscious mind that our conscious minds are able to eventually receive it.

So how do we gain access to those answers? Again, it is a very simple self-hypnosis programming process. And remember, the more you practice, the better you will get at it, and the more reliable your answers may become.

Think of a question that you have about something. It must be a question whose answer is possible to know. Answers to questions that are of high emotional impact to you will be less reliable because you may interpret your answers through the colored lens of your hopes and fears. For instance, if you are terribly upset with your spouse and you suspect they are cheating on you, your dream may reveal your fears, not the truth. However, the answer to a work-related issue might be a good place to start.

Once again, think of the problem that you want answered, as you go to bed. Continue to ponder the question, with as much curiosity as you can muster while staying relaxed. Just think about the question, telling yourself that you want to receive the answer in your dream and that you will remember it when you wake up. It will be helpful if you have been practicing the techniques to remember your dreams outlined above.

This seems almost too simple, but that's really all there is to it. Just do it, and practice frequently. Remember that the answer may come in the form of a symbol. In that case, simply go through the steps outlined for dream interpretation.

Dream On!

Dreams are a wonderful and fascinating aspect of life. They can be entertaining, informative, and mysterious. They give us insights into our lives and can reveal our deeper motives and feelings. Dreams give us access to unconscious patterns, connections, and symbols, divulging information that we might otherwise never become aware of. Cherish your dreams as they are valuable, and completely personal, aspects of you.

CHAPTER SIXTEEN

Remarkable Stories about the Power of Self-Hypnosis

The power of self-hypnosis is often best told from the people who have experienced miracles or dramatic changes in their life. The stories in this chapter are all shared in the words of the person who lived the events. In all cases, Mary Lee and I know the contributors and we are excited for you to hear about their success stories. Some are simply . . . miraculous!

Eye Sight Improvement Without Laser!

The first story we want to share with you comes from my (K.H.) good friend Mair Llewellyn Edwards, of the United Kingdom. I've known Mair for many years and if this story had come from virtually anyone but Mair, I probably wouldn't have believed it! Read on to see the contribution that self-hypnosis made in the improvement of Mair's eyesight. I'm still amazed!

My partner and I were planning our second trip to Romania and we were excited. We really enjoyed travelling overland last time, and this was to be a similar trip. Nothing blurred the horizon except my eyesight. I was finding it increasingly difficult to read the maps and look at exactly where we were going, even while wearing my prescription lenses. In desperation, I visited my optician, who assured me that what I was experiencing was quite a normal problem for someone of my age. The answer to my problem was to have varifocal lenses in glasses instead of using the contact lenses, which I had used for some twenty years. I admit I did not like the sound of this. I guess I am vain and would prefer to use contacts. However, seeing was more important, so glasses it was and the trip to Romania was wonderful!

My prescription details in 1997 were: right eye, -2.50, and left eye, -2.00.

On my return home I found I really disliked wearing my glasses, yet, when we went out my contacts made it impossible for me to see people across the room and also to read the menu. So, I forced myself to stop using both my glasses and contact lenses because I was really fed up. Neither option worked for me. This was difficult because I had been seeing through a lens of one sort or another since I was seventeen years old. I had lived with them constantly and now I was in my 'fifties.

I decided there must be better ways of coping. I could find other things I could do to help myself. I have been a practicing hypnotherapist for twenty years. My very first experience of using self-hypnosis was for the birth of my fourth baby over twenty-five years ago. I thought, *"If I used hypnosis then, and it worked so well, why not use it now with my eyesight."* Why was I being so shortsighted about this? I am passionately excited about the mind-body relationship, so this challenge was really beginning to be fun.

My journey had begun. I did a bit of self-analysis about my beliefs and about my eyesight. I asked my optician how my eyes worked. I read *Eye and Brain* by R. L. Gregory. My imagination began to work overtime. I always love it when this happens. I was beginning to understand a little of what needed to happen physically in my eyes in order to improve them. When I asked my optician about exercise and using my glasses less, he told me that books such as *Perfect Sight Without Glasses* by W. H. Bates had been discredited. Instead of this information stopping me in midflight it made me even more determined. For me and my eyesight this time could just be a miracle waiting to happen.

I discovered that the treadmill at the gym was a great place to start eye exercises. Fellow joggers looked at me quite strangely! I still could not focus well enough to see, but it did not matter, as I was on the way to slimmer thighs and better vision in no time at all! At least if I bent down double on the scales I could see my weight was shaping up. Did I imagine it, or was I really less doubled up each week when I weighed myself?

Somewhere I had read suggestions that hypnosis using age regression could help in improving my eyesight. I decided to approach this quite gently and I realized that the time my eyesight began to falter was during quite an upsetting time in my life. My then boyfriend, somewhat older than me, was horrible when I was trying to navigate for him. On returning home from a trip he told my Mum and Dad in no uncertain terms that I needed to have my eyes tested (he wore glasses!). I had made no connection between that incident and my eyesight, but I have always felt useless at navigating ever since. I now firmly believe that I could actually see okay, but was frightened to give directions. That fear and his suggestions could have affected me in my belief in my ability to see, or of finding my way. (By the way, I can now navigate well, or so my loving, biased current partner says.) That was the regression completed and it was so good being loving to myself about that time in my life anyway.

One day, whilst I was waiting for the telephone to be answered, I was looking out of my office window, focusing on an object in the distance. Then, I closed my eyes and hallucinated that point and put in the detail I knew was there more clearly, more sharply focused, and looked again. I then screwed up my eyes and relaxed them and the muscles around my eyes, just experimenting a bit I guess. As I did this, I mused that waiting for my telephone connection to be made was no longer a waste of time. Playing with my eyes was getting to be real fun. I love playing and I was getting to play more each day. "Hello," I said to the answering machine that suddenly kicked in, "I can *see* you are not there at present. I'll ring you again tomorrow."

That night, in bed, I imagined all sorts of bizarre things—window screen wipers cleaning my vision, seeing things bright and clear, and bringing imagined things closer, then putting them into the distance with more clarity. I also did some more serious work of imagining more accurate physical projections to the back of my eye and my eye muscles being flexible and adapting well. I was loving every minute of it, and I found myself getting so excited about the possibilities that it became rather difficult to actually switch off and go to sleep. I realized it was more fun than being in a sweet shop! The only side effects with this type of play was possible improvement in vision, and I had hours of time enjoying myself.

My youngest daughter is a beauty therapist and fortuitously embarked on a course of eye massage as part of her professional development. I volunteered early on for treatment with as little indecent haste as I could muster. At around the same time we took a trip to China and our courier shared with a whole coach load of travelers how she used pressure points to help with eyestrain and headaches. I was rapidly becoming an expert in what to do with your eyes when you have nothing else to do. Was I imagining it or were they really rewarding me by becoming noticeable brighter. I still used my glasses and contact lenses occasionally, but had found a very old pair far more comfortable for my eyes to wear. I was considering asking my optician for a more up to date frame for these old lenses.

My partner is a homoeopath and he happily obtained Euphrasia mother tincture (known as "eyebright") for me to use as part of my eye journey.

When my yearly eye check came up in November 1998, my optician was very helpful—he said my eyes were changing quite considerably and suggested that I try out all sorts of combinations of contact lenses to see how I got on. He told me, in effect, that I would know what felt right for me and, provided I used the recommended prescription for driving, he was very happy to be led by me. This was such a refreshing experience and the playing continued. I discovered that the low power lenses at -1.00 were the most comfortable for both of my eyes except when driving. When I was driving I used my new prescription, which was now right eye, -1.00, and left eye, -2.00. I am wearing my lenses a lot more now, obviously every time I drive, and two or three times in the week when I need a little help to see better. This was a massive change for me. Not long ago, I was totally dependent upon lenses, and now I use them only when necessary.

From November 1998 until the present, I have continued to be more relaxed and positive about my eyesight, as well as other areas of my life. The process of greater self-acceptance has not just been regarding my eyesight and my skills in navigation, but about myself generally.

On the November 12, 1999, I went for my yearly eye check up. My optician seemed puzzled as he examined me. During my eye test, he said, "You should not be able to see that," a couple of times. I told him I had been working at self-hypnosis, as well as eye exercises, and he said, "Eye exercises do not work. They have been discredited."

I asked if there could be another explanation and he said changes frequently occur at my time of life. Then he went on to say the changes in my eyes were not phenomenal but he could not understand why they had changed so much. His answer to why, essentially, was that I was a witch! I asked if he would be willing for me to work with some of his clients in a double blind test. He said he was interested in diseases of the eyes, not something like this.

We parted the best of friends and the prescription he gave me was right eye, -0.50, and left eye, -0.50, general day to day wear and right eye, -2.00, and left eye, -0.50, for driving. As he discussed this new prescription with me I noticed he had a twinkle in his eye as he said, "I hope we are not tempting providence giving you this." I smiled back and thought, "It may not be phenomenal to you, but it has had a miraculous effect on my life."

Live Well Longer

One of the first people that I (M.L.) met when I moved to Seattle was my friend Sam C. Zeiler, M.S., Clinical Nutritionist and Lifecoach. I can personally testify to the effectiveness of Sam's nutritional guidance, and in his story below you will see that he, too, agrees with the connection between the mind and the body. In Sam's own words, his story.

In the beginning there was the thought. When we were young, we seldom thought of aging or being infirm. It is only as we gain in years that we build constructs or thought patterns based primarily on the experience of others.

As long as we accept these thought patterns as the "Truth" for us, be they healthy or unhealthy, we become the physical manifestation of these thoughts. Over time, these physical manifestations provide the pathway to develop habits, again, healthy or unhealthy.

It has been stated in many ways, "a thought held in mind produces after its own kind." Patterns of thought grow and either become constructive or destructive. Your experience will provide evidence as to the character of your thought patterns to this point.

What does this have to with longevity and health? Everything!!!

The Bible states: "As a man thinketh in his heart, so is he." Longevity may find definition in at least these six criteria: How and what you eat, drink, sleep, play, work, and think.

All of these factors fall under the category of nutrition. In other words, nutrition is anything that helps you sustain life and grow. To a certain degree, we accept the construct that thought occurs only in the brain or mind. Recent research provides evidence that every cell has a memory and is part of the collective brain.

This means that under certain stimuli, the whole body responds, not just the mind. This gives new meaning to: "As a man thinketh in his heart so is he."

Living well longer is, in essence, application of conscious intake of healthy thoughts, actions, food, water, and etc., with regard to the six factors mentioned earlier, at the minimum.

The good news is that, at any point, one can improve their longevity through awareness, and begin a process of changing them where necessary. There exist many modalities to bring this change into reality. From the physical aspect, nutrition offers essential support for the physical body to undergo significant change on the emotional, mental, and spiritual planes.

Life's Journey in a Journal

My (M.L.) path has crossed with that of my friend, Jo Ann Sunderlage, in so many ways since I have lived in the Seattle area. She has done remarkable work in her personal life through regression, past life regression, and writing. In her own words, her story.

Writing in diaries and journals, and penning poetry and prose, has always been part of my life. To tell you how much it means to me as I near a half-century on this earth means I must go back to my childhood. My mother saved a little scrap of paper, printed in my childlike hand, which said, "when I grow up, I want to be a mommy and a sekketary [sic]." I was eight. Funny, I've done just that in my life.

My first short story was written when I was also eight, and I remember calling it "The Robber and the Red Purse." Mom also showed me a poem I wrote as a teenager showing my confusion over which boy I liked best.

At 13, I received a diary as a birthday gift. Those empty pages were like heaven to me, and I began writing in it with fervor. I knew just how much my diary meant to me when our town was hit by a tornado that next spring. Along with saving my Beatles records, my diary was the most important thing to me. I didn't care about my clothes, my bed—nothing but the music and that little pink diary. I remember writing in it with a flashlight as my sister slept in the bed next to me, pouring out my heart and my young adolescent feelings. I wore the key on a yarn chain around my neck, pink to match the diary. I read it now with tears in my eyes for the innocence and the starry-eyed hope of the young girl I was then.

At 19, poetry and prose became my fascination instead of diaries. I was a true hippie, I thought, and, having met the man I later married, I wrote pages and pages of love poems, over and over. I wrote my thoughts, such as, "together we are one, yet together we are also two—maybe we are three." I thought that was quite deep. Twelve years later, my journals became full of my feelings, worries, and concerns about my divorce and the effect it was having on our children.

When I married for the second time in 1993, I found inner peace and serenity writing in journals wherever we traveled. My husband respected that part of me. I would, for instance, sit on the deck when we went to a cabin on the coast, and just write and write. This was my therapy—the blank pages filled with the words of my heart were more therapeutic than any psychiatrist. Sometimes I can't write the words fast enough, as my mind overwhelms itself with thoughts. I soon found, while going through my well-worn boxes of old journals, that I was honestly writing my biography without realizing it—about my upbringing, memories of my father who died way too young, and working my way through my emotions as I grew as a daughter, as a woman, as a sister, as a mother, as a stepmother, and as a friend.

In 1996, my journals seemed to become more spiritual as I learned more about the metaphysical world and began reading tarot cards. Today, I'm on my tenth spiral-bound tarot journal, and I write my readings faithfully every day. This brings its own reward—for not only are the cards a true indicator of what is really going on in my life, they force me to look at myself when sometimes I would rather not.

Not too long ago, my mom (who had her first short story published when she was 69) showed me *her* mother's journal. In it were recorded the words, "Born to Marge and Orlo, a girl, Jo Ann." That was me. I hope someday, as a grandmother, to be writing those types of words in my journal, for my daughter to pass on in future years. Mom told me recently that *her* great-grandmother also wrote in journals.

The story of me as recorded in my diaries, journals, and poems will be there for future generations—it' is my legacy, which, to me is much more important than money.

Now I say when I grow up I want to be a writer. I think that had I not written in my diaries and journals, I would not be the person I am today. I can look back and see how they helped me through periods of depression, through periods of incredible happiness, through the stress of divorce, through the trials of being a single mother, and through simply tracking daily tarot readings. I'm still growing, and I'll always be writing.

The Case of the Disappearing Headache

Monica Piechowski of River Falls, Wisconsin, is a certified hypnotherapist and recently experienced a long bout with chronic headaches. That bout is now over, thanks to the power of hypnosis and her mind. Here is Monica's story in her own words.

Several years ago, during high school, I had the chance to learn self-hypnosis, and through the years have utilized it for several personal things, including control of high blood pressure. In March 1998, while at work as a ski instructor, I was skiing on an advanced run. I accidentally wiped out the wrong way, causing me to hit the back of my head. I suffered a concussion.

Following the accident, I went to the local clinic at college and got checked. The doctor told me to take Tylenol™ for the headache. I was worried, though, because my vision wasn't clear, my balance was off, and earlier that day I had a professor single me out to ask if I was going to make it through class that day because I looked like I was about to pass out.

Up until a few weeks after the appointment, I had never experienced a headache at any point in my life and laughed his statement off simply because of that fact. Then, it happened, driving home one day, I had the type of headache that one feels clear through to the nerves within the teeth, and I wanted it to go away *now*! The discomfort was intense, and if I had to rank it, it would have been about an 11 on a 10 scale.

One of my personal decisions has always been that medicine should only be used as a final resort. I am aware of the placebo effect for many over-the-counter medicines, so I decided that if my mind could create it, my mind could get rid of it. After repeatedly giving myself relaxing suggestions for the muscles in that region, the headache diminished, and eventually went away. Beginning the next day, however, the headaches began happening more and more frequently. Eventually nausea came into the picture with the headaches. Within a few weeks, the headache and nausea developed into a morning, noon, and night occurrence.

Less than a month prior to the accident, I had completed a hypnotherapy certification course. I was able to look at this problem from the perspective of what I would do if a client came to me with this problem. First on the list was to meet with a medical doctor. Over the eighteen months of headaches, I had gone to the doctor three times, with the third one being to my regular family physician, which finally helped to eliminate the constancy of the problem.

For days, in self-hypnosis, I focused on every aspect of the headache I could think of. This helped to eliminate the headache from bothering me during the day because, eventually, I became incredibly bored with the headache. I switched gears to almost negotiating with myself to discover what the positive intent behind this wretched headache was, and what it would take for me to get it to go away.

During this phase, my patience was beginning to wear thin. I did not notice this at first, but eventually found myself taking out my frustrations on a friend. I knew that something needed to be done, and soon. I began to focus on different petty annoyances that would put my attention elsewhere in the environment. This proved relatively successful, and along with the self-hypnosis, I was able to go for short stretches of time each day without the headaches or nausea. Through building upon each success through self-hypnosis, I was eventually able to go for longer periods of time without the problem, and, increasing the time without the headache, I achieved much success.

In May 1999, during spring break from college, I again went to the doctor, only this time it was to my regular family physician. After doing a case analysis, it was determined that the headache, most likely, was being caused by a buildup of scar tissue from some previous injuries to the same area. The doctor was surprised when I told her that I had only given in and taken four Tylenol™ during the eighteen months, and was incredibly excited when I told her how I had utilized self-hypnosis. She offered many alternatives, but I decided to go with the least intrusive method first. I decided to begin the stretching routine that had been developed with the physical therapist. The problem eventually went away.

To this day, the headaches still come back once in a while, but I am able to perceive them in a unique way. The funny part is that when they come back, I actually can smile or laugh because I have been free of the headaches for whatever length of time I have gone (sometimes weeks, sometimes months), and if I can go that length of time without them, a few minutes was nothing compared to the time that had been wasted during the eighteen-month run of the headache. I still spend a considerable amount of time on the ski slopes during the winter months, and enjoy every minute of it as though it is a taste of heaven on earth. I now do not push myself to perform movements beyond the ski equipment or my body as I did then, but am able to have just as much fun.

The significance of self-hypnosis through this entire process is that whenever the headache would begin to flare up, I would utilize self-hypnosis instead of taking any over-the-counter pain reliever, which may have taken a long time to activate. This also helped me to develop empathy for individuals experiencing problems such as these headaches. Having learned advanced hypnotic techniques in certification training, and how to apply these myself, would I want to go through this experience again? Absolutely not! Would I recommend learning self-hypnosis to anyone experiencing this? Definitely!

Healing Shame

We met Rose Rockney this year at our certification training in Minneapolis. She displayed excellent skills at hypnotherapy and was comfortable to share her past abuse with us. Now she shares with you a small part of her healing process, in her own words.

One of my earliest memories of using self-hypnosis to make a significant change in my life was when I was doing some work from the book *Healing the Shame that Binds You* by John Bradshaw. You can probably guess the reason I was reading the book. One of the meditations I did was go down a path, through a curtain, and see myself at an earlier age, an age where I was very small. I was able to use the entire exercise to get in touch with the little girl I was at about three or four years of age. As per the instructions, I went to the little girl and told her I was from her future and I wanted her to know she would never ever be alone, because I am always with her. I held her, and loved her, and told her she would survive. That was the start of my road back.

Since that time, I have used self-hypnosis regularly for relaxation, dealing with stress, processing grief, changing habits, and just plain going to sleep. Practice makes perfect, and each time I do a progressive relaxation technique it is easier and easier. I can take a nap at work no matter who is with me and what is going on around me. I can tell myself to wake up in 29 minutes and be punched back in at exactly one-half hour from when I punched out for lunch. I can go to sleep in a hotel and tell myself what time to wake up in the morning and I will be awake and drinking my first cup of coffee before the desk calls for my wake up call.

I also use visualization (another form of self-hypnosis) to change my personal paradigms into success and confidence. I honestly do not know where I would be today without this valuable tool. Because of this skill, I am so much more aware of the words that I say out loud and how they have the power to change my life. Visualization is a tool that anyone can learn. I would strongly encourage people to learn to use this wonderful technique to communicate with themselves, and ultimately to change their destiny.

An Ability Suit

We met Liz Heidenger at our certification training in Seattle in 1999. Liz is quite a woman. She has a grand sense of humor and is extremely bright. This story illustrates how one simple trance experience can change your life. Here's Liz in her own words.

It was a small church, just starting up. Our attendance was only perhaps 40 people. We met in a conference room at a budget hotel chain in the western suburbs of Chicago. However, this little start up church changed my life, or perhaps I should say that the minister did. It was at a difficult time in my life. I was in a job I hated but one that paid well. When I was working the night shift, going to church wasn't easy, but it was well worth it. I had just divorced and was seeing a man who was threatened by any successes I might have. He laughed at the church and it's beliefs. At the time, I believed life was totally about luck and out of our own control. Thanks to this little church, that belief was changing.

New concepts were being presented to me. For the first time, I was hearing that life is, in large part, in our control. I was also learning about positive belief systems, manifestations, and conscious choice. Over and over again, the minister had preached to us "Don't sacrifice the 'better' on the altar of the 'good.'"In other words, he said don't let fear of loss stop you from exploring new horizons with even greater good.

Gradually my self-confidence grew and I started making choices to change my life. I didn't know it at the time, but my life was about to change, one day, when the minister did a particular meditation. Each service had time set aside for a meditation. This one particular Sunday we were meditating on the "ability suit." We were induced into a trance state and were told to enter a peaceful place, or a sacred place. Then we were told that in that peaceful place, there was a closet, and in it was the "ability suit."

We were encouraged to dream big. At first, nothing came of the admonition. Again we were told to have no limits, and that nothing is impossible that has been done before by someone else. At the time, I wanted to be an airline pilot but that was very far off. I didn't even have my private pilot's license. But I went ahead and tried on the "ability suit" anyway. I felt as giddy as a child going to Disneyland. It felt so unreal at first, but then eventually I mentally and emotionally "grew into" my new suit (a crewman's uniform).

A couple of years later, I got a temporary assignment of training newly-hired maintenance technicians at the airline where I was working as a maintenance technician. I wanted to go into training, but little did I know that was a small step on a big journey. Not too long after that, I broke it off with the boyfriend who was very controlling and emotionally abusive. My small success on getting into training was more than his ego would tolerate. The breakup was a big relief for me. I finally felt things were moving. Then, a couple of years after that, I got a transfer into the flight crew training division. I was thrilled. I moved to Denver for the new position. I wrote the minister to thank him for his meditations and his believing in me. He liked my story so much, he asked permission to use it as his next sermon.

The transfer to flight crew training was a mixed blessing. I got laid off right before my household goods arrived from Chicago. I had to make a choice then, go back to maintenance in Chicago or brave facing a job loss. I had fallen in love with Denver and didn't want to leave. Something told me that going back would have equated to giving up.

So I took the layoff. After working temporary crew training assignments I found myself working for a small charter airline out of Tucson, Arizona. I was hired to conduct both crew and maintenance training. The owner of the airline wanted to encourage employee loyalty so he announced he'd be offering Flight Engineer positions to the maintenance personnel. I was thrilled, but still faced the problem of having no licenses. There was one employee there who was a forward thinker, and convinced me I was qualified to take the tests for these licenses. That involved submitting documented proof of your experience in aviation to an FAA inspector. I gathered up all my documentation and since the FAA inspector was already familiar with the work in training I had been doing, he signed the necessary papers for me.

A year later, I was back at my original job in Denver. I had taken the signed FAA documents and passed the Flight Engineer written exam. I had two years to finish Flight Engineer training before the written exam expired. Another obstacle faced me—after nearly two years of sporadic employment, I didn't have the money for flight engineer school. I kept inquiring and a few months later I got a tip about one of the local flight schools offering flight engineer training. I later learned they were running a class and had two guys training to be captains and would have to pay someone to "play" flight engineer. So I got accepted into the course, at cost. Again I was thrilled.

While teaching pilots by day, I was training to be a flight engineer by night. And in November 1995, I finally earned my Flight Engineer License. Not quite an airline pilot, but darn close! It all started quite a few years before back in suburban Chicago at a small church, trying on that "ability suit."

Managing Visual Floaters

I (K.H.) met Craig Lang in 1998. He is an engineer at Medtronic in Minneapolis. He has a brilliant mind and has a fascinating hobby. In his free time he investigates UFO sightings, interviewing those making claims of close encounters. However, his story of managing visual floaters is something many people will find very down to earth. Here's Craig's story, in his own words.

Very common among we 30- and 40-somethings, visual floaters are those annoying dark spots that occasionally appear to swim into one's field of vision. At their most benign, they are merely the result of the normal aging process of our eyes. For many years, these have come and gone from my visual field, usually lasting a few days to weeks, and then vanishing. However, during the fall of 1998, one particularly annoying spot appeared, permanently fixed at the center of the visual field of my right eye. This very large dark spot occasionally interfered with my ability to focus—and occasionally even caused a degree of pain.

Several trips to the ophthalmologist established that there was no actual problem with my eyes—no retinal damage, no degeneration, etc. The good news was that that my eyes, like the rest of me, were merely growing older. The bad news was that there is no treatment for the problem. Floaters are just something you have to live with—even this large obnoxious one swimming in the very center of my vision.

During the months prior to this, in preparation for my upcoming hypnotherapy certification class, I had been reading many books on NLP, hypnotherapy, self-hypnosis, etc. Inherent in many of the techniques suggested by the authors was the use of metaphor and guided imagery. An example might be to control pain by imagining a device, perhaps with a control knob, which could be turned down to decrease the pain. Since I am an electrical engineer by trade, being both visual, and analytical, such a device metaphor seemed useful in dealing with my annoying visual companion.

Also, during this time, I had become very dedicated to the study and practice of meditation, spending approximately an hour in trance each evening before retiring. In the practice of meditation, affirmations are also very significant tools. Many authors (Peterson, *Creative Meditation,* Leichtman & Japiksi, *Active Meditation*) describe them as a means to accomplish useful change through the meditative process. The idea immediately suggested itself, that my normal mediation time could be used to install a simple self-hypnotic pattern, reinforcing it using affirmations, to help me manage the obnoxious floater problem.

That evening, during meditation, as I was going into trance, an image formed in my mind of an optical filtering device, which I imagined in place between my retina and my brain. This device was "programmed" to filter out unwanted "garbage" images, such as my floater. I mentally switched it on and reinforced it with the affirmation: "You have a filter in your mind that removes unwanted spots from your field of vision." In addition, I installed an anchor on my left hand by touching my left thumb and middle finger (convenient when driving, with your hand around the steering wheel). Descending into meditative trance, while holding my thumb/finger anchor in place, I silently and continuously repeated this affirmation in place of my normal unspoken meditative cue words.

The next day was sunny and bright, a perfect opportunity to test my imaginary filtering device. While stuck in traffic on my way to work, the familiar spot appeared. Gripping thumb to finger around the steering wheel, and silently repeating to myself, "You have a filter . . . " the spot abruptly vanished. It remained delightfully absent for several moments—until I moved my eyes. As it reappeared, I again repeated, "You have a filter . . . " placing thumb to finger. The spot again obediently faded to oblivion. Each time the spot appeared I repeated my affirmation and the spot vanished.

The next several days were clear and bright, affording lots of additional practice opportunity. Within a few weeks, I found that the mere appearance of the spot would trigger thought of the affirmation, thus invoking the filter. Now, the moment the spot appears it triggers the filter, which suppresses it. Thus, the spot has become its own demise.

World Class Swimming Speeds!

Our final story of success with hypnosis is a bit different than the rest in this chapter. This story is from Mary Lee's friend John Sayre. John is a world class swimmer and national record holder. He is someone who knows how to validate the success of self-hypnosis! When you come to the end of this story you may see just how powerful the power of your mind truly is. Here's John's story in his own words.

At age 13, I learned in a workgroup the basics of using mental imagery to enhance performance with my age group swimming program. During the class, we were instructed to take 3" x 5" cards and write out our times for specific swimming events. We were also taught to write affirmative goals, and post them somewhere where they could be seen each day. We were told that this could cause these goals to manifest. Finally, we were taught to ritually imagine the swim race in as much detail as possible.

During the next year, I used these techniques regularly, and integrated them into my daily workout routine. I had set a goal to win the Northwest Regional Championships in four different events. I also noted the times early in the season on 3" x 5" cards and posted the times and these goals on my mirror. Weeks prior to the swimming meet in Lake Oswego, Oregon, a pool I had been to the year before, I would envision each of the races, the lane ropes, the smell of the chlorine, the splash of the water, the starting gun, the turns, the crowd yelling, and the finish. I was able to see in my mind touching the wall, looking up, and seeing the clock to see my time. This would coincide with the time on my 3" x 5" card.

At the meet, at age 14, I ended with four Regional Championship Gold Medals, four new Regional Records, and three times that qualified in the Top 10 National swims for the year, placing highest in the 400 IM at sixth in the U.S. I had surpassed my times in all four races, and felt a glory and accomplishment, as if it were a prophecy.

Later in my career, when I had achieved a status of racing within the World Class caliber swimmers, I had a similar experience. In December each year, there was a classic "mid-season" competition called the Husky Invitational at the University of Washington. At this meet, as other swimmers around the country posted their pre-Christmas "Best Times," one could count on having the competition and excitement to post times that could rank with the best.

I had previously set a goal time for my 400 yard Individual Medley, and engaged the visualization techniques to practice my swim nearly 100 times before the event. I'd also practice turns as if in the race, during practice. I continued to see the time posted on my mirror of 3:55.50, which I figured would be the top swim in the nation to date during the season.

At the meet, with anticipation on high, and time to reflect, I jotted my splits and final time on a heat sheet of one of the nearby parents of a swimmer on our team, and asked them to take my splits and watch me hit 3:55.50. When the gun went off and I hit the water, it was as if my mind was a machine. I felt as if my body was a finely tuned instrument that flawlessly exercised each stroke, each breath, each turn in all four strokes, butterfly, backstroke, breaststroke, and freestyle. I was racing others, but had a comfortable lead and finished first, then turned to look at the clock with a time of 3:55.49.

I later wondered if I should have set my goal to a quicker time given how accurate and intense the manifestation techniques work!

Goal Setting

To conclude this book, we asked Kim Johnson, a fine hypnotherapist and a colleague of ours to help us out. We asked Kim to write a little bit about goal setting and how hypnosis helps us meet our goals. Without further ado, here's Kim!

Goal setting has long been the standard by which we accomplish tasks. It is that constant reminder to ourselves what steps we must take to get to where we are going. In this way it is embedded into our subconscious what we want to become or get done. Setting realistic goals, and their incremental stages toward realization, takes careful planning and attention to detail. First, define the end result. It can be a physical or psychological outcome. It could be to lose weight or build a house.

Create the image you desire in your mind, visualize it, and draw it or write it down. Set a time that is realistic to accomplish the goal, make a note of it or create a time line. Break down the goal into easily accomplishable tasks.

Establish an order to initiate and to complete each task. Write it down and display it in an area that you will see it each day, and especially on critical days. If losing weight is your goal, make sure your posted notes are highly visible before holiday parties, group gatherings, or any time to celebrate.

The plan needs to be acknowledged as frequently as is reasonable. One individual developed several detailed long-term goals spanning many years. He wrote letters to himself. He had them mailed and delivered at critical times during his plan. He used these to check on his progress in attaining his goals, and was able to evaluate where he was according to his preset long-term goals. The evaluation was made and new sets of letters were posted to help keep him on track. He was without a formal education and was able to create a successful career for himself through this highly effective method.

Like a squirrel in the fall, the time to start preparing is in advance of the desired goal. You can plan and plan and plan, but nothing gets realized unless the journey begins. Once you start, and remind yourself where you are going, it becomes increasingly difficult to not get there. The accomplishment of each task shapes you into a new being. Stopping a flower from blooming once it starts is impossible, unless you pluck it. To realize your dreams, start setting goals and making plans, now.

Bibliography

Bandler, Richard. *Using Your Brain For a Change.* Moab: Real People Press, 1985

Barber, Joseph. *Hypnosis and suggestion in the treatment of pain : A clinical guide.* New York: Norton, 1996

Binswanger, Harry, ed. *The Ayn Rand Lexicon: Objectivism from A to Z.* New York, N.Y.: Meridian, 1986

Cheek, D. B. *Hypnosis. The Application of Ideomotor Techniques.* Needham Heights, MA: Paramount, 1994

Dossey, Larry. *Be Careful What You Pray For . . . .* San Francisco: Harper Books, 1998.

Frankl, Viktor. *Man's Search for Meaning.* New York, N.Y.: Washington Square Press, 1984.

Hilgard, E. R. and Hilgard, J. R. *Hypnosis in the Relief of Pain.* Los Altos, CA: William Kaufmann, 1975

Hill, Napoleon. *Think and Grow Rich.* New York, N.Y.: Ballantine Books, 1960

Hill, Napoleon. *The Laws of Success.* Evanston, Ill.: Success Unlimited, 1977

Hogan, Kevin. *Miracles of Hypnosis: Advanced Techniques and Strategies of Hypnotherapy and Hypnoanalysis.* Eagan, Minn.: Network 3000 Publishing, 1998

Hogan, Kevin. *The Gift: A Discovery of Happiness, Fulfillment and Love.* Eagan, Minn.: Network 3000 Publishing, 1998

Hogan, Kevin. *The Hypnotherapy Handbook: Hypnosis and Mindbody Healing.* Eagan, Minn.: Network 3000 Publishing, 1999.

Hogan, Kevin. *The Psychology of Persuasion: How to Persuade Others to Your Way of Thinking.* Gretna, La.: Pelican Publishing Company, 1996

Holy Bible. King James Version

Horton, William. *Primary Objective.* Chicago, Ill.: Eschaton Books, 1998

Lozanov, Georgi. *Suggestology and Outlines of Suggestopedy.* New York, N.Y.: Gordon and Breach, 1978

Rossi, Ernest. *The 20 Minute Break.* New York, N.Y.: G. P. Putnam and Sons, 1991

Sumner, Holly. *The Meditation Sourcebook.* New York, N.Y.: Lowell House, 1999

Wolinsky, Stephen. *Trances People Live.* Falls Village, CT: Bramble Company, 1991

Ziglar, Zig. *See You at the Top.* Gretna, La.: Pelican Publishing Company, 1984

Resource Guide

Hypnotherapy Certification Training

If you are interested in further information about this subject, you may contact either of the two associations listed below.

Hypnosis Research and Training Center
1960 Cliff Lake Road #112-200
Eagan, MN 55122
(612) 616-0732
website: http://www.kevinhogan.com
e-mail: meta@ix.netcom.com

National Association and Convention

World's largest hypnosis association for certified hypnotherapists. The NGH provides a multitude of benefits to their members including three publications, a video rental library, legislative support and a national convention in Nashua, NH, in August of each year.

National Guild of Hypnotists
Box 308
Merrimack, NH 03054
(603) 429-9438
ngh@ngh.net

Author and Contributor Contact Information

To contact any of the authors or contributors featured in this work, please send correspondence to their attention (don't forget to mention the title of the work), c/o:

Pelican Publishing Company
P.O. Box 3110
Gretna, Louisiana 70054-3110

or you may E-mail them at editorial@pelicanpub.com.

We will forward your letter or E-mail to the appropriate person.

THE PSYCHOLOGY OF PERSUASION:
How to Persuade Others to Your Way of Thinking

By Kevin Hogan

How do you ethically direct others toward your point of view? Understanding precisely what they are thinking is the first step. Using techniques from hypnosis, neurolinguistic programming, the Bible, and the greatest salespeople in history, Kevin Hogan teaches you the skills of persuasion. This knowledge will empower you to improve loving relationships, get the best price on an automobile, save thousands on a home, and increase sales in dramatic fashion!

Share the most powerful tools, strategies, and techniques of persuasion already used by winning political candidates, multimillion dollar television ministers, and some of the world's most powerful people. Begin your journey to understanding why we do things and how to persuade others to our way of thinking.

ABOUT THE AUTHOR

Kevin Hogan is a national public speaker and founder of Success Dynamics Foundation, a nonprofit organization that strives to teach schoolchildren about making correct choices about drug use. An expert on body language, he is sought after by the media and even has interepreted President Clinton's demeanor during a televised speech for the *New York Post.* He holds a doctorate of clinical hypnotherapy from American Institute of Hypnotherapy (Irvine, California) and a Ph.D. in metaphysics from the American Institute of Holistic Theology (Youngstown, Ohio). Dr. Hogan has a clinical hypnotherapy practice and sees clients daily. He resides in Eagan, Minnesota.

288 pp. 6 x 9 Charts
Appendixes Biblio. Glossary
ISBN: 1-56554-146-4 $22.00

Also available on audiocassette:
Narrated by Kevin Hogan
Two audiocassettes Total running time: 120 minutes
ISBN: 1-56554-431-5 $18.00

Readers may order toll free from Pelican
at 1-800-843-1724 or 1-888-5-PELICAN.

TALK YOUR WAY TO THE TOP:
Communication Secrets to Change Your Life

By Kevin Hogan

" . . . as instructional as it is rousing. Even for the professional communicator, there is something to be learned from the insights offered by Hogan." *ForeWord* magazine

Drawing on more than two decades of experience, Kevin Hogan explains how to communicate interpersonally, talk to yourself, and transcend physical experience into the realm of idea and thought.

He does so by revealing such communication secrets as reinforcing verbal messages with non-verbal cues. He also instructs readers how to interpret the body language of others and to then modify communication strategies accordingly.

By implementing these easy-to-follow instructions, anyone can become a better listener, a better speaker, and a better communicator, which will yield great dividends, both personally and professionally.

ABOUT THE AUTHOR
Body language expert Kevin Hogan has frequently interpreted the demeanor of President Clinton and other notables for the *New York Post*.

208 pp. 6 x 9 Illus. Biblio.
ISBN: 1-56554-426-9 $21.00

Also available on audiocassette:
Narrated by Kevin Hogan
Two audiocassettes Total running time: 120 minutes
ISBN: 1-56554-703-9 $18.00

**Readers may order toll free from Pelican
at 1-800-843-1724 or 1-888-5-PELICAN.**